D1596738

HITLER'S PSYCHOPATHOLOGY

HITLER'S PSYCHOPATHOLOGY

Norbert Bromberg, M.D.

Verna Volz Small

INTERNATIONAL UNIVERSITIES PRESS, INC.

New York   New York

Library of Congress Cataloging in Publication Data

Bromberg, Norbert.
  Hitler's psychopathology.

  Bibliography: p.
  Includes index.
  1. Hitler, Adolf, 1889-1945—Personality. 2. Hitler, Adolf, 1889-1945—Health. I. Small, Verna Volz. II. Title. [DNLM: 1. Mental disorders—History. WZ 313 B868h]
DD247.H5B727 1983   943.086'092'4   83-261
ISBN 0-8236-2345-9

Manufactured in the United States of America

Contents

". . . the facts are eloquent enough."
Alan Bullock

in *Hitler, A Study in Tyranny* (1964)

Acknowledgments

Many have contributed to the development of this book: patients, colleagues, friends, and the families of both authors.

One of the first to stimulate Norbert Bromberg's thoughts about the puzzles of the subject, as early as 1960, was Dr. John Frosch, whose studies of the psychotic character first alerted Dr. Bromberg to the congruence between Adolf Hitler's behavior and that more disturbed form of the borderline personality. Other colleagues contributed in discussions of papers on Hitler presented by Dr. Bromberg at psychoanalytic meetings. Drs. Otto Kernberg and Arnold Richards thoughtfully and most helpfully reviewed this manuscript in its first version; later versions of chapters benefited from the critical reviews of Dr. Mark Kanzer and Professor Robert G. L. Waite. Conversations with Professor Waite about

Hitler over recent years were especially illuminating. Dr. William Niederland offered thoughtful comments. Gregory Halpern was a source of encouragement and help.

Sarina, Charney, and David Bromberg and most especially our spouses, May Bromberg and Leonard Small participated with the authors at every stage of our joint work for well over a decade. We are grateful to them for their great patience and their direct help in shaping the manuscript. For careful typing and enthusiastic interest in the subject, we are grateful to Sylvia Krohn; we also thank Charles Flanders.

Preface

At a time when the publication of works on Adolf Hitler has become a virtual industry, why another Hitler study?

One of the most puzzling questions of history is this: how did this odd, awkward man, full of rage and hatred, hold a civilized nation in thrall and lead it to the conquest of most of the European continent and a systematic annihilation of millions of innocent lives? One part of the complex answer has to do with the nature of the personality of the man himself.

Historians who have pondered the enigma of Hitler's personality have shed light on but one or another of its aspects. Some have simply admitted failure. Thus, for example, the distinguished historian, Sir Alan Bullock (1958), finds it unreasonable to believe that the youthful Hitler was the stuff of which future Caesars and Bonapartes were made. Yet a present-day student of personality development knows that significant influences in the early years of a child which yield no consequences immediately apparent emerge years later to shape his acts as an adult. This study further contends that the youthful Hitler clearly revealed the shape of his personality, and that its very pathology played a role in his rise to leadership and power.

Such personalities are now understood much more precisely than they were five decades ago. With few exceptions, however, those who specialize in the study of human personality have not shown much interest in understanding Hitler. After Norbert Bromberg (1960, 1961, 1962, 1971, 1974) read one of his papers on Hitler at a meeting of the American Psychoanalytic Association, one colleague objected that no diagnosis of a human being could possibly encompass the personality of Adolf Hitler. Apparently he would not want to elevate Hitler, nor to denigrate himself, by admitting him to our species. Another commented, "Why write about Hitler's personality? Everyone knows he was crazy."

The first response leads to the acceptance of Hitler's own grandiose myths about himself; it isolates him in our thoughts as some nonhuman embodiment of the mysteries of nature. But Hitler is part of our humanity. Our myths helped to produce him and we cannot get rid of him so easily. He lives openly at every cross-burning of the Ku Klux Klan and in every American Nazi who vows to complete what Hitler started. Myths, we know, do not die spontaneously. Nor can their heroes safely be dismissed by denigration or trivialization. The danger of the Hitler myth was stated by Robert Hughes: "Only if Hitler is anchored in human reality will he stay dead. If not, he will continue as he has been since 1945: a nightmare of history from which we cannot awake" (1973, pp. 81–82).

Can we anchor Hitler in human reality? The answer is that his life record as now known makes this possible. A comment by Freud (1900, p. 621) is relevant.

> Action and consciously expressed opinions are, as a rule, enough for practical purposes in judging men's characters. Actions deserve to be considered first and foremost, for many impulses which force their way through to consciousness are even then brought to nothing by the real forces of mental life before they can mature into deeds.

Hitler, moreover, showed psychopathology of a kind that reveals in behavior almost as much about his fantasies as would his direct reports of them in therapy. And what Hitler said and did is extensively documented. We have surveyed his acts, utterances, and writings, official documents and findings of historians amassed and winnowed over half a century since his emergence in politics, and have made deductions based upon the clinical findings of psychoanalysis.

A hypothetical diagnosis is presented, useful as a framework for consideration of the psychological roots of Hitler's personality. Certainly, it is in no sense an excuse for his acts. And it addresses only one part of the Nazi phenomenon: what manner of man embodied it?

NORBERT BROMBERG
Tarrytown, New York

VERNA VOLZ SMALL
New York City

CHAPTER I

Enigma Examined

This book presents a psychological study of the personality, and a diagnosis, of Adolf Hitler. Whereas psychology alone cannot fathom the Nazi chapter in history, it can explore the personality of the man who devised and dominated Nazism and was therefore one of its key elements. A summary of the record of Hitler's behavior is offered, to enable readers to reconsider his biography in light of the diagnosis and evaluate its probability.

Understanding the man has a pressing purpose. Adolf Hitler was among the first politicians to exploit microphones, amplifiers, and radio for manipulation of the masses. Now electronic techniques expose even larger populations to control of their thoughts, emotions, and actions. Since a Hitler with present communication technology would be more deadly in potential than the Hitler of fifty years ago, we consider the man a subject not safely dead despite the abundance of books about him during the 1970s.

Adolf Hitler's character is often regarded as a unique phenomenon or one too monstrous for examination by ordinary methods, beyond the pale of humanity. But Adolf Hitler was not psychologically unique, however extraordinary the dimensions of his drives and destructiveness. Our study shows how the man whose life made the name Hitler infamous belonged to a group of disturbed people with a definable personality organization. The diagnosis here hypothesized has been identified in recent decades by some psychoanalysts as referring to a distinct pathological syndrome.

This pathological personality structure itself can be highly adaptive for emerging political leaders, especially in stressful social conditions like those of late twentieth-century America. Since this personality is especially dangerous in a person who attains sufficient political power to attempt actions derived from its drives and fantasies, the syndrome should be described clearly so that the public can recognize it. Otherwise, it could again threaten humanity in a new leader who might at first be seen as Hitler was as a savior, or as just another unprepossessing crackpot.

One purpose of this work is to contribute to a general public understanding of the existence and the nature of this readily overlooked personality disorder. An electorate so informed would at least scrutinize with extra care a candidate who shows the disorder's hallmarks: that is, who presents himself as an omniscient simplifier of complex issues, who ignores obvious realities to promise the clearly impossible, whose oratory brims with rage, who charges one single enemy with responsibility for all difficulties. In the absence of public understanding of this pathological pattern, many of its elements are readily accepted as evidence of forcefulness. Others are welcome because they permit the campaigner to relieve frustrations among the electorate by offering sanction for aggressive feelings and hostile acts. Still other aspects of the personality are welcome because they permit a demagogue to offer a simple panacea for an all too confusing reality. In short, the very nature of the personality can be the key to political success if not recognized as abnormal.

Can any diagnosis be related meaningfully to the long-dead dictator? Over the past quarter-century voluminous detail about Hitler's early years has become available for study. His contemporaries in a position to know portions of his personal history have set it down. These contemporaries include his sole teenage friend; a professional archivist from the district where he grew up; his family doctor; fellow vagrants of Vienna; and close associates who witnessed his political rise and his exercise of power. Historians in Europe and America have exhaustively surveyed the record. Today many of Hitler's personal and public documents, with the reports and comments of personal witnesses, are available to illuminate his life.[1]

---

[1] Most of the sources on Hitler are in books now readily available in English for the reader who wishes to examine the cited behavior in more detail.

Some of the witnesses are adulatory, some hostile; some
seek self-exculpation, some strive for objectivity.

   Aspects of Hitler's life were examined for psychological
meaning during World War II when the American Office
of Strategic Services requested Walter C. Langer to review intelligence data on Adolf Hitler. In 1943 he and
a team of fellow-psychoanalysts made the pioneering and
until now sole attempt at a total psychological assessment
of the man (published in 1972 as *The Mind of Adolf
Hitler*). When the secret document and its source material (Langer, 1942–1943), were declassified, we were
able to examine its data for congruence with the hypothesis of this study. All the available data and inter-
pretations were examined with care taken to weigh fairly
every detail that might not fit.

   When re-examined and compared to the hypothesized
diagnosis, the life record of Hitler is seen in a clearer
light, and its puzzles and paradoxes are reduced. Essentially, the diagnosis here postulated clarifies commonly
occurring psychological pictures previously found puzzling in many people less deadly than the German dictator. It now is considered a combination of two closely
related disorders (Kernberg, 1967) or the overlapping of
contiguous sections of a continuum (Adler, 1981).

   Like many diagnoses, that of Hitler can be postulated
in his absence as a living subject, just as strongly probable
diagnoses of patients are now postulated every day when
consultant psychiatrists are called upon to decide the
diagnostic meaning of data supplied by other profession-
als.

   One inevitable question is not addressed here: why
did a civilized nation follow this man in carrying out such

wide and cruel destruction, ultimately resulting in its own collapse? How Adolf Hitler was able to win over millions of Germans and lead them through frightful hate to catastrophe is a study in history, economics, and sociology beyond the scope of this inquiry into his individual psychology, long considered an enigma.

CHAPTER II

A *Diagnosis of Adolf Hitler*

Adolf Hitler's life record, so baffling to historians faced with his accomplishments and his crimes, is strikingly similar in its details to the features of a psychoanalytic syndrome which began to be more sharply delineated around the mid-sixties. His behavior as an adolescent and a young adult are strongly indicative of a diagnosis more clearly formulated long after his death. His behavior when he sought and wielded power confirms it. The condition happens to be one in which the patient reveals much of the nature of his psychopathological state by his observable behavior, unlike many other conditions diagnosable with the help of direct revelation of fantasies and dreams as well as emotions. For this diagnosis his overt behavior, which includes his statements and language, is most telling. Since Hitler's behavior is extensively recorded, the significant elements for proposing a diagnosis are available even in the absence of a living patient.

Careful study of the now abundant biographical data leads to the conclusion that Adolf Hitler was a *narcissistic personality* with *paranoid* features, functioning on a *borderline personality* level, hereafter more briefly referred to as a *narcissistic-borderline personality* or *narcissistic-borderline personality disorder*.

In 1918 Hitler doubtless showed features that would today be subsumed under this diagnosis when he was treated for gas poisoning in an army hospital. There the diagnosis *"psychopath with hysterical symptoms"* is said to have been made. It was, however, long concealed by the disappearance of Hitler's army records. The old designation "psychopath" was used for patients in whom almost complete absence of conscience is a major feature, patients who are now often considered among the borderline personalities.

The two main components of the present narcissistic-borderline personality diagnosis can be described separately. Otto Kernberg, in two early studies (1966, 1967) and subsequent studies, was one of the authors who in recent years contributed notably to their understanding. Others include Maxwell Gitelson (1958), Edith Jacobson (1964), Roy R. Grinker, Sr., Beatrice Werble, and Robert C. Drye (1968), John Frosch (1970), Heinz Kohut (1971), Ben Bursten (1973), James Masterson (1976), John G. Gunderson and M. T. Singer (1975), Peter Hartocollis

(1977), Gerald Adler (1981), and Michael H. Stone (1980).

In the following summary of the syndrome, the reader familiar with Hitler biographies will find point after point recalling acts and expressions of the Nazi dictator. A condensed version of Hitler's life record is given in the next section for comparison with the diagnosis.

THE NARCISSISTIC PERSONALITY

The concept of excessive narcissism is now much discussed in both technical and popular discourse. Degrees of narcissistic investment range from a healthful self-esteem to the extreme self-preoccupation of the schizophrenic, who constantly fantasizes about himself. The narcissistic personality is a disorder in which there are both conflicting feelings about the person's worth and specific severe difficulties in his relations with other human beings. Yet such an individual is often someone whose life outwardly appears to be a successful one, even one of achievement or celebrity.[1] Although the narcissistic personality openly reveals his megalomania, his needs to be admired, praised, and flattered are marked. Great ambition often accompanies his grand fantasies, driving him to strive for preeminence in wealth, wisdom, beauty, leadership, power, or whatever. Lack of initiative and lack of decisiveness often interfere with effective work. He is aware of feeling shame and embarrassment.

[1] Narcissistic and borderline personalities occur in either sex. Because we are here concerned with a male, and for the sake of simplicity, the masculine pronoun will be used in what follows.

He complains of a feeling of emptiness. He has little if any sense of humor. He tends to lie. Even if very intelligent, he can be most literal in understanding of concepts. He often has neurotic symptoms. Most importantly, the narcissistic personality cannot make significant relationships, being at most times arrogant, contemptuous, and denigrating, as well as demanding and exploitative. Blows to his self-esteem often elicit violent anger. Frequently he reveals paranoid distrust. He may show hypochondria, exaggerated preoccupation with his body generally or more specifically with moderate malfunctions of some organ system. His interest in normal sexual relations is often slight or lacking, but perverse fantasies are found and sometimes acted out.

With so much of his psychic energy devoted to himself, the narcissistic personality has little understanding of complex feelings in others; he has little empathy for them, or even interest. His emotional life is shallow and his feelings are undifferentiated in quality; he may find these aspects of himself to be a deprivation, something to complain about. Although often seen to be engaging and charming, he usually makes the effort to be perceived in this way for an ulterior purpose, such as to manipulate others. Behind the benign appearance is usually a cold, ruthless determination to gratify aggressive drives.

Two interests in others the narcissistic personality often reveals are voyeurism and exhibitionism. Promoting the exhibitionism is the intense need for admiration and praise, which the male especially tries to elicit by showing off, sometimes to the point of recklessness. He exhibits his body, clothes, aggressiveness, and masculinity. One way to demonstrate his idea of masculine fearlessness is by reckless acts. The narcissistic personality usually takes risks, expecting to be magically saved by a powerful, miraculous fate and to emerge unscathed.

The showing off and boastful self-praise emphasizing virile qualities often occur before a woman whose admiration is sought. But the narcissistic man has contradictory attitudes toward women. Whereas he usually speaks of them in derogatory and contemptuous terms, he often poses as the defender of motherhood and the sanctity of womanhood because he wants to appear wise, heroic, benign, or commanding.

The grand boasts and lofty behavior of the narcissistic personality make him appear self-confident and secure. But his inflated self-esteem and fantasies of omnipotence alternate with feelings of abject shame, insecurity, and inferiority. Indeed, these sharp differences in self-concept are often the first indications to the psychiatrist of the patient's condition. Fantasies of embarrassment, humiliation, and shame are particularly prominent in narcissistic personalities with paranoid trends. These people are not to be confused with psychotic individuals designated as paranoid. Unlike the true paranoid, the narcissistic personality with paranoid trends may lead a fairly productive occupational life if he works in a field where his suspiciousness, secretiveness, or tendency to very exacting criticism is useful, since his hold on reality is at most times, though not always, relatively undistorted.

When confronted with situations which arouse intense envy and jealousy and when he can no longer deny the marked disparity between his fantasies and reality, equally intense feelings of shame emerge to plague him.

Since any narcissistic personality secretly harbors a shameful concept of himself, he suffers greatly. Grandiosity, obviously, is not tolerant of shame. When plagued by fantasies of embarrassment and humiliation, the narcissistic personality, using paranoid maneuvers, tries to rid himself of a shameful self-concept by projection. With his excessive self-importance he is suspicious, hypersensitive, jealous, envious, and rigid, and accuses others of evil motives. These traits promote constant searching for shameful behavior in others. Projection of rage and aggression is particularly marked. The narcissistic personality especially deprecates those from whom he does not expect to benefit. Much of the denigrating attitude toward others results from the projection onto them of his own shameful self-image.

Hostile and insensitive behaviors are abetted by the marked deficiency in empathy and capacity to be concerned about others, to say nothing of loving them. These deficiencies limit the narcissistic personality's capacity for enjoyment of life to the praise and admiration he can get from others. Thus in his relations he often appears clinging and demanding; he becomes exploitative, at times even parasitic. He behaves as though he has the right to exploit others without a qualm. He is markedly jealous and envious of those who enjoy life or succeed in the areas of his own ambitions, and suffers an additional pang from the inferiority that his envy implies. He is not, however, truly dependent because he is too distrustful of others. The very idea of dependency on anyone evokes fear of becoming especially envious, with that concurrent painful feeling of inferiority.

The narcissistic personality is driven to control and

manipulate others. His great striving to advance his own interests, reinforced by grandiosity, demandingness, exploitativeness, and parasitic traits and uninhibited by empathy or concern for others, makes the need to control and manipulate them obligatory. For manipulation, many narcissistic personalities freely use lying and deception, either unconsciously, protected by denial, or even consciously, especially if the preceptors who reared them held appearances more important than truth.

When the narcissistic personality does not receive the gratification of praise and admiration, strong feelings of boredom, emptiness, and restlessness drive him to seek new stimuli to feed his self-regard. Life seems to lose its meaning, to become empty and hollow. Lacking empathy, the narcissistic personality cannot enjoy human experiences even vicariously. Still, his feeling of emptiness should not be confused with the feeling of loneliness related to a longing for friendship with others. Devoid of capacity for significant relationships, he does not have a strong feeling of missing others.

With his paranoid features he can avoid this emptiness and even feel deeply engaged when defending himself against imagined enemies. Paranoid tendencies may be perpetuated exactly because the presence of fantasied enemies to be conquered gives the narcissistic personality that intense feeling of purpose so rare in his experience. This struggle is preferred to the desolate emptiness he feels when no enemies can be conjured up and no gratification from admiration is available.

Finally, he experiences frequent flare-ups of narcissistic rage. It erupts often when, inevitably, unrealistic wishes are frustrated or exaggerated self-esteem is

wounded. This rage can be unbearable. Again, he can
project the rage onto someone else and feel as though
the anger originated in the other person, thereupon seen
as a great threat. Controlling, manipulating, and grandiose actions are often justified by the narcissistic personality as ways of coping with such unrealistic threats.

THE BORDERLINE PERSONALITY

The borderline personality can be considered an especially severe character disorder. Its pathological organization is close to that of a psychosis (Frosch, 1970),
but unlike the psychoses, it does not involve hallucina-
tions or gross delusions. The borderline personality's
capacity to appraise the real world is distorted only in
limited areas and at limited times. Hence he is not
blocked as the psychotic usually is from success in the
real world. The diagnosis of this disorder largely depends
on finding typical defects in object-related functions and
in certain ego functions. The most telling aspect of the
characteristic ego weakness is the presence of primitive
defense mechanisms, i.e., infantile defenses which have
not evolved or been abandoned but persist beyond their
appropriately phase-specific time. Less effective than
other defenses, they also weaken other ego functions.
Most important is the use as a defense of splitting, a
normal occurrence only in the months of infancy, when
the child for a short time experiences the mothering
person in separate part-images—"all good" when his
needs are met and "all bad" when they are not. Without
significant impediments to development, splitting dis-

appears. The synthesizing function of the ego gradually merges these disparate images of the mother into an image of the whole real person. She is recognized and regarded at times as both good *and* bad. Under unfavorable circumstances of the infant's health or care, the separation or "splitting" of the two part-images persists. The split later prevents the development of realistic concepts of other human beings. Equally important, the development of a normal concept of self is distorted by the prolongation of splitting because the infant identifies himself, not with a single image of the mother, but rather with the two contradictory images. He also keeps his conflicting self-images separated from each other.

Injudicious management of the infant, as when the mother strongly encourages the toddler to persist in pleasurable clinging to her and to deny the reality of the need for psychological separation, has other consequences for mental functioning in the borderline personality disorder. In the early phases of development, it is apparent that the pleasure principle motivates the primary process, dominating the thought and behavior of the young infant. His inevitable failure in always avoiding pain and in always having pleasure gradually impels him to function on the basis of what is real as well as what is pleasurable, even if the real is somewhat disagreeable. His purely pleasure-motivated ego gradually changes to a reality-motivated ego. In the borderline personality, however, a considerable part of the ego apparently does not succeed in making this transformation and remains pleasure-dominated, like the infant ego. A separation into a reality-ego and a pleasure-ego results. A diagnostically important implication of this separation is that the persistence of the pleasure-ego means the persistence of some measure of primary-process thinking which the pleasure principle motivates. The individual with a borderline personality disorder does indeed use primary-process thinking at times, though it is not always clinically detectable. A further effect of the persistence of the pleasure-ego is a willfulness which is often mistaken as a strong will or strong ego when in fact it denotes the opposite.

In the everyday behavior of the adult borderline personality, persistent splitting manifests itself in the separation of others into all-good or all-bad people. An individual consigned to either category by the borderline may suddenly become the subject of a complete reversal of perceptions and feelings. Further, when the borderline struggles with some conflict, he may show splitting in his alternating expressions of both sides of the conflict and in his total lack of concern about contradictions in inner experience or outer behavior.

The splitting and the ongoing failure to synthesize contradictory identifications result in a failure to establish a stable, integrated sense of self, i.e., in identity diffusion. The contradictory identifications remain dissociated from each other, and tendencies to behave in accordance with first one and then the other of them persist in the ego. A manifestation of either of these partial and contradictory identifications is possible to the borderline when useful for his adaptation to a situation. At one moment he may act the rageful, aggressive attacker, whereas at the next, if it seems desirable to him, he may act the charming, benign appreciator, even the benefactor, of another person.

Finally, splitting results in lapses of impulse control. The borderline personality has episodic outbursts of primitive impulses of aggression or of the sexual drive, momentarily acceptable to him although not acceptable before or after the impulse. These violent outbursts often terminate as suddenly as they start.

The defense of denial is used by the borderline personality to reinforce splitting; it results, for example, in the bland acceptance of two emotionally opposite aspects of consciousness. The awareness that at a specific moment his ideas, perceptions, and feelings contradict those he held before has no emotional significance for him; the contradiction does not influence his present attitude or his stance of the moment. Swift reversal, with the same lack of awareness of contradictions, is just as possible. Denial also makes it possible for the borderline personality to disregard an obvious emotion related to a certain external reality or inner experience. In other areas of consciousness he is intellectually aware of what is denied, but he cannot integrate those awarenesses with the emotions connected with them. The emotional relevance of a reality of which he was once aware is denied, as are the emotions which he experienced and still remembers.

A defense mechanism continually used by the borderline is projection, chiefly to externalize his images of himself as aggressive and all-bad. The narcissistic personality also uses this mechanism, but the borderline often brings into play a more complicated projective process, projective identification. It becomes available because of his weakened capacity to maintain ego boundaries, especially when aggressive impulses are involved. The borderline, by identifying with the other person, feels that he still has the aggression he has projected onto him. The frightening aggression reacquired in this way is then again reprojected and increasingly feared. Projective identification obviously does not achieve the relief sought but rather tends to perpetuate and increase the borderline's fear and hostility. To cope with this intensifying imagined danger, he is driven to try to control and attack the other person before the anticipated attack on himself. Impelled by projective identification, he is very likely to act on his aggressive feelings, especially when he can safely do so.

Another mechanism closely linked to splitting is an idealization resulting from the tendency to regard an individual unrealistically as entirely good, often as powerful. This primitive idealization serves to make the idealized person temporarily immune from harm by the borderline's aggression. At the same time, if the idealized individual is also seen as all-powerful, the borderline becomes a protector of the idealizer. Such idealization contains no real human concern or regard, nor does it imply permanent absence of aggression toward the person idealized. This mechanism merely serves the borderline personality's narcissistic needs by providing him someone in whose greatness and omnipotence he can share. As a consequence, a demanding, clinging relationship with the idealized person may form temporarily. The borderline personality identifies with the individual he has endowed with omnipotence and therefore sees himself too as magically omnipotent. As the boundaries between the two blur, the borderline sees the idealized person as an extension of himself. He then uses him without concern, possessively and ruthlessly, trying to manipulate the idealized protector so that he will destroy the borderline's fantasied enemies for him.

Since the borderline is unable to feel love or even concern, inevitably he will lose interest and devaluate the idealized person when that person fails to continue as a source of gratification or protection. His vengeful destruction may be sought if this failure is especially frustrating or if the borderline fears that the idealized person may become an enemy to be dreaded and hated.

Just as weaknesses of the ego are found in this syndrome, so too are deficiencies in the superego. Freud described the superego as the precipitate of the ego. Since a flawed superego develops inevitably from a defective ego, a defective conscience is conspicuous in the behavior of borderline personalities. The conscience develops by identification with moral attitudes of parents and other important people near the child, as well as with standards of his society and of his heroes as he grows older. Since the borderline personality's perception of others including his parents is distorted by projection of his own aggressive feelings, he fails to come to terms with their realistic demands, seeing only his hostile, aggressive, and destructive projections with which to identify. This in turn facilitates his adoption of similar features, real and projected, which he perceives in others in his environment. In short, his superego is distorted and his conscience is defective.

The borderline personality's inferiority feelings, revealed from time to time, reflect his negative self-images, but these feelings are relatively superficial. They may reflect some perception of real limitations but usually serve to mask the more prevalent marked optimism,

based on denial, and the fantasied omnipotence and right
to exploit others and to be gratified as a privileged person—all rooted in the coexisting megalomanic self-images.

Another pathological consequence worsens all human
relationships. The borderline must eschew close emotional involvement with others, lest it lead to the necessity to use the primitive defensive maneuvers with
their limitations and threatening painful side effects: projective identification, with its fears of attack, and primitive idealization, with the need to submit. To avoid
these dangers, the borderline maintains a shallowness
in all emotional relationships. Unchecked by a normal
superego, he can all the more easily exploit and make
unreasonable demands upon others, whom he perceives,
in any case, largely as objects. The manipulation of others
is also promoted by the need to maintain control over
everything around him. Such control keeps submerged
those paranoid fears that arise from constant projection
of aggressive urges and concepts of the self. When efforts
to control are not successful or when strong wishes are
frustrated, many borderline personalities physically
withdraw from others. In this isolated state, free of in-
sistent contradictions by reality, they can evolve without
hindrance fantasies in which their wishes are gratified.

The presence of depression is an ambiguous feature
in this syndrome. Paradoxically, either the absence of
depression or its excessive manifestation may be found
in the borderline personality. Neurotic depression is
characterized by feelings of guilt and low self-esteem.
But guilt suggests the operation of an integrated superego, with standards of behavior that have been trans-

gressed. Given the poorly integrated superego, guilt is not prominent enough to produce true depression in the borderline. And since he cannot establish warm, close interpersonal relations, his reaction to the loss of a relative or an associate, for instance, is usually not a depression, but rather a sense of isolation and angry demandingness. However, since the borderline's ego is weak, a loss that greatly deprives him may overwhelm him for a time and disorganize his ego functions. He may suffer a temporary breakdown of his omnipotent and other grandiose fantasies, experience feelings of helplessness and hopelessness, and withdraw from emotional relationships of all kinds; he manifests, in short, what appears to be a brief, severe depression.

The major differences between the borderline individual and the psychotic can be recognized fairly readily: the borderline has a better integrated ego than does the psychotic. He maintains his capacity for recognition of reality except for occasional lapses in limited areas. He can differentiate between self-images and non-self-images to a greater extent since his ego boundaries are firmer than those of the psychotic. Even careful clinical examination may fail to reveal any disruption of thought processes in the borderline, so that psychological tests may have to be used to uncover primary-process thinking. In general, the borderline personality, unlike most psychotics, functions in the real world.

The ways in which the borderline disorder differs from a neurosis, however, are not so easily discerned, since the borderline patient shows typical neurotic symptoms. But these symptoms have specific features which lead the experienced examiner to suspect the more serious pathology of an underlying borderline personality. Especially indicative is a combination of the following neurotic features.

Conspicuous anxiety is one of the first indications discernible, often evident on inspection. Exploration reveals it to be chronic, diffuse, and free-floating. Since symptoms serve to cope with anxiety, when marked anxiety continues to exist in addition to other symptoms, the quantity of anxiety experienced is obviously greater than the capacity of the symptoms to relieve it.

A key symptom, ubiquitous but not always readily apparent, is marked anger. In a study of hospitalized borderline patients, Grinker, Werble, and Drye (1968) found that anger, expressed more or less directly, was the chief if not the only emotion these patients experienced. In less disturbed borderlines with better control, anger is not allowed to surface so readily, but perception of almost all other people as hostile makes anger inevitable and pervasive.

Along with markedly abnormal anxiety and anger, the addition of at least two of the following neurotic symptoms make a borderline diagnosis very likely: multiple phobias, obsessions, compulsions, and dissociative reactions.

One symptom that should particularly alert the examiner to the possibility of an underlying borderline personality disorder is polymorphous perverse sexual behavior. Indeed, bizarre forms of perversion in a person who is not psychotic are definitely indicative of the borderline syndrome.

Many narcissistic personalities have an underlying

borderline personality structure. The hypothesis here put forward is that Adolf Hitler was such a personality who also had strong paranoid trends. Most narcissistic personalities manage at least superficially adequate human relationships and ego functions, in spite of their primitive defensive operations. Those who, like Adolf Hitler, are shaped to a greater degree by the borderline personality disorder reveal the more morbid features of that syndrome. These more disturbed people function poorly in social relations; they cannot tolerate increases in anxiety; they have poor control of their impulses; and they have little capacity to divert their drives into socially acceptable channels. Easily frustrated, they have frequent outbursts of intense rage and become ever more relentlessly demanding and deprecating in their relationships.

Adolf Hitler's life, traced in the next chapters, is strikingly congruent with the pathological patterns of this syndrome. The contradictions and mysteries about him, often increased as extensive new data are published, become more understandable in light of this diagnosis.

THE LIFE RECORD

CHAPTER III

Progenitors

About his antecedents as about so much else, Adolf Hitler lied. He sometimes stated grandly that he had no family but belonged to the nation. Yet in 1930 he was driven to enough concern about one family matter, the rumor that his father's father was a Jew, to have that rumor secretly investigated. Hitler actively discouraged Nazi Party zealots from memorializing his early life. His references to family in *Mein Kampf* (1943) are the barest description of a stern but respected father and a few conventional mentions of the beloved mother. He spoke of his father as a drunkard who beat him yet falsely

27

ascribed to him the titles "Justizrat" and "Chairman of the Assizes." In describing his youth as a struggle lacking means or help, Hitler created a myth of his family history and biography.

A different understanding of the characters of his parents and of their economic status emerges from the public records of their lives and deaths and from direct testimony.

THE ANCESTRY

Although we now know more than he wanted known of Hitler's origins in the remote Austrian backcountry, the annals are short. His known ancestors were peasants, notable for their poverty even there. Many family members died young. Langer (1972) reported World-War-II Intelligence information to the effect that many were disturbed individuals. His father's line is a tangle of names and relationships, traceable definitely only on the maternal side. It starts in a tiny primitive Upper Austrian hamlet called Strones, in a family of peasant farmers and weavers. There, in 1795, was born Maria Anna Schicklgruber, one of eleven children. We know only a little more about her, but that includes the fact that at age forty-one she bore an illegitimate son, Alois Schicklgruber, the future father of the Chancellor of the Third Reich. When the little boy was five years old she married a drifter named Johann Georg Heidler, the man Alois later would claim, not as just his stepfather but as his true father. When Alois was ten his mother died.

The Nazi Party lawyer Hans Frank (1955, pp. 320–321)

in his confessional book states that on Hitler's instruc-
tions in 1930 he personally investigated a rumor that
Alois' grandfather was a Jew. Maria Anna had been, he
found, a cook for a Jewish family in Graz, and the head
of this family paid maintenance to her for fourteen years
on behalf of his young son as the putative father of her
baby. Without proof, the facts of this report remain a
mystery.

Hitler's mother was Klara Poelzl. Klara's mother belonged to the same Heidler family that Hitler's father
claimed since she was the daughter of Johann Nepomuk
Heidler, brother of Alois' stepfather Johann Georg Heidler. If Johann Georg and not the Graz Jew was in truth
Alois' father, the parents of Adolf Hitler were second
cousins.

THE FATHER

When Alois' mother died the stepfather dropped out
of sight. At that time or perhaps earlier, Alois was taken
in by Johann Georg's much more prosperous and stable
younger brother, Johann Nepomuk, to live with his family at the Heidler farm in Spital. The Heidlers treated
Alois like any illegitimate child in the village. By local
custom the illegitimate child could not expect to inherit
land. His accepted lot was a few terms of elementary
school and, if he was fortunate, some introduction to a
trade. Alois was given just that, a brief training with a
shoemaker and no more.

Alois left the home village very early in his teens. He
had learned enough there to read and write correctly;

his written German was far better than his son Adolf's
would be. He earned his own way as an apprentice cob-
bler in Vienna for a few years but as soon as he was
eighteen made a shrewd choice of a surprising vocation.
In 1855 he went to work for the Austrian Finance Ministry, in the Imperial Board of Inland Revenue of the
Customs Service, which maintained frontier guards. In
taking this step toward a new life, he found one of the
few occupations available to him to make possible a social
transformation. The job's demands were stiff for a youth
with minimal schooling, but it promised definite status.
In five years he became the equivalent of a noncom-
missioned officer in the Imperial Civil Service and
stepped out of the peasant class.

In fact, Alois lived two contrasting lives: the one
that of his work, responsible and conforming, and the
other his personal life, self-centered and uncaring. His
emphasis on the career over the personal is dramatized
in his photographs. Each memorializes an increase in
rank; none marks any of his three weddings. In nine
years Alois left the clerical grade and became an official.
He donned an officer's uniform and gained the respect
of his fellows and the privileged status he was to flaunt
for the rest of his life. Secure and, after 1875, prosperous,
Alois rose by 1892 to the highest rank permitted without
more education, "Higher Collector," roughly equivalent
to army captain.

In 1876, when he was nearly forty, he managed to
have his birth registration records changed to read that
he was the son of Johann Georg Heidler. Biographers
agree that deception was essential to accomplish this
change. Johann Georg was dead nearly twenty years, but

the priest by law had to believe him living to avow his paternity. Nearly twenty years after the name change, the ever-surprising Alois elected to retire at the unusually early age of fifty-eight. His pension and benefits provided decently for his young pregnant wife and three children; the pensions put him at about the middle of the salaried class, far above the worker category.

Alois' personal life was far less regular than his career. His relations with women were numerous and active. He had an illegitimate daughter when about thirty, the first of his nine children. He married three wives in swift succession. His active sexual relationships were sometimes concurrent. None of his three wives was near his own age. At thirty-six, he first marriage was an advantageous match with the fifty-year-old daughter of an official, a woman of means named Anna. His second and third wives were each twenty-three years younger than he. Contemporaries report that his wives were unhappy women.

Alois conducted two simultaneous extramarital affairs with teenagers while living with his wife Anna in rooms over an inn. One was with his relative Klara Poelzl, whom he brought in 1876 from Spital to Braunau as a domestic, and the other with Fanni Matzelsberger, who worked in the inn. Anna became ill early in the marriage and finally separated legally from Alois in 1880. He installed Fanni, by then nineteen, in his home and at her insistence sent Klara out of it. After Fanni bore Alois' first son in 1882, Alois legitimized the boy as Alois, Jr. When his estranged wife died in 1883 Alois did not attend her funeral. Six weeks later he married Fanni, two

months before she bore their second child. Soon Fanni
fell ill of tuberculosis, and Klara got another chance.

Alois summoned her back into his home, and they
renewed their liaison. Klara was pregnant when Fanni
died. Alois was then willing to marry Klara. Having established that his father was Johann Georg Heidler, Alois
was too closely related by blood to marry her without
a papal dispensation, which he secured without fee by
pleading poverty. His petition stressed his two moth-
erless children.

After Alois married Klara on January 7, 1885, he spent
little time in the home. Rather, he frequented the tavern
when he was not off pursuing his hobby, which was
beekeeping. After a few years Alois began to be known
by neighbors as harsh, exacting absolute obedience to
his wishes. Klara's extreme compliance and respect for
him were remarked by all. Yet increasingly she displayed
an air of great disappointment. Ten years later, even a
friend sympathetic to Alois remarked that "his wife had
nothing to smile about" (Jetzinger, 1958, p. 51).

A rupture in 1896 with his eldest son, Alois, Jr., indicates his harshness. The boy then left the home at
fourteen. Decades later his son, William Patrick Hitler,
described to American investigators his father's bitter
memories of the older Alois' brutality (Langer, 1942–43).
As William Patrick reported, "Alois, Sr., frequently beat
[Alois, Jr.] unmercifully with a hippopotamus whip. He
demanded the utmost obedience . . . every transgression was another excuse for a whipping." Brigid Hitler,
first wife of Alois, Jr., said that her husband described
his father as a man of "a very violent temper" who "often
beat the dog until the dog would . . . wet the floor. He

often beat the children, and on occasion . . . his wife, Klara." One account alleges that he once beat Alois, Jr., unconscious and once beat Adolf until he left him for dead. Some who knew him said Alois' children never dared to speak in his presence without permission and were required to address him as "Herr Vater." He would call Adolf by whistling for him as he did for his dog. Close observers interviewed by the Gestapo in 1940, not to be expected to criticize the Chancellor's father, nonetheless had negative views of his disposition. His cook testified that he was a man with a terrible temper.

Yet the town mayor insisted that Alois "never touched" Adolf, his bark being "worse than his bite." Konrad Heiden (1944), interviewing the Hitlers' neighbors during World War II, could find no substantiation of violence in the Hitler family life. Many fellow villagers had found the old man "amusing," according to American Intelligence. Alois made and kept good friends among men, one close association lasting for a quarter century until his death. The mayor of Leonding, his last home, was his friend and served as Adolf's guardian when Alois died. A younger colleague at one of his posts who enjoyed Alois and who was for a time his daily tavern companion said of him:

> Always cheerful and good company, interested in anything to do with agriculture, beekeeping was his specialty. . . . he got along well with everyone, the priest included, . . . a restless individual, always taking something up and dropping it again [Jetzinger, 1958, p. 44].

Adolf Hitler's statements about his father are also con-

tradictory: he once told his secretaries that his father
lashed him unmercifully, but that he bore the beatings
in silence. Yet he usually, though not always, mentioned
him most respectfully, as in the *Mein Kampf* story of his
struggle against his father's effort to make him a civil
servant.

Fellow workers said that Alois was efficient and devoted and filled all requirements, being especially careful
to stay on duty every required minute, rigid, precise,
even pedantic. One used the words "unsympathetic, inaccessible, hard to work with." Alois himself stressed in
his letters how hard he found the strict devotion to duty
in work where "drinkers, debtors, card players, and
other types that lead immoral lives cannot last." Evidently pompous, Alois insisted upon being addressed
with his full long title; he used it to sign personal letters
to his cousin. The heavy official at all times, Alois was
constantly acting a part, wore his uniform like a costume,
and even developed an artificial way of speaking as part
of the character he willed himself to be (Smith, 1967,
pp. 25–27).

Alois impressed his ideas forcefully upon his neighbors, and his readiness to discourse upon any subject
figures in his obituary. He was not an observing Roman
Catholic, yet he insisted that the women of his household
attend church regularly. Progressive-minded always, he
was an ardent advocate of public education and thus
opposed to the role of the Catholic church in schools.

How much Alois drank is of interest. As Chancellor,
Hitler told of being sent as a boy to bring his drunken
father home from the taverns. But the Leonding mayor
recalled the opposite, that the father often had to go

searching for the boy. He pointed out that Klara would never have dared to do such a thing as send the boy for his father. While Alois was always a regular drinker in respectable gatherings, a young crony stated flatly, "I never saw him tight, and he always started back home in good time for supper." His steady career, substantial savings, and laudatory obituary are also evidence that the father of Adolf Hitler was no sodden drunk, however regularly he imbibed. On January 3, 1903, during his usual morning visit to an inn for a glass of wine, he suddenly collapsed and died of a lung hemorrhage.

Thus, at age sixty-five, Adolf's father died a man of substance and recognized status. The epitome of the lower middle class, he left his family with real property, savings, and income. His standing was such that the province newspaper of largest circulation gave him a long laudatory obituary (Jetzinger, 1958, pp. 52–53).

THE MOTHER

Of Hitler's mother biographers can tell us less than of the father. The accounts deal gently with her; the bare outline of events in her forty-seven years of life is a litany of misfortunes. Yet its sequence suggests a personality more complex than that of the submissive sufferer.

Klara was slim, as tall as her husband, at least five feet seven. Her photograph shows regular if undistinguished features, dark hair, and notably staring light-colored eyes. Born August 12, 1860, Klara was the eldest surviving daughter of Johanna Heidler and Johann Baptiste Poelzl of Spital, a man whose misfortunes were chronic.

They lost their farm, and while they were not destitute, their house is described as poor and crowded. Only three girls among their eleven lived to maturity. One was Klara, another Johanna, born in 1863, who lived out life as a spinster, a hunchback with an irascible temper. Hitler's aunt Johanna was often present in his childhood home. A Gestapo affidavit attests that she probably was schizophrenic. The third surviving daughter married a peasant named Anton Schmidt, who prospered and kept his Spital farm holding; Adolf as a child visited them in summer.

What happened to Klara in her humble home in Spital before age fifteen is unknown, but her young life was transformed approximately in 1875 by an invitation. Her mother's relative, Customs Officer Alois Schickelgruber, asked Klara to come to help his wife in their household at Braunau, beginning a relationship that ten years later made her his bride, four months pregnant, the mistress of a household in which two active stepchildren had been born to her rival. In a few months, care of her own firstborn was added. Here one of the strongest indications that Klara had likable personal traits appears; she earned the friendship of the mother of her dead rival Fanni. The grandmother of Klara's stepchildren stood as godmother to Klara's first baby, Gustav, and later to her second child, Ida. Then came a third child, Otto, in the summer of 1887. He died within a few days and shortly thereafter both Gustav and Ida were dead of diphtheria, although Klara worked desperately to save them. Still another girl might have been conceived and born in the thirteen months between the birth of Otto and the conception of Adolf Hitler, Klara's next recorded child. But the only trace of her is the recollection of the physician who treated the family more than a decade later. He was certain than an imbecile daughter, older than Adolf and always kept hidden when he visited the Hitler home, was named Klara like her mother (Langer, 1972, p. 106). Concealed in the home and a constant worry to Klara, an afflicted child might account for a puzzling report of her behavior: her unvarying habit of hurrying home from her rounds of shopping, and, although a very friendly woman, resisting all temptations to pause for conversation (Jetzinger, 1958, pp. 51–52).

Only sixteen months after the last in her succession of losses, on April 20, 1889, Klara gave birth to Adolf Hitler in the crowded quarters. An interval of five years followed without a recorded birth, a break in the series of frequent conceptions significant for Adolf's childhood. Then in March, 1894, came a little brother, Edmund, followed in two years in 1896 by Paula. Edmund died in 1900 at the age of six, leaving only Paula and Adolf of Klara's children to grow up. Paula, described as probably retarded, lived out her life of sixty-four years as a recluse and a spinster, never connected publicly with the Nazi dictator. She died in Vienna in 1960.

Hitler's mother was only forty-two when her husband died, leaving her alone to care for the fourteen-year-old Adolf and the seven-year-old Paula and to watch over an unmarried stepdaughter of about twenty. The home she kept for Adolf, Paula, and Angela appeared to have few if any visitors in her last years, 1906 and 1907, when Adolf was a youth. Klara had almost entirely lost any personality of her own. She forgave everything but told a visitor, who called her a "wretched woman" with a sad demeanor, what a hard time she had when she was young and added that "what I hoped and dreamed of as a young girl has not been fulfilled in my marriage" (Kubizek, 1955, pp. 28, 34).

CHAPTER IV

Child and Youth
(1889–1907)

The future dictator was born into an inauspicious family situation. His mother was spent by fruitless exertions and grief for two children recently dead. Klara had reason to fear that her sickly newborn would also die. Adolf never became a robust infant, and her solicitude for him was notable. Even after he began to develop adequately physically, she continued to indulge him until her death, when he was eighteen. Klara's extreme devotion could also have been due to Adolf's monorchism or other genital anomaly or deformity, about which more will be said below. It is well known that a child's physical defect will usually elicit special solicitude and love from the mother. In *Mein Kampf* Hitler remembered his childhood as that of a "mother's darling" living in a "soft downy bed."

For Adolf's first three years his father was at home only rarely because of his long working hours, beekeeping, and tavern visits. Much alone, Klara could concentrate upon her sole surviving child. Details of her infant care are unrecorded, but her stepson and neighbors agreed that her children were always the center of her attention. His father's concerns were elsewhere. In pursuit of Alois' interests, the family made seven shifts of domicile during Adolf's childhood, the first when he was three. His father's promotion in rank meant a move, after twenty years in Braunau, to the Bavarian city of Passau. During the next eighteen months Adolf faced the stern presence of his father in the home more frequently than heretofore.

The next year Klara became pregnant again. Adolf, at five, lost his status as family baby to a brother, Edmund. The next month the father was transferred to Linz and left the family for an entire year. Adolf began a year of unrestricted rough play. He became immersed in daily war games and cowboy-and-Indian fights, an activity that totally absorbed him for at least ten years, well into his adolescence. As he grew older and his peers lost interest, he staffed his troops with younger boys. A description of Adolf before age seven comes from his older stepbrother (Gilbert, 1950, p. 18):

> He was imperious and quick to anger from childhood onward and would not listen to anyone. My stepmother always took his part. He would get the craziest notions

and get away with it. If he didn't have his way he got
very angry. . . . [H]e had no friends, took to no one and
could be very heartless. He could fly into a rage over
any triviality.

The lack of supervision ended abruptly around his sixth
birthday. The father reunited the family on a nine-acre
farm he bought in Hafeld, and Adolf began to attend the
easygoing one-room primary school a half-hour walk
away. His first teacher recalled the new pupil as pale
and sickly, very docile, and orderly. Another account
called the new boy alert and obedient, but lively. Just
as Adolf started school, his father again loomed large in
the crowded home, when he retired from duty.

As Adolf approached seven in 1896 the birth of a sister,
Paula, and additional claims on the mother increased the
stress in the home. The oldest son, Alois, Jr., fourteen
in 1896, left home after a violent controversy permanently estranged from his father. Despite the family
storms, Adolf did excellent work in his first school, a
good record which he maintained for the first five grades.

After two moves in Lambach Adolf found some
younger boys with whom to continue his constant battle
games, now to his mother's bitter anguish, as he himself
wrote. Here he also absorbed the popular and gory tales
of Karl May and became addicted to them—an addiction
which he, unlike most of the many other young devotees,
was never to outgrow. Hitler persisted all his life in
cherishing seriously the exploits of "Old Shatterhand,"
a hero who justified by Bible quotations his right to
exterminate inferior races, and followed his butcheries

of Redskins with megalomanic shouts of how great and marvelous he was.

The Hitlers moved again in 1899, to a one-story house bought in Leonding, just outside Linz. A surviving pencil drawing by Adolf at age ten indicates that again the Hitler family lived in crowded quarters. Entitled "Our Bedroom," it shows a symmetrical arrangement of two beds, mirrors, and wardrobes. The title suggests that one bedroom may have served all the children or even the entire family. His sister Paula (1959) reported a memory, probably from around 1900 when he was eleven and she perhaps five, that Adolf was wildly terrified at the thought that a girl, even a little girl, might kiss him. That that feeling went beyond the repugnance small boys allege for girls, especially their sisters, is hinted by his extreme response to the mother's frequent suggestion that Paula give him a kiss to awaken him in the morning. The request, made just loud enough for Adolf to hear, would bring the sleeping boy out of bed instantly, Paula remembered.

Signs that all was not well with Adolf became clear as he approached puberty and entered secondary school. The aging father, whose hopes now centered in Adolf, undoubtedly chose Adolf's secondary school for him. The classical *Gymnasium* was the usual route to the civil service; the technical *Realschule* offered a more modern, practical curriculum but was not the usual entree to his father's prized official status. The father's social status as an imperial official and Adolf's excellent work in primary school would also have indicated the *Gymnasium*. Hitler in *Mein Kampf* and elsewhere contended that Alois tried to force him into the civil service, but Alois' having permitted his entry into *Realschule* belies the story of a fierce struggle between them. From the beginning of his classes at the *Realschule* in nearby Linz, deterioration in his school performance was striking and never to be reversed. In *Mein Kampf* Hitler falsified this sorry school record, but the facts regarding his grades and behavior at Linz were documented by Franz Jetzinger (1958). In school five more years until age sixteen, Adolf was never able to bring his work up to standard. He dropped out of school without credentials for more advanced education. Some Linz classmates, as he complained, may have snubbed him as countrified, despite his father's respectable social standing. But all could scarcely have been "spoiled," as Adolf charged in explaining why he had no friends among them. Most important for his performance, the *Realschule* was the first level in the Austrian school system requiring sustained application of the student. Here Adolf for the first time confronted a demand that he exert himself to develop real competence.

At the time he began the first form around twelve years of age, Adolf's physical maturation was lagging, as photographs show. When his school failures began he became sullen and withdrawn from both his fellows and his family. He had to repeat the whole first year. On his second try, he just managed to get through, subject to re-examination in mathematics in the fall of 1902.

Hitler contended in *Mein Kampf* that by age twelve he had chosen painting as his metier. But although drawing was an important subject at Linz, no evidence of a commitment to an art vocation is found in grades of "excellent" for Adolf. "Good" was his best grade in art in four years there, and none of his drawings was pre-

served in the school collection of outstanding work. A
surviving drawing from age twelve reveals sexual preoccupation rather than remarkable talent. Dated September, 1900, his first month in Linz, it depicts a professor
fully dressed, holding in his right hand what appears to
be his erect penis. Werner Maser (1973), a German biographer, wrote that the teacher is holding an ice-cream
cone in his hand. The ice-cream cone, however, was
nonexistent at the time of this drawing. It first appeared
four years later, at the 1904 World's Fair in St. Louis,
as Robert Waite has noted (personal communication).

Early in 1903, when he was thirteen years and eight
months old, his father died unexpectedly. Later Hitler
claimed that this death left his family financially in need.
That this was his self-created legend of poverty is attested, among much other evidence collected by Jetzinger, by the fact that at fourteen he boarded during the
week with a Frau Sekira in Linz, an arrangement paid
for by his mother presumably to spare him the effort of
commuting. Other boarders remember him as reading
and drawing, reserved and polite, usually alone, and
never using the familiar form of address, as they did. On
weekends at home he still played the childish battle
games with younger boys or read by himself.

The adolescent of 1903 was remembered for baiting
his teachers, especially the religion teacher. Four decades later Hitler recalled the intense rage he felt toward
a priest who then taught him, a fury that made the boy
see red whenever he looked at him. Other 1903 memories Hitler reported in his *Secret Conversations* (1953)
were that he sought some sex instruction in a wax museum and that he turned away from the Christian faith

during his fourteenth year, being convinced then that one should blow up the whole show with dynamite. With less than good marks in conduct and diligence, Adolf passed to Form III only on condition of re-examination in mathematics. Hitler told an ear specialist years later that at age thirteen or fourteen his teacher's voice would sometimes seem very loud, while his head would appear bigger and bigger and seemed to be moving closer, making Adolf anxious (Waite, quoting Dr. Erwin Geissing, typescript).

During school vacations from 1903 on, Adolf's family made visits to the family farm of Klara's sister and her husband in Spital. Adolf came alone in 1908 after Klara died. His grandmother, Johanna Hiedler Poelzl, and her spinster daughter Johanna, Adolf's eccentric and crochety aunt, lived there. In Spital Adolf played with his cousins, but they remembered that he did not share their work in the fields. He was permitted by his mother and relatives to draw and read instead.

When his older half-sister, Angela, married Leo Raubal, a young assistant tax collector, the new brother-in-law pressed Adolf about his school and work plans. Adolf ignored his advice and accused him, falsely, of being a drunkard. No exhortation improved his school performance. In 1904 his Linz years came to a premature end; he was passed only on condition that his mother enroll him in a less exacting school.

The Linz school provides reports on Adolf's behavior from about twelve to fifteen. Fellow students and teachers interviewed by World War II American Intelligence testified that he never applied himself, that he usually seemed bored. He hid his Wild-West books under his desk, brought bowie knives and hatchets to school, talked "big," and tried unsuccessfully to lead the others into Indian games, but his fellows were not impressed (Langer, 1972, p. 114). The testimony of his professors at the time of his trial in the 1920s after the Munich *Putsch*, based on notes and record books as well as recollections, was surveyed by Jetzinger: "solitary," "resentful," "sullen," "uncooperative," and "hostile" were among the words used. One who taught Adolf throughout the Linz period deposed as follows:

> I can recall the gaunt, pale-faced youth pretty well. He had definite talent, though in a narrow field. But he lacked self-discipline, being notoriously cantankerous, willful, arrogant, and irascible. He had obvious difficulty in fitting in that school. Moreover he was lazy; otherwise, with his gifts he would have done very much better. In freehand sketching he had an easy, fluent style and he did well in scientific subjects. But his enthusiasm for hard work evaporated all too quickly. He acted with ill-concealed hostility to advice or reproof; at the same time, he demanding of his fellow pupils their unqualified subservience, fancying himself in the role of leader, at the same time indulging in many a less innocuous prank of a kind not uncommon amongst immature youths [Jetzinger, 1958, p. 69].

Another of Hitler's teachers said that he was not drawing on imagination but definitely remembered Hitler holding dialogues with trees stirring the wind (Jetzinger, 1958, pp. 68–69).

In *Mein Kampf*, Hitler sought political capital in two distortions of his years at *Realschule*. He wrote that at

Linz he took an important political step and became a fanatical German nationalist; he also wrote that there he learned to grasp the meaning of history. Adolf's last grade in history at Linz was "fair." A fellow-student who became a Nazi told the Party that the young Hitler had not voiced political ideas about joining organizations and was not a member of any of the numerous anti-Semitic organizations there. He did remember Adolf's calling another student "you filthy Jew" (Jetzinger, 1958, p. 71).

One direct manifestation of the fifteen-year-old's feelings in May, 1904, is a detailed account of Adolf's behavior on the day of his confirmation as a Roman Catholic, an occasion both serious and festive. His sponsor was his late father's young friend and fellow official, who with his wife gave the presents and arranged the usual celebration. (Klara asked them not to give Adolf a watch because he already possessed two.) The sponsors describe Adolf's rudeness, saying that despite the efforts and expense they went to in giving him a fine prayer book, a bank deposit, a lunch, and a drive in a carriage and pair, Adolf sulked the whole time, scowling and noncommunicative. Back at Leonding he promptly joined a group of boys who were waiting for him and charged around the house, playing Red Indians. The sponsors never heard from him again (Jetzinger, 1958, pp. 74–76).

For his term in a smaller and less exacting secondary school at Steyr, fifty miles from Leonding, Klara rented a room for him in the home of a family that boarded students. Ugly stories are in the record about his rudeness, even cruelty, to the landlady's elderly husband. Adolf called his stay "purgatory," Steyr "conservative and clerical"; again he complained that some of the students made him an outsider. A fellow pupil made a portrait sketch of him at sixteen, the only likeness from this period. He appears sickly looking, with thin cheeks and neck and untidy hair.

In the first semester at the easier Steyr school he failed three subjects, making good marks only in drawing and physical exercises. A teacher later described him as shy, withdrawn, and a bit depressed. In the spring of 1905, he rallied to achieve his first and only "excellent" in drawing in any school and improved in five subjects. But losing ground in physics and failing geometry and geometric drawing, he faced re-examination in the fall to get a completion certificate or be permitted to enter the next level of schooling.

Adolf carried this depressing realization with him when he rejoined his mother and sister and went to the homestead in Spital for the 1905 summer holiday. Here, according to his cousin, Adolf had a bout of physical illness whose nature and extent were not clear but which was serious enough to require a physician from nearby Weitra. Hitler called it a lung infection. Relatives remembered that his mother brought warm milk to his bedside each morning. By December, Dr. Eduard Bloch of Linz pronounced that Adolf showed no sign of lung trouble. But Adolf did not apply for advancement to the next school level. Rather, he left school forever. Hitler himself sounded the final note of his education: when he got his report, he went out carousing to celebrate and lost the precious paper. He stated that he was going to lie to Klara, saying that it had blown away out of the train window, but his landlady suggested that he ask the school director for another copy. The director sternly presented him with the badly soiled original, which had been found and returned. Adolf had used it for toilet paper. When he repeated the story as after-dinner conversation, Chancellor Hitler said that he still felt the humiliation (1953, p. 160).

With the petering out of his schooling, the sixteen year old did not try to move into work, either to help his mother or to support himself. He seems to have chosen a role, that of dilettante, as a full retreat from the real problems of his peers. He set himself up for reading, writing, and drawing in his room, the only private bed-chamber in a new *Humboldtstrasse* apartment taken by Klara. These activities he pursued at his whim, without supervision or challenge, for two years.

Late in 1905 he met August Kubizek, later the source of an extended close-up portrait of Hitler as an adolescent. The two youths met in the standing-room section of the Linz opera house, probably in November. They were close companions until summer, 1908, when Adolf cut off all communication without a word. Kubizek was the older by almost nine months; he had had only primary schooling and worked in his father's upholstery shop. His great interest was music; he played violin, trumpet, and trombone and worked seriously at viola lessons. By his own account, he was soon enthralled by Adolf and remained at his imperious beck and call until Adolf abandoned him. The two had no contact whatever until 1933, when Kubizek wrote Hitler three days after his appointment as Chancellor. Eight months later he got a cordial answer. After five more years of silence, Kubizek in humble admiration sought out the German

Chancellor after he took over Austria. The dictator received him, and Kubizek was thereafter invited by the Nazi Party to contribute recollections of Hitler's youth to an official biography (Jetzinger, 1958, p. 87). Long after Hitler's defeat and death, Kubizek greatly expanded that original memoir of thirty-some pages into a book entitled in English, *The Young Hitler I Knew*. In this testament Kubizek remained to the last word totally protective of Adolf Hitler. Yet he gave to history, unwittingly, abundant details of the pathological personality already evident in his idol.

Kubizek is explicit that Adolf let his mother keep him, giving the grand excuse that he was an artist. This assertion was supported largely by drawings, which after 1905 were mostly copies of pictures of buildings. Soon the two met nightly to attend the theater, to stroll the town promenade, or to seclude themselves in a rustic hideout they created on the bank of a stream, where Adolf made drawings and wrote poetry. Sometimes Adolf led restless wanderings into the early morning, although August had to rise early for his hard workday. Kubizek found that neither the countryside or the town contented Adolf. As Adolf read his poems and showed him what Kubizek called confused and confusing designs, Kubizek concluded that Adolf belonged to an exalted species: that of artists who despised work for mere livelihood. Surprised that Adolf had so much spare time, the industrious August early in their acquaintance asked him whether he had a job. The gruff and contemptuous reply was that Adolf did not consider a bread-and-butter job necessary for himself. August refrained from more questions, having found that Adolf was annoyed with any question that did not please him. Only later did Kubizek learn that Adolf was supported by his mother.

When August brought their conversation around to school, he provoked a temper outburst. Adolf was no longer concerned with school and hated both the teachers and his classmates, who were being turned into idlers by the school. But when this discussion revealed that August had not performed well in school either, Adolf evinced disapproval, a paradox that August put down as one of Adolf's ever-recurring contradictions.

Klara now managed to satisfy Adolf's luxurious tastes, including, besides regular opera-going, an impressive wardrobe. At sixteen, Adolf dressed like a man of means, invariably spruce and smart, even elegant with a broad-brimmed black hat, black kid gloves, white shirts, and black overcoats silk-lined in winter. To his two watches he now added another accessory, an ebony walking stick with a shoe-shaped ivory handle. This costume, perhaps appropriate for the opera, was hardly everyday dress for an unemployed Linz adolescent. He kept his clothing clean at all costs, partly, perhaps, because he was most sensitive about anything concerning his body. Because he was contemptuous of sports, his sole physical activity was restless walking.

Adolf was already aware that the outstanding feature of his face was his eyes. Kubizek's mother, on meeting Adolf, remarked his eyes with some fear. Others also were struck, characterizing them as "shining," "blank," "cruel," or "extraordinary."

Another attribute was what August termed extraordinary eloquence. Adolf not only liked to talk but talked without pause; indeed, he had to talk. The portrait is also full of observations of Adolf's anger. Terms such as "red with rage," "exceedingly violent and high-strung," "furious," "temptestuous feelings," and "like a volcano erupting," form a conspicuous thread running through these memories. Compulsive speech was both the expression of his anger and the safety valve for his tensions. The effect on his gentle audience of one was hypnotic, as it would be on other audiences later.

As his father had required, Adolf always used the full title of a person in speaking to him. He adhered strictly to correct behavior toward those in whose good graces he wanted to remain and punctiliously observed social rules when it suited his purpose. Adolf also always held himself straight, reminiscent of his father in uniform. To Kubizek, rigid inflexibility seemed Adolf's outstanding character trait. He explains that because of Adolf's "inflexible nature" he simply could not avoid adding to his mother's burdens, despite great grief at her worry. As though realizing that the behavior he described belied his contention, Kubizek chose phrasing that seems unduly strong, swearing before God that Adolf really loved his mother.

Adolf's attitude toward people generally was a riddle. He rarely spoke about his family, saying that it was well not to mix too much with grown-ups. Their peculiar ideas—such as his guardian's outlandish idea that he ought to learn a craft—would only divert one from one's plans. His opinion of contemporaries was no better, and his rage was less controlled with them. Once, when a former classmate greeted him and asked cordially how he was getting on, Adolf became red with rage, pushed the baffled young man sharply, and continued on with

August. On another occasion Adolf became violently agitated upon seeing some young men through the win-
dows of a café, charging that they were exhibiting
themselves and wasting time in idle gossip. Kubizek specifically noted how much Adolf's indignation was contradicted by his own life and that some of those
denounced may have been, unlike Adolf, gainfully employed.

August frequently referred to his friend's turbulent
nature and tensions. An aid to Adolf in enduring these
appears to have been Wagner's music, with which he
had become acquainted at about age thirteen, and which
was to move him profoundly all his life. Wagner seemed
to stimulate grandiose fantasies in him. Kubizek devoted
a chapter to this effect in which he described Hitler's
response to the first performance he had heard of *Rienzi*.
After the performance, the story went, Adolf strode to
a peak near the town and in a trancelike state poured
forth a torrent of words identifying himself with the hero
as a political leader. In reality, however, he undertook
no political activity for at least fifteen years after the
display.

Young Adolf gave his daytime hours at home to drawings of buildings, a mania for imaginary building that
received two chapters from Kubizek. As the two youths
strolled through Linz, all quiet and harmony, Adolf
would suddenly be seized by a passion to change everything in sight. Later he expressed the same angry urges
to remake Vienna, and ultimately, parts of Berlin. Once
Adolf conceived an idea, he was like one possessed. The
fantasied reconstructions were so real to him that his
hearer also confused fact and fantasy. Yet Kubizek saw

that Adolf was totally unrealistic about limits to his capabilities or proper concerns when he took as his responsibility everything built and every defect he found in society. Hitler's memories included one reported in his dinner-table discourses in the 1940s: that he was at fifteen already so original a thinker that he began to "dictate" (*sic*) a play about divorce reform to his sister. If the report is true, the family as well as Kubizek fed his sense of uniqueness and limitless scope.

Adolf's ideas and projects were prodigies of originality to his worshiper, who marveled that some were later realized. In addition to ideas for structures, Adolf had an idea for what is now called a "living museum," with a permanent population recreating the costumes, trades, and activities of the past. Another idea was for a non-alcoholic "people's drink," because he detested the lack of control alcohol induces. His grand plans were in his fantasy realized as soon as he "roughed them in" and thought them through.

In May of 1906 Adolf first saw the buildings of Vienna, when Klara treated him to a four-week sightseeing holiday. He sent four postmarked picture postcards to Kubizek which meticulously included polite greetings to his parents but contained many errors in spelling and grammar. The Vienna stay may have cost Klara more than a month's income. After the summer holiday in Spital, Klara bought Adolf a costly piano and engaged a private teacher for him. But practice soon bored him, and although Adolf's memory for music was remarkable, Kubizek considered him incapable of playing an instrument.

Back in Linz, Adolf's fantasy teemed with new projects for rebuilding the town and one for designing a huge national monument. Asked how he proposed to finance it, he gave as solution the purchase of a lottery ticket. For Adolf, winning was a certainty from the moment he bought the ticket, even in the face of his careful calculations of his slim chances. His sole problem was how he could spend the winnings. Abandoning his plans for the monument, he decided he and Kubizek would spend the money on themselves and he spun an elaborate fantasy, so vivid and detailed that its realization was unquestionable to both. For their new life on their winnings, Adolf had an idea delightful to his admirer: they would dress exactly alike, so that people would take them for brothers. It should be recalled that Adolf's nickname for August Kubizek was Gustl, actually the nickname for Gustav, which was Adolf's brother's name. When the day of the drawing ended his fantastic dream, Adolf was in a rage rare in intensity even for him, furious at the state lottery, the state, and the entire Hapsburg dynasty, never reproaching himself for assuming the prize was already his. The shock threw Adolf briefly into what seemed to be a deep depression. For the first time Adolf's willpower had failed him, something far worse than the loss of all he planned. When he emerged from gloom, he resumed his grand designs for projects, still ignoring their financing.

During these months Adolf was immersed in another vivid and extended fantasy, an entirely imaginary love affair from afar with a young woman of Linz to whom he never spoke a word. Kubizek's novelistic account of Adolf's love for this "Stefanie" (a pseudonym) is the only trace of interest in a girl during Hitler's youth (Kubizek, 1955, pp. 56–69). It began one spring evening as the two

youths were taking their usual stroll along the Linz promenade. Among the customary pleasures was flirting, at
which young army officers were particularly successful.
Adolf suddenly announced that he was in love with a
slim blonde girl walking with her mother. The two youths
thereafter stood waiting for her every day. When the two
ladies were accompanied by young officers, Adolf gave
vent to jealous rage, quickly generalized into enmity
toward the whole officer class.

As the months passed no words were exchanged, but
Adolf insisted that he and Stefanie communicated without them, even on complex matters, because what was
"in him" was also in her. He was sure that she deliberately masked tempestuous feelings for him by pre-
tending attention to the officers. When Kubizek discovered
that she liked dancing, Adolf was equally sure that she
would not care to dance once she became his wife. Certain that her sole wish was to await his proposal, he drew
up a plan to ask her for her hand in four years. But when
Stefanie's glance did not seem to fall his way for some
time, he shifted to a plot to kidnap her with Kubizek's
help. Kubizek's question of how the pair would live sob-
ered him, and he dropped the kidnap idea for a detailed
scheme to kill himself and have Stefanie die with him.
The suicide-murder was forgotten as soon as she happened to look again in his direction. He began at once
to design a house for her. In a short time the fantasy
ended. Adolf and Stefanie never met.

An even more bizarre fantasy was a search for actual
memories of centuries-old events in living people. On
more than one visit to the site of an historic battlefield
Adolf questioned residents, expecting confidently to find

in them traces of actual memories of a great battle of the Peasants' War hundreds of years before.

The terminal illness of Adolf's mother was manifest by January, 1907, and Dr. Bloch's diagnosis of breast cancer led to immediate surgery. In May the ailing mother moved the Hitler family to the Linz suburb of Urfahr, taking an apartment on the first floor. Adolf's aunt Johanna stayed with them again to look after Paula, now eleven, and kindly neighbors interested themselves in Klara's situation. Adolf began to be depressed, inaccessible, and distant to Kubizek and often wandered alone in the countryside. He said that he didn't know what was wrong with him, not mentioning his mother's grave state. Then he announced that he must leave Linz and urged Kubizek to move with him to Vienna. He secured his mother's agreement to apply for the small personal legacy of over six hundred kronen left him by his father so that he could study at the Academy of Art in the capital. His mother was pleased that he would be in a school of some kind, although a career in the arts seemed to her frivolous and insecure. By this time she was in the last months of her life and in extreme pain.

In September Adolf departed, with an extensive wardrobe provided by Klara and an additional twenty-five kronen each month in pension, a substantial increase in his resources for the year. No one heard from him for more than two weeks. The usually unprotesting mother expressed her worry and complained to Kubizek that Adolf went his way as if he were alone in the world. Yet although she had been advised to enter the hospital, she did not want Adolf to be told or taken away from his hard work at the Art Academy.

Actually the eighteen-year-old Adolf was not the art-academy student she believed him to be. He had failed the 1907 examination for admission. He sought an interview with the director to learn why his test drawing was rated unsatisfactory and was told that he lacked the talent necessary to be a painter and should instead apply for architecture. Adolf said later that he accepted that idea in a few days. But he did not face up to the elementary realities of preparing for the profession. His solution was another flight. He simply retreated to his lodgings and told no one. He went on with his self-directed "studies" as though nothing had happened.

These activities and his excursions around Vienna ceased only upon word from Linz of his mother's grave state. Accounts of his actions conflict. Kubizek alleged that Adolf returned to Linz at least three weeks before Klara's death and became a paragon of service to her in her suffering. He wrote, too, that when Adolf was informed that his mother suffered from an incurable disease, in a characteristic transformation of personal anger into a general charge, he exclaimed that it was not that his mother had an incurable disease but that the doctors were not capable of curing it. In fact, the family physician, Dr. Bloch, a Jew, was admired as an excellent physician and a man of great kindness who sacrificed himself for his patients, especially the poor. Dr. Bloch wrote later in an American magazine that Adolf was in Linz with his mother when she died and that the youth drew a portrait of her dead face (Bloch, 1941, p. 37). To the contrary, Adolf's presence with his dying mother was denied by witnesses in Jetzinger's personal investigation in Urfahr and is belied by a neighbor's account quoted by Smith (1967, p. 110f.) to the effect that she and Johanna alone nursed Klara; she pitied the son because he arrived too late.

Whatever the facts of his presence or absence, Adolf was eighteen years and eight months old when his mother died on December 21, 1907. Dr. Bloch described his grief as the greatest he ever saw in a son for a mother. The physician cited this unusual degree of feeling as the explanation for having kept in his files for decades the cards and letters of thanks he received from Adolf Hitler. Adolf claimed that the death left him with no one to help him. Kubizek revealed his contrary perception: that Adolf's isolation was self-imposed. Several people, in fact, offered concrete help as well as guidance. He was not homeless during his mourning; Aunt Johanna continued to run the household while the heirs made their plans and pension applications. *Mein Kampf* describes a quick decision made under pressure of poverty. Actually, Adolf was secure and knew his intent; he remained in the Urfahr apartment until at least mid-February, 1908.

No will is recorded; Klara must have divided her assets into gifts to avoid inheritance taxes. Adolf's likely share, in addition to his capital, was not less than five hundred kronen, and perhaps as much as a thousand, according to Jetzinger. Beyond this, Adolf was entitled to part of the regular orphans' stipend and applied for it on February 10. The amount of this payment is a matter of public record. Together, Paula and Adolf were to have fifty kronen per month until the elder was either self-supporting or reached age twenty-four. Thereafter only twenty-five kronen monthly would come to the younger

child; until then the pension authorities left the division
of the monthly payment to their guardian. He assigned
one half to each, apparently on the assumption that Adolf
was an active student at the Art Academy and would
need income (Jetzinger, 1958, p. 110). Far from destitute, Adolf in the year 1908 thus had a lump sum from
his mother's funds plus his patrimony and the regular
monthly payment. The last two items alone gave him an
income equal to that of a junior barrister.

Adolf moved promptly to escape forever from his work-
aday relatives. For his continued charade of a life in art,
he wanted his faithful audience to accompany him to
Vienna. He forcefully, even rudely, persuaded August
to put aside the upholstery trade and come to Vienna to
study music and persuaded the senior Kubizeks to agree.
Adolf went to the capital and impatiently waited for Kubizek's arrival.

Elegantly dressed, Adolf met the travel-weary Kubizek at the station, ate the feast he brought, and then
forced him out into the dark cold mist to view Vienna's
scarcely visible glories until early the next morning. This
was the first of many incidents of thoughtlessness Kubizek recounted, as though oblivious of their implications.

In their small rented room, Adolf slept late every day
while August left early for the Academy of Music. Their
life was one of stringent economy. Adolf never confided
the actual facts of his income, and August's allowance
was small. Their expenses were large, not because of
rent or food, but because they attended the theater or
opera almost every night. August as a registered music
student could get free or low-cost concert tickets, but

theater and opera were expensive because Adolf insisted on the pit, where women were not allowed. Cheap meal tickets were available for the university canteen through Kubizek, but Adolf's use of them was delayed because the student body included a few Jews. Their very presence was enough to keep Adolf away until his great love of the canteen's nut cakes overcame his anti-Semitism. Kubizek was explicit about Hitler's attitude toward Jews. Adolf's anti-Semitism was already confirmed when they first met in Linz. He regarded as false Hitler's implication in *Mein Kampf* that only his experiences with the many Jews of Vienna made him an anti-Semite and insisted that Hitler's father was an anti-Semite, not the cosmopolitan liberal Hitler depicted. Hitler was a woman-hater, too. When a woman music student being tutored by Kubizek came to the youths' quarters for help with a written assignment, Adolf, infuriated, did not even acknowledge his introduction to her. She was hardly outside when he went after August wildly, first objecting to women music students spoiling their room and finally to women studying at all.

Music for Adolf seemed limited. Wagnerian operas, which reinforced his fantasies of grandiosity and omnipotence, pleased him; his favorite opera was *Lohengrin*. (The composer called its hero a symbol of the man who seeks the woman who would love him with an unconditional love.) Non-German music, such as Italian operas, he consistently denigrated. Toward books, Adolf's attitude was the same as his attitude toward the world in general: he was a seeker only for confirmation of ideas he already had. He could tolerate nothing, according to Kubizek, that might put him to the test. Kubizek's suc-

cess with music gained him entree to the houses of cultivated families, to which he took Adolf. But Adolf
preserved a rude silence at these gatherings and came
to be considered an eccentric, presumptuous and arrogant. Kubizek insisted that despite Adolf's refusal of so-
ciability and his misogyny he was most attractive to
women of all kinds. Adolf, he said, was absolutely normal
in physical as well as sexual respects, his abstinence from
all sexual activity, including masturbation, the result of
high-minded and complete self-control. Yet he concluded by wondering what it was that held young Adolf
back from doing what was normal for others.

Sexual subjects produced many lofty moralizing hom-
ilies from Adolf. But his fascination with prostitution led
him to take Kubizek late one night to explore the pros-
titutes' district, not once but twice. Adolf also deplored
homosexuality, a subject new to Kubizek but not to
Adolf. The two once accepted a stranger's invitation to
supper, but Adolf afterward scorned his sexual proposition, declaring that he had known all along the man
was a homosexual.

One day Adolf exploded in a diatribe against the Art
Academy, his eyes full of hate. The outburst was followed
by the first admission that he was not studying there. As
he furiously cursed its bureaucracy for not understanding
true artistry, he said that tripwires had been cunningly
laid to ruin his career. Adolf even turned his friend's
progress in music into a conspiracy against him; he said
that he could not earn any money. To every suggestion
as to ways he might earn money, perhaps doing illustrations for a publisher or a newspaper or writing drama
reviews, Adolf found objections. An especially furious

refusal came when a possible employer suggested to him proved to be a Jew. Feeling persecuted, Hitler persisted only at his self-training in drawings of architecture, avoiding any contact with practical steps toward that profession. In Vienna in the spring of 1908 he translated every problem of whatever kind into a political one, insisting, even more than he had earlier, that the most difficult problems became easy when transferred to the political plane. He had discovered the Austrian Parliament and often dragged August there to listen to debates, frequently not understandable to either of them. But this intense political interest had no practical focus at the time.

The sole political idea in relation to which Adolf took a positive step in his teens was anti-Semitism. Adolf stated often that he was a convinced follower of the brutal anti-Semite politician Georg von Schoenerer and admired the skillfully anti-Semitic mayor of Vienna, Karl Lueger. One day in that spring of 1908 Adolf came to the youths' room with a startling announcement. He had that day actually joined the Anti-Semite Union and gratuitously had also enrolled Kubizek's name.

As the spring of 1908 came, Kubizek was increasingly puzzled by Adolf's self-imposed ·isolation and his demands for Gustl's exclusive attention. The disorganization of Adolf's activities alarmed him but he was too cowed to protest. Adolf became uncharacteristically self-critical, then suddenly in a "crazed" manner changed his self-accusations into accusations against everything and everybody: mankind did not understand him and persecuted him. Kubizek feared for Adolf's sanity. By summer August's marked success at the Music Academy was in sharp contrast to Adolf's total failure to advance. Adolf's intense envy did not escape his friend, but he excused it.

The two youths made specific plans to continue their joint living arrangement in the autumn when they would both return. August assured their landlady that whatever happened, he would remain with Adolf as her tenant, and Adolf went off to his family at Spital as usual. Kubizek kept the brief letters and postcards he received that summer from Adolf. They were bitter in tone, with complaints about hard work and irritation directed at his little sister Paula, bedbugs, an attack of "bronchial catarrh," and the stupidity of the Linz city fathers. Then silence. Having notified Adolf, Kubizek returned to Vienna on November 20, 1908, expecting Adolf to meet him at the station as always before. But Adolf was not there. Adolf had moved out of their room, with no word about his new quarters and no message for the devoted August, now deserted.

CHAPTER V

Young Adult
(1908–1918)

When Adolf returned to Vienna, nineteen years old, he had done no paid work or systematic study, completed none of his projects, begun no career. His military responsibility loomed, demanding that he face up to the necessity to take orders from superiors. Sexual drives had been repressed for some time. His several inheritances steadily drained away in daily expenses. Still he persisted in isolation; according to his sisters he turned away from them for years. For the next six years, the period he later called his unhappiest, history has no close chronicler like Kubizek. The writings and depositions of witnesses drawn together by Smith (1967) and police, court, Art Academy, and Austrian Army documents collected by Jetzinger (1958) are the sources here.

Adolf applied to the Academy of Art once again. In October, 1908, the notation with his name is "Not admitted to examination." Regulations permitted special admission for those showing marked talent but lacking a school leaving certificate. His excuse that he lacked only the paper credentials is untrue. His deterioration thereafter was rapid. With his self-esteem so damaged, he could not long sustain his old fantasy of the artist's life in the nineteenth-century style. He relinquished the designation "artist" in his 1908 police registration, substituting "student." This "student" stayed holed up alone in a rented room with no visible occupation, seldom leaving the house, until August of 1909. Hitler in *Mein Kampf* claimed that he worked as a laborer in Vienna, suggesting misery; he described the hovels of laborers as making him shudder with horror at the memory. The facts are that Adolf was still too prosperous in early 1909 to resort to manual labor and that he consistently avoided it later.

During this solitary period Hitler did find an approach to life and society acceptable to him, probably on a nearby newsstand: a magazine called *Ostara*, a melange of the mystical, occult, and erotic, full of explicit racist propositions, the creation of one Joseph Lanz. *Ostara's* message was that any Aryan is a hero by right of blood. *Ostara* gave the Aryan a single enemy responsible for all his trouble: the dark, hairy, ape-man. Noble blonde and blue-eyed Aryan heroes struggled with them, especially to protect the Aryan females, carriers of the

Aryan blood. Their all-powerful female sexuality made them vulnerable to the dark and potent menacers. Notions such as these were supported by occult elements drawn from old Germanic magic spells and a form of number mysticism. Lurid illustrations made vivid the perils of the heroic blonde Aryan woman. Adolf bought the magazine regularly and during 1909 sought out the publisher personally to complete a collection of back issues, which he carried with him to at least three new homes.

Hitler later outdid this thinker; he came to feel that Lanz equivocated about Jews and was not firm enough about German nationalism. The magazine probably led Adolf to the ideas of Guido Von List, a theoretician who justified German ascendancy with a special version of ancient history and with racial anti-Semitism. Adolf also seemed to have dipped into the abundant religious literature on anti-Semitism and race at hand for anyone in Vienna. During his last period of subsidized leisure, the twenty-year-old probably pieced together from these fragments his lifelong personal philosophy.

That poverty was impending seems to have dawned upon him; this was probably when he began to pawn his clothes. Two moves to rented rooms and the shift to "writer" as his occupation appear in his police registration in late 1909. These are the months when Adolf Hitler should have registered for military service with the age group born in 1889. Adolf ignored the notices posted on every street corner. Required military service may have been among the factors soon to render him almost totally incompetent. Before the year ended, he could not meet

his most basic necessaries; his inheritance was used up
and he did not seek work to supplement it.

After only a year of solitary pretense at being an artist-
prince, Adolf Hitler became a denizen of Vienna's flop-
houses and residences for homeless men. In the unusually cold, wet November of 1909, at age twenty, he
was a homeless vagrant said to have begged and slept
in the streets and huddled in public warming rooms. He
was remembered as remarkably deteriorated physically
and emotionally, pale, thin, unshaven, with sunken
cheeks and very bad feet. His fellow vagrants saw him
as extremely shy, almost crawling, with jerky movements. His wardrobe and possessions gone, he had no
coat. What use he made in late 1909 and through 1910
of the monthly pension, enough for basic food, is a mystery.

He lined up seeking shelter in a new, large flophouse
despite its Jewish philanthropic auspices. It gave tran-
sients sleeping space, providing fumigation and a wire
cot for five nights. Here he was exposed to the enforced
camaraderie of the destitute, some of them experienced
tramps; he was in close contact with a group of strangers
for the first time in his life. According to one of the
experienced vagrants, young Adolf was by this time half
dead, so battered that he elicited spontaneous help and
protection from his fellows. They shared with him and
taught him about the bread lines and soup kitchens and
buying unused portions of dormitory cards to circumvent
the rules and remain longer.

Reinhold Hanisch, a vagrant then using the name
"Fritz Walter," took hold of Adolf. This man, four years
older, lent his abundant energy and aggression to the

lethargic youth. Hanisch wrote later that Adolf said he did not know what he wanted to do with his life, so great was his helplessness and despair, a report the diametric opposite of Hitler's later description of his resolute and purposive view. In the bitter winter of 1909–1910, the two developed a system for surviving together, confirmed by the accounts of other derelicts. Hanisch reported that Adolf was too weak to haul luggage or shovel snow, the casual work they first sought. Moreover, even in such straits, Adolf resisted hard manual labor and sometimes simply refused to look for work at all. Hanisch said he constantly worried about Adolf, especially about his health. He questioned his protégé closely about any work he knew how to do and learned about his "painting." Disappointed that it was not house painting, Hanisch rallied with a way to make them some money from little watercolor pictures Adolf would paint and Hanisch would peddle as postcards. The indications are that at his insistence Adolf wrote to his aunt, Johanna Poelzl, for money for his "studies" and received fifty kronen by mail. Hanisch said part went for art supplies and part for a warm overcoat from the government pawnshop, since Adolf feared being cheated in the Jewish shops. Because the flophouse provided no place to work on the postcards, after two months they moved to a model institution providing minimal housing for single men. Adolf Hitler's home for the next three years, this Men's Hostel was not mentioned in his account in *Mein Kampf*. In its dayroom he painstakingly copied the popular scenes of Vienna from photographs on postcards using a grid he devised to transfer the shapes. The limits of his ability in drawing made him avoid human figures, and his style was stiff,

fussy, and detailed. "Fritz" hawked his work in the cheap
taverns and at fairs. Little pictures placed in frames or
sized to be fitted into wood frames taken from the backs
of sofas and chairs proved more profitable, although Adolf
could not draw angels or goddesses, motifs that would
have sold especially well.

Descriptions of Adolf's appearance in the spring of
1910 mention whiskers, long hair, greasy derby hat, and
a shirt notoriously dirty even among the destitute. His
meticulousness of the Kubizek period gone, he was once
in danger of expulsion from the Hostel as too unkempt.
He still had an evasive manner and was described as shy,
never looking a person in the eye. The sole exception
was during ecstasies when he talked politics.

He claimed later that he read widely and deeply at
this time, but in fact his interests were in unrelated
subjects picked up and abandoned: ancient Roman history, Eastern religions, yoga, the occult, hypnotism, and
astrology. Only newspapers sustained his interest. The
Deutsches Volksblatt earned mention in *Mein Kampf* as
part of his transformation into an anti-Semite. That publication notoriously exemplified the strong pornographic
element in Viennese anti-Semitism. Adolf admired the
successes of Vienna's anti-Semitic mayor, Karl Lueger,
who used the Jew as scapegoat to exploit the anxieties
of classes most threatened in the changing society. Hitler
later adopted a Lueger principle that politics is the art
of using human weaknesses. Hitler later also praised and
emulated Lueger's example of marshalling existing institutions, especially power blocs, on his side, and he
adopted his use of emotional slogans and humanitarian
platitudes about the little man.

But Adolf soon found Lueger's brand of anti-Semitism too "indulgent," too feeble, just as he had come to find that of Lanz inadequate. He preferred the ideas of the aged Pan-German Nationalist Georg von Schoenerer, although he was in decline as Adolf gathered his bag of political notions at the Men's Hostel. Adolf cherished Schoenerer's vicious, maniacal hatred of the Jews and responded fully to its frank racial basis and emphasis on blood. Two framed Schoenerer mottoes are said to have hung over Hitler's Hostel bed.

Among the Vienna derelicts a new captive audience served him to release his raging hates: the House of Hapsburg, Marxists, Social Democrats, Slavs and members of other minorities in the empire, as well as Jews. Waiting in line at soup kitchens, he would erupt with heated diatribes expressing these feelings as ideas. In the Hostel his shouting and arm waving sometimes caused the porter to intervene. The Hostel director remembered Adolf Hitler as one of the oddest residents. The word "odd" also turns up to describe the respect accorded him by some lodgers: others laughed at him, and many considered him a fanatic. He would cite his late father as authority on disputed points. He brooked no contradiction but lost control and showered abuse on any who attempted discussion. He was incapable of reasonable debate, as he was of ordinary companionship. If he could not dominate an argument, his wrath would be followed by sullen silence. His irritability and hatreds caused the atmosphere around him to be uncomfortable, even hostile.

An experience that affected him deeply was viewing a huge Social Democratic Party parade. He recognized

at once the emotional power of planned mass demon-
strations. He credited that detested party with mastery
of political control through showmanship and later
frankly used the model.

In early 1910, as he attained his majority, his actual
activity was directed toward schemes for milking the
public with worthless products and making vulgar advertising posters. He dreamed of grand marketing
schemes, based upon the idea that human susceptibility
is so great that anything can be promoted. Toward summer in 1910, Adolf's manager found that the lazy artist,
unless he needed money for cream cakes, greatly preferred newspaper reading to painting. His fellows noted
that his ambitious plans, demands for attention, and
spurts of energy alternated with indolence, withdrawals,
and short disappearances. One of those disappearances
involved a brief episode with a part-time art dealer and
old-clothes seller, a Hungarian Jew. This Josef Neumann, who shared Adolf's interest in things German,
had given Adolf an old black overcoat that became his
trademark. Despite his anti-Semitic outpourings, on
June 21 Adolf actually left the Hostel and rented a hotel
room with Neumann, but after five days returned out
of money, ready to resume his partnership with Hanisch.

The end of that fragile relationship came soon. Hitler
attempted a fairly large picture of the neoclassic Parliament Building. The price it brought was later verified
as ten kronen, divided with Adolf as usual, but Hitler
alleged that Hanisch got much more and pocketed the
difference. In his first formally recorded act as an adult,
Adolf Hitler turned on his protector and, knowing Hanisch's dread of the police, had him arrested. By exposing

Hanisch for living under an assumed name, he brought the man who may well have saved his life a few days in jail. It had no practical issue for Hitler himself.

Alone, Hitler that autumn resumed his dreary picture-production routine at the Hostel, now selling his work himself. He expended very little energy and accepted very low prices, often three or four kronen. Most of his paintings were bought by just two dealers, both Jews; two other regular customers were also Jews. For nearly three more years—into 1913—he confined his world to the Hostel and his life to this low level of output and aspiration. Working alone was more profitable than the partnership. One of the dealers reported that his appearance greatly improved and that his clothes, though old and worn, were always clean and neat. But through these years of his young manhood Hitler chose to remain in the very cheap and almost monastic Hostel.

Adolf may well have had three thousand kronen from his aunt Johanna Poelzl during this parsimony, as Jetzinger established by investigating her bank account and public records in Spital. Within two months of her death in March, 1911, a court in Linz assigned Adolf's share of his father's pension to his younger sister, because he had received considerable sums of money for his art training from his aunt. By early 1913, Adolf began to talk about great plans for a future in Munich, plans that included attending the Art Academy there, which Johanna's bequest could have funded. A reason he did not avow would have sufficed, however: he was in violation of the Austrian requirement of military service. He had avoided the matter since late 1909 but was still subject to induction.

At twenty-four Adolf abandoned Vienna, but he was to carry with him some of his responses to it for the rest of his life. He would long rail against what he called Vienna's hybrid quality and yet also paradoxically call it the embodiment of incest, certainly the opposite of hybridization. One aspect of Vienna in the earliest years of the twentieth century he eschewed completely: the revolutionary changes then emerging in all the arts. Hitler claimed to have learned all he would ever need in the "hard school" of his Vienna years, without, of course, mentioning that he had ever been a lodger in such an institution as the Men's Hostel. The historian Bullock (1958) and the biographer Fest (1970, 1973, 1974) have stressed one theme he averred lifelong after his stay there among the destitute: a crude notion of Darwin's survival of the fittest, applied to society and used to justify any harsh means.

Hitler began his life in Germany with a lie. In Munich he registered himself as "stateless," not Austrian. He now grandly stated his occupation to be that of "painter and writer." Later, in *Mein Kampf*, he would lie to the effect that he had emigrated a year earlier, and he would prevaricate elaborately and self-servingly with the claim that his reasons were primarily political. The personal reason for flight that he concealed was that by 1913 the Austrian military might well be on his trail. In fact, seven months after he crossed the border, police appeared at his door to arrest him.

In the interval, however, he played a new role in a new scene as an artist-Bohemian political philosopher. Commentators note that a sense of a vocation in politics would have led him straight to Berlin rather than to

Munich, "The City of the Muses." In Schwabing, then a poor Munich suburb with many taverns, tolerant of eccentricity, he found a room over the tailor shop of Josef Popp. There he lived in quiet isolation; "studious" was the description Frau Popp gave later to researchers assigned to investigate Hitler's early years by the Nazis. The Popp family was never intimate with their tenant, but Josef Popp received some of the very few letters Hitler wrote during World War I. The Chancellor had an aide trace the family in 1935 and arranged a small stipend for the surviving widow.

Adolf at the age of twenty-five again barely eked out a living, according to his tax report, most of it from making advertising posters. He pored over newspapers in beer halls and cafés and became known in the cheaper cellars for periodic outbursts of extreme but popular prejudices, readily acceptable to an audience described as prone to relish calamities and welcome saviors. Again, acquaintances describe him as sickly, haggard, frightened in manner. No indication is found that, as he later alleged, he seriously tried to find a job with a well-known architectural-design firm. Rather, he drifted as before. And in Munich he was again oblivious of the contemporary ferment in the arts so close to him.

On January 18, 1914, Hitler was arrested by the Munich police as a deserter from the Austrian Army. He then wrote a long letter of apology to the authorities, setting forth excuses for failure to report. It was forwarded with a mysterious note from the Austrian Consul, who made a plea for leniency in terms still unexplained: "he claims to be suffering from a complaint which rendered him unfit for military service and at the same time removed all motive for evading it." The burden of Hitler's own letter of excuse was his extreme poverty. Moreover, he contended, without support, that he did request registration in Vienna in February, 1910 but through error was somehow overlooked. The upshot was that Adolf was twice lucky: he was allowed to report to nearby Salzburg and found too weak to bear arms even unfit for auxiliary duties (Jetzinger, 1958, pp. 146–155).

Only a few months later, at the outbreak of World War I, he petitioned the King of Bavaria to be accepted as a volunteer in the German Army. The onset of the war, Hitler wrote, was a release from the painful feelings of his youth. In actuality the war promised to solve his problems of failure, frustration, and lack of status. And further, fighting, and especially the German Army, had been the center of his admiration since childhood, when he pored over its exploits, saying he felt them to the depths of his being. Three days later he was in the Sixteenth Bavarian Infantry Regiment, a unit made up largely of volunteers like himself, many of them university students and many considered the flower of Bavaria's intellectual youth. He was there exposed for the first time to men of status and education superior to his own. His wish for combat was soon realized. The regiment, rushed into action, became renowned for shocking losses.

In ten weeks, Hitler was under heavy fire. He wrote at great length of his zest for the slaughter in a letter in which he also announced that he had already received the Iron Cross Third Class. The letter's many pages, full of detail if not quite accurate historically, dwelt upon wounds, deaths, corpses all about him, sounds of gun and artillery, struggles of men hand to hand, dirt, even a decaying horse. He recounted without a trace of mourning the reduction of 3,500 men to 600. No fear was expressed, only an excited enjoyment and a confidence in his miraculous protection that grew even stronger. A later letter concluded with the political, the hope that this "stream of blood" will not only "crush" (*sic*) Germany's enemies but also break "our internal internationalism." In a twelve-page communication to an acquaintance, a lawyer named Ernst Hepp, he reiterated fears of the enemies on his old list. The letter contained a rare expression of attachment, albeit an impersonal one, to another human being. He wrote that "we worshipped Lieutenant Colonel Engelhardt," evidence of his reported extreme though short-lived respect for officers during the early part of his army years (Payne, 1973, pp. 109–111, p. 112; Toland, 1976, p. 60; Waite, 1977, p. 201).

Hitler was set apart from his fellows, or set himself apart, in many ways. He was older than many recruits. He gave himself the exalted and unusual occupation of "architectural painter" when asked as to his work. He had no home ties and admitted he did not know what had become of his sister. He received very little mail, renounced his furloughs, shared neither the soldiers' worries nor their amusements, cared nothing for women. He followed every military regulation with pedantic rigidity and was so obliging to officers that he was at first thought to be bucking for stripes. Worse, he never complained; he was sometimes cursed for eschewing griping, the soldier's safety valve. As isolated as ever, he was consistently described by fellow recruits as odd, brood-

ing, eccentric, strained looking, even crazy, a pipe drea-
mer, a "white crow." In a memoir published in 1931, an
orderly named Hans Mend remembered Adolf as "apart"
from the rest. His only manifestation of humor was an
occasional bizarre mockery of another. He refused to
share amusements or delicacies from home, would sit
"unreachable in thought" in the dugout. He might leap
up suddenly to run around in an excited harangue that
ended in an equally sudden return to withdrawn silence.

Other conspicuous ideas and feelings setting Hitler
apart were a certain Puritanism, a contempt for physical
comforts, and late in the war a scorn for his superior
officers, both high and low. And always his hates: he
hated Masons, and he hated Jews most wrathfully. When
his comrades laughed at his anti-Semitism, he told them
that he would rule over them all and get rid of the Jews.
The warm feelings of fellowship of the front that Hitler
often cited during his rise to power were not in fact his.
That he held apart from the others is shown in his position
and his posture in extant photographs of his military
group. Yet at the pinnacle of his achievement and to the
end of his life, Adolf Hitler chose for his preferred re-
laxation the ways of the barracks and barracks company.
It was in the army at war that Hitler found a role at last.
Quite literally, he was at home there; he had no other
home address. He said decades later that the only period
in his life when he had no worries was his six years as
a soldier (Hitler, 1953, p. 45). Most basic, the quarter-
master corps did for him what he had not been able to
do on his own: it fed and clothed him adequately. Figuratively, too, Hitler was at home at war. He enjoyed
the possession of his gun and bayonet. He was not ap-

palled by war's blood and dirt; he "passionately loved soldiering" (*ibid.*, p. 12).

Hitler was sustained through both the boredom and the danger of the World-War-I trenches by his sense of important personal participation in a glorious mission for Germany. As the war went on, he criticized its conduct by officers and by the supreme command and freely stated his own ideas of how he would command it personally. He ran great risks without show of fear in his dangerous task of running dispatches. Carrying orders and messages between the front and the command headquarters fostered the idea that he set the forces in motion. It also removed him from the grime of trench warfare, although he called himself a "front-line soldier." His job was close enough to the front, however, and he did it well, making unusually careful use of maps to plot his routes. "Exceedingly brave, effective, and conscientious" are the words used by one officer who recalled how Hitler and another orderly had shielded him with their bodies from machine-gun fire.

An unusually dangerous message run for which he volunteered resulted in October, 1916, in a wound that sent him first to a hospital near Berlin and then to a reserve battalion at Munich. Exposure to the citizenry in back of the lines enraged him. Hitler had earlier developed a disdain for German propaganda efforts and an admiration for the Allied leaflets rained down on German troops. Hearing the complaints of civilians in Berlin and Munich aggravated his contempt for the masses. He was so inflamed by the public disaffection he blamed on the "Hebrew Corrupters" that in 1924 he wrote in *Mein Kampf* (1943, p. 679) that thousands of them should be

held "under poison gas." He volunteered in March,
1917, to return to the front, there to excoriate defeatism
and the government's toleration of critics and dissenters.
He saw the Jews as the focus of all treachery and was
certain of an alliance between the Jews and the English.
With the rank of lance corporal, comparable to private
first class in the American Army, he took part, certain
of victory, in his company's heavy fighting in the last
German offensive. One October night in 1918 chlorine
gas temporarily blinded him and put him in the military
hospital at Pasewalk just a month before Germany's surrender.

His "great experience" ended. In the killing he had
been at home, his rage and aggression sanctioned. He
remembered every detail of four years in combat, including the name of every man in his company. What
he himself recalled so vividly he was less eager to have
remembered in detail by others. Hitler's military records
are far from complete, and his army medical file disappeared from them before 1933. Those lost medical records would establish facts of concern to him as a rising
politician. One of these was the precise nature of his
injury in October of 1918. Another, of psychological im-
port, was the truth about his genital anatomy, a consideration that alone might have impelled him to arrange
for the disappearance of the file. The facts were not
recorded anywhere else during his lifetime because of
his implacable refusal to submit to a complete physical
examination. During the early 1920s a story was current
in Munich that fellow-soldiers had observed in the wash-
house how his genital organs were almost freakishly
underdeveloped (Hanfstaengl, 1957, p. 137). A third set

of missing facts were the circumstances of his being decorated three months before the war ended with the coveted Iron Cross First Class, a distinction rare for a common soldier. Hitler, usually so expansive about his war experiences, was always silent on the topic of how he got it. A fourth matter: American Intelligence in the 1940s was told that the record included a court martial for "pederastic practices" with an officer.

Adolf Hitler in the First World War never rose from the ranks despite the German Army's shortage of officers, a puzzling fact much discussed as he rose to power. Explanations are found in how he was regarded by superiors. His regimental adjutant testified at the Nuremberg War Crimes Trial, after Hitler had led and lost the Second World War. "We could discover no leadership qualities in him," Hitler's long-ago superior recalled and added that Hitler had never wanted promotion (Fest, 1974, p. 69). With "his" Great War ended in defeat, Hitler nonetheless clung to the army and under its postwar auspices found a way to rise at last.

CHAPTER VI

Politician
(1919–1933)

Hitler wrote that upon news of the 1918 German defeat everything went black as he wept into his hospital pillow, overcome by hatred for the perpetrators of this "dastardly crime." Thereafter, violent rage always erupted at any mention of November, 1918. This extreme emotion has suggested that his blindness was hysterical, and indeed, there is evidence that it was (Lidz, 1976). In 1923, referring to the 1918 hospital episode, he said that "voices" called him to rescue the Motherland. That he equated Germany with his mother and The Jew with her violator has been suggested by Langer (1972) and other authors.

In *Mein Kampf* he repeatedly castigated Jews as Germany's violators (1943, pp. 193–194), ending, ". . . I, for my part, decided to go into politics" (*ibid.*, p. 206). In fact, he promptly went to Munich to take one of the prized civilian jobs in the shrunken army, a lucky break for an untrained man without civilian associations.

Hitler became involved in a political program with private armed units devised by army officers to encourage Rightist and Nationalistic movements against the new Weimar government. During extreme turmoil in Bavaria, Hitler was completely inactive against the Red government, docilely doing the most routine army chores. Later he volunteered for a new role as an informer who would turn in for execution fellow soldiers sympathetic to the Reds. The Propaganda Department of the Army Political Program placed Hitler in "civic-thinking" courses, where a professor noticed that he fascinated fellow students with his guttural outpourings. He recommended more training for the speaker and reported a strange feeling that the man fed on the excitement he himself generated. Made an undercover agent in an "Enlightenment Squad" at a returnee camp, Hitler soon found that his old hates matched the prevalent fears of a Red revolution.

An early assignment called for Hitler to report on the tiny "German Workers Party," a drinking club of lower-middle-class men. This group had two unusual aspects: its encouragement of the aims of the influential anti-Semitic Thule Society and an unusual formula, Socialism with Nationalism. Hitler's notes on the group were scornful. Irritated by the session that he had attended, Hitler burst out with angry oratory so overwhelming that the members begged him to join. He later claimed to have agonized a long time over giving up art for politics but in actuality he promptly joined the executive committee of the little group he would soon transform into the Nazi Party.

His first preserved political statement was a guide to army instruction on "The Danger of Jewry," requested by his superior officer. The position paper declared that politically useful anti-Semitism, not emotional but based on reason, must move toward "the removal of the Jews altogether" by "the ruthless intervention" of national leaders with profound inner feelings of responsibility (Fest, 1973). "Ruthless" was frequent in his utterances. In a sense of his own mission thus asserted, Adolf Hitler began to work for the first time. Still on army pay, he wrote, typed, delivered invitations, talked. Of his first address to an audience of more than one hundred, he wrote ecstatically that he electrified them.

But he was not alone, as he would later allege. His emergence was personally encouraged by two men. A well-known old writer, Dietrich Eckart, found embodied in Hitler the savior of Germany, about whom he had earlier written a "prophetic poem." He introduced Hitler to Munich society and provided him with money, books, and advice on dress. Hitler's army superior introduced him to Captain Roehm, then Chief of Staff to the Military Governor and political adviser to the victorious Free Corps. The prominent Roehm promptly followed Hitler in joining the insignificant German Workers Party and backed him with influence, money, weapons, and men. The dull secret club became within months a vocal public political party.

Its founders had lost control to Hitler by 1920. Protected by the Bavarian Justice Minister, Franz Guertner, and Wilhelm Frick, a police official, Hitler staged big public meetings for which admission was charged. Subsequently he falsely portrayed himself as the central figure of the first of these—in fact a routine event, but his first success. The relative newcomer also put his stamp on the twenty-five-point party program announced there, the major elements of Nazi doctrine. He was important enough to be flown to Berlin in 1920 as a liaison officer from Bavaria when Rightists briefly seized power in the capital. In the same year Rudolf Hess, a well connected Nazi convert who had been an officer in the same regiment as Hitler, assured the Bavarian Prime Minister that Hitler would lead the workers back to the Nationalist cause. He wrote that Hitler was one of the rare individuals who was honorable and of pure character, full of profound kindness, a good Catholic, and a selfless man.

Hitler moved out of the barracks in April, 1920, but not back to his prewar room. His new landlady had another view of the politician of whom so much was expected: he was extremely moody, sometimes for weeks looking through her family as though they were not there. And Hitler's ever more forceful public outbursts were now largely attacks on the "antiquated" or "useless" ideas of others. His contempt for ideas was lifelong, the single exception concerning ideas that could function as weapons: these he regarded as useful. In *Mein Kampf* he insisted not that an idea requires force to support it, but that force always needs the support of an idea. His very vocabulary was always rich in words for extreme force, as well as for blood and the fear of blood.

Throughout 1920 his speeches, given almost weekly, drew crowds as large as 3,500. Reports of hearing him with detachment are rare indeed. He deeply moved Germans of all kinds, and not merely the hysterically inclined, who often were conspicuous in his audiences. His oratory drew to him his most useful followers—for example, Speer, Goebbels, Ludecke. Dr. Ernst Hanfstaengl, a Harvard-educated German with a degree in history, joined the Nazis in 1921 because of "enormous excitement" on first hearing Hitler and went on to serve as his foreign-press secretary for fifteen years.

By thirty-two, Hitler was becoming the man whom Alan Bullock (1964) termed "the greatest demagogue in history." He then had an unequaled command of phrase, and a voice capable of extraordinary shrillness and penetration, described variously as tremendous, squeaky, rasping, hoarse, and sweet, capable of such feats as a five-minute reproduction of an artillery barrage. A skilled mimic, he habitually used this gift to mock his fellows. Hitler wrote in *Mein Kampf* that the orator follows the lead of the masses to find in the living emotions of his hearers the apt word which he needs. One convert saw evidence that the small, sweating orator felt the exalted response rising up to him from his hearers, having created a "hypnotic spell" that swept away every critical faculty (Ludecke, 1937, p. 13). Yet Hitler's speeches were not spontaneous; he worked on them as on nothing else. Spending as many as eight hours in the preparations for a given speech, he wrote large pages of cue words, rehearsed pacing up and down, and received telephone reports on audience moods virtually continually. He staged dramatic arrivals, heavily guarded.

Master promoter as well as star performer, he applied in publicity work the traits he displayed consistently: harshness, lack of scruple, and willingness to take boldly that last step from which many would recoil, along with preoccupation with minute details. He freely made use of brawling, scandal, terrorism. He risked huge party debt to buy himself a weekly newspaper with a down payment from Roehm's backers. The daring plunger ,fussed over every small detail of propaganda, even badges. He personally drew up the Nazi version of the ancient swastika to symbolize invincible machinelike power and terror.

Hitler displayed his conviction as to his own personal uniqueness by resisting his colleagues' strong· wish to accept an invitation that called for the Nazis to head a coalition of rightist groups. Instead, he demanded that the other groups disband and that their members join him personally. He also faced down severe intraparty criticism. An anonymous pamphlet, later revealed to have been prepared by his own propaganda assistant, accused him of intent to take over Germany for unknown backers, spending large sums on women, having an ungovernable temper, and always being enraged by members' inquiries about his income or former occupation. The protective Munich police forbade display of these accusations from what Hitler called "foreign elements," and he weathered the attack by threatening to resign if the members did not support him. His reward for total audacity was the statement that "the committee is prepared in acknowledgement of your tremendous knowledge, . . . selfless service . . . and your rare oratorical gift, to concede to you dictatorial powers" (Fest, 1973, p. 141).

The army's protégé then moved to set up an armed force in his own party, at first, with the ostensible purpose of organizing various sports activities. The force was known by its initials "SA." These soon came to represent, not "Sports Troop" but "Storm Troop." Hitler began to emphasize brute terror as an attraction openly and publicly, because, he said, cruelty impresses and the masses need something to dread. He stated as the SA's great appeal two qualities that unite men: common ideals and common scoundrelism. The Storm Troopers were to be reliable fighters for his own personal use in whatever political shifts he might elect.

The violence of his own disposition erupted when Hitler, flanked by his personal bodyguards, "silenced" a Monarchist by assaulting him on a public platform. After serving a month in prison of a three-month sentence for the assault, Hitler began to speak openly of a Messianic mission. He said his punishment paralleled Christ's, compared himself with Napoleon, and spoke of "the next war" and of seizing the grain of the East. Somewhat chastened by a threat of deportation, he did not apply for German citizenship although it was readily available to him, given his war record (were he willing to have that examined). Instead, he argued for a citizenship based on blood rather than mere papers. Blood and race were now a main theme. The effective party was to be one, not of class struggle but of racial struggle. Racial fears and antipathies enlisted worker, bourgeois, and aristocrat alike, he insisted.

Off the platform, Hitler showed personal oddities:

unpolished manners, a dirty coat, an uncomfortable appearance, almost comical servility with superiors. Hitler at first struck Hanfstaengl as a modest, friendly man, but the Hanfstaengls soon found Hitler more secretive than friendly. They noted his marked food peculiarities, including a passion for sweets in huge amounts, his elaborate fears of being poisoned in unrealistic and exotic ways, his refusal to swim or to wear swim garb, and his dread of the water and of small boats. Always evident was implacable rigidity, manifest in refusal to entertain ideas new to him. An early exception was the automobile; he quickly perceived its tactical use to make his forces more mobile than the police. He developed a lifelong addiction to being driven fast in ever-more-costly personal cars.

For a long time Hitler refused to be photographed, fearing murderers everywhere and glaring angrily and suspiciously at anyone who spotted him. Later, with more bodyguards, he welcomed attention. He was observed to dress oddly and conspicuously, as though "to make himself memorable" (Fest, 1973, pp. 134–135). He carried a whip with a weighted handle and wore a cartridge belt with a revolver, even at evening parties. He said that his odd little mustache was setting a fashion (Hanfstaengl, 1957, p. 67). As to his interests and pleasures, he was still observed to scan books voraciously; he owned a few war books, histories, and well thumbed semipornographic works. In 1923 he would postpone a conference to see a film. In one that entranced him Frederick the Great threatened to behead his own son. The beauties of nature moved Hitler little. Music was now important to him largely for the release of tension; Hanfstaengl gained the post from which he was able to observe Hitler closely by being drafted to play the piano to calm him.

Except in his preparation of speeches, associates despaired that Hitler would ever develop any decisiveness, orderliness, or punctuality. Always guarded, he wandered Munich with his whip and his fierce dog, talking all day as he dropped in at the party office, newspaper, and certain cafés. Now he abandoned all detail to underlings, implying he needed only attend to imminent great events. A then-devoted aide noted that he was almost impossible to keep on one point, prone to interrupt aides' careful reports with long speeches "as though to an audience," and yet he somehow exploited the disorder that his work habits and lack of administrative method created, in that others did the work for him (Ludecke, 1937, p. 58).

Withal, by 1923 Hitler was surrounded with veneration. Ludecke wrote, "I had given him my soul" (*ibid.*, p. 16). He noted times when Hitler "gave an impression of unhappiness, of loneliness, an inward searching" but added that Hitler would turn abruptly to the next "frenzied task" (*ibid.*, p. 91). Hitler's thin, pale face was often seen by women as tragic, and he was taken up by a number of genteel older ladies. Motherly patronesses cared for him early in his rise, some as indulgently as his own mother had. All but one of the older women who mothered and fed him were very rich: one had been born a princess and another was the wife of a famed Berlin manufacturer of pianos. The latter expressed her motherly interest by suggesting his clothes, pawning her jewels to fund him, and trying to marry him to her daugh-

ter. The climbing politician would sit beside her and lean
upon her bosom. After he became Chancellor, he merely
kept her on the list of those to whom he regularly had
birthday flowers sent, a niggardly remembrance that
spurred the lady to call him "shabby" to his face in 1936.

Hanfstaengl, after fifteen years of close observation,
decided that Hitler's relationships with women were limited to "passionate declarations," or at most some fon-
dling and petting. Seeing in him "a lot of Lohengrin with
its German connotations of impotence," he explicitly
called Hitler "impotent, the repressed, masturbating
type," and wrote, "I do not suppose he had orthodox
sexual relations with any woman," being "probably incapable of a normal reaction to their physical proximity"
(1957, pp. 123–124). His wife concurred in placing Hitler
in a sexual no-man's land, although she was herself embarrassed by some of his declarations of desire for un-
available wives of colleagues or outbursts to other
inappropriate women.

Most of Hitler's hours were spent with a small chosen
circle, all armed bullies: an ex-convict who later served
successively as secretary, chauffeur-guard, and, finally,
valet; a barroom bouncer; a handsome wrestler, a
butcher's apprentice; and two other ruffians who served
to protect him lifelong. The low atmosphere of his am-
bulatory headquarters never changed as Hitler rose. But
for all the guarding of his person, Hitler did not rely on
personal loyalty for his safety or control. He had Hess
set up a card index on the weaknesses and potential
dangers of all his followers, a fear-impelled device attributed to his having turned in ex-comrades, his exten-

sive knowledge of political murders, and his own promises of "lampposts full of corpses" and "heads rolling."

By 1923 he had chosen many followers whom he would enrich and take with him on his rise, controlling them absolutely. These included glorifier and amanuensis Rudolf Hess; business manager Max Amann; photographer and majordomo of entertainment Heinrich Hoffmann; liaison to the High Command Hermann Goering; idealogue Alfred Rosenberg; and chief anti-Semitic pornographer Julius Streicher. Hess and Amann had been in the List Regiment with Hitler in World War I; Amann was privy to his war records. Streicher and Rosenberg were notorious for sexual depravity, Hoffmann for tolerance of it, Goering for violence. The personalities of the chosen are, of course, revealing of the chooser. Speer, who long worked close to men around the Nazi Chancellor, observed that each had "some flaw in the weave." Hitler consistently encouraged their rivalries, maintaining control as well as his "mania" for secrecy by keeping all associations in separate watertight compartments.

Secrecy was strictest about money and about his personal history and life. His policy was to conceal the identities of all financial backers; he forbade the recording of contributions, and any traces that became court records in his several libel suits were removed after he became Chancellor.

At this time, Hitler's ruthlessness was evident even to the devoted Hess, who in a portrait of Hitler wrote prophetically that he would "trample" people to achieve his goal (Heiden, 1944, p. 99). His patron Eckart said that Hitler was developing "an incurable case of *folie de grandeur*" and would ruin them all "if he lets this Messiah complex run away with him" (Hanfstaengl, 1957, p. 83). Believing that it was possible for him to accomplish a coup, Hitler was willing to use any means and said the Nazis must compromise supporters so they would have to march with him.

His chance seemed to come with the devastating German inflation of late 1923. He welcomed the misery it brought about, declaring the need for pride, will, defiance, and "hate, hate, and again hate!" So high was Hitler's excitement by mid-autumn that a *Times* of London interviewer thought him a lunatic. He raved about "clearing out" one-quarter of the Nationalists and finding enough trees in Germany to hang all its betraying Socialists and Democrats. He declared that people would fall on their knees before a German Mussolini. Hitler tried to force upon his Bavarian protectors collaboration in a National uprising, ignoring his recent pledge to them never to make a *Putsch*. His grand tactic was to arrest the Bavarian leaders in public and force them to agree to his *coup d'état*. For all the violence Hitler promised his followers, his actual method was not to destroy authority but rather to make it sanction him. He failed in Munich on November 8, 1923, because of his unrealistic and diffident execution of his unrealistic and incompetent design.

When the authorities clamped down on his march the next day, he was not heroic under fire which killed and wounded fellow Nazis. He grabbed his companion's arm, tumbled to the ground when his supporter was shot dead, crawled with a dislocated shoulder to a car waiting with a Nazi doctor, and sped thirty-five miles to safety at the

Hanfstaengls' country retreat. Frau Hanfstaengl said he was "almost incoherent" during two days of hiding in her attic. As the police vans closed in, he threatened suicide, but she was able to wrest his pistol from him. Taken to a maximum-security prison and charged with high treason, he was first described as in shock, but he was easily dissuaded from the suicide he threatened because, he said, "of the deaths on his conscience."

In February, 1924, Hitler was rested and ready for his trial. His guardian angel, Guertner, still Bavarian Minister of Justice, provided every opportunity for the accused to manipulate the trial process and gave him an unparalleled stage for a political miracle, in that he turned the charge of treason into a public indictment of the government of Germany. In his climactic four-hour peroration, which the presiding judge said he could not bring himself to interrupt, Hitler declared that the *Putsch* had *not* failed, because no mother had charged him with the death of her son. In his final outburst he declared that ". . . the Goddess of the Eternal Court of History will smilingly tear up . . . the verdict . . . and set us free!" The stunning speech brought him world notoriety. He simply stepped over and above the accusations with the assertion that he was born for a mission: to destroy Marxism. He was not, like lesser politicians, compelled to seek power or to excuse himself for his climb, because such a man as he simply *willed* power as his calling and his duty.

Hitler received the minimum sentence for treason, which in fact amounted to a highly restorative eight months and twenty days during which he rested in great comfort, his only real punishment his genuine terror of incarceration. He received extraordinary privileges—a sunny cell and extra rooms, and the presence of his rough bodyguard, first as secretary, then as valet. When Hess was sentenced he shared Hitler's prison suite and took over as secretary. Like a man of wealth in a well-run hotel, Hitler had breakfast in bed. He was allowed to keep gifts of flowers and delicacies, and eventually his quarters came to resemble a shop. Although he was getting fat, he refused to exercise or take part in games because he thought that a leader could not afford to be beaten. These and other incredible details of Hitler's princely confinement are documented. His treatment and the adulation of his guards could only confirm Hitler's extraordinary estimate of himself.

Hess put his university education to work at typing out Hitler's autobiography, largely from his dictation. Each chapter was approached as a speech. Begun in 1922, its original title was "A Reckoning." By 1924, with rage added to feelings of persecution, Hitler wanted to call it "Four-and-a-Half Years of Struggle Against Lies, Stupidity, and Cowardice." His publisher avoided this disaster, choosing instead "My Struggle" (*Mein Kampf*). When the first volume of the work was finally released and widely sold in 1925, Hitler's personality was publicly revealed. But few read the book carefully. Its political frankness masked by its turgid style, *Mein Kampf* set forth Hitler's plans to destroy existing society, eradicate a portion of mankind, and conquer the world. But in its jumble, most readers, including statesmen, overlooked the messages as to the author's intent and character. Although Hitler aspired to present himself as a theoretician, the ideas he fastened upon early in Vienna are scarcely developed systematically: Jews to be hated; men contemptible; the pure German race superior; Germans entitled to living space in the East; Marxism, an enemy; the ruthless superior to those checked by conscience; the fundamental law of the universe "a merciless struggle of all against all." According to Hermann Rauschning (1940), the book revealed that Hitler believed in nothing and respected nothing. Rauschning thought that the style was understood by no one. Style is the man, however, as a French sage long ago noted. The style in *Mein Kampf* was the essential Hitler, Hanfstaengl (1957) wrote, specifying Hitler's grandiosity, stilted attempts to achieve elegance of expression, fantastic energy, and single-mindedness. The book bares the range of Hitler's hates: the aristocracy, the bourgeosie, workers, and most nations, excepting only Italy and Germany at the time of writing. It revealed some of his mistaken notions, e.g., that Russia was dominated by Jews and that Teutonic knights once ruled there. The book derides workers and the middle class, but Hitler soon emulated the tactics of both. He was able to ignore the contradiction and to get others to ignore it with him, as in so many other matters.

The volume includes ideas on propaganda sometimes cited as evidence of Hitler's intelligence, among them ideas about the manipulation of people that now are among the commonplaces of advertising. Most are rooted in his fundamental contempt for mankind. He stressed the primacy of emotions over reason, especially in the responses of groups and called crowds feminine in nature. In the writing of propaganda he abjured any qualifications or shadings in feeling or ideas, insisting upon

endless repetition and extreme simplicity. Especially did
he stress the importance of the single target, even if two
enemies, e.g., the Jews and the Russians, had to be
artificially combined into one. But these concepts were
in all probability not original. A French sociologist, Gus-
tave LeBon, had expressed most of them in an influential
study of crowd psychology (1895), published in German
in 1908 as *Psychologie der Massen*. Robert Waite called
Hitler's indebtedness to LeBon close to plagiarism, so
similar to LeBon's ideas are the specifics in the famous
propaganda chapter in *Mein Kampf*. The propaganda
techniques equated with the very name of Hitler, the
effectiveness of violence, and the Big Lie appear in
LeBon. In the Vienna libraries haunted by Hitler for
over five years, he could scarcely have missed a new
work so directly connected to his then-new interest. But
he never credited this or any other source for them.

After prison Hitler seemed tense, irritable, and nervous. His tension manifested itself at a small private dinner at the Hanfstaengls when, striding up and down,
Hitler suddenly screamed out a tirade, threatening to
"reduce Paris to rubble." He displayed his fixed views
of the world, narrower than ever; for example, he simply
denied America's part in the First World War. He vented
his passionate dislike of the officer class. He delivered
anti-Semitic opinions of a now heavily racial kind, defending Rosenberg's ponderous racism. His hosts tried
reason but met a blank wall. Later in 1924, Hitler suddenly turned away for an entire year from General Erich
Ludendorff, a man revered by Germans because of his
exploits in World War I, whose support had been so
useful to Hitler in politics. He also replaced his chief

bodyguard, although that loyal aide had just recovered from wounds suffered in shielding Hitler during the *Putsch*, a second dramatic change in behavior toward an individual.

After the success of *Mein Kampf*, Hitler promptly bought a large supercharged Mercedes-Benz. Although he frequently went on picnics for amusement, he still would not learn to swim, having an unreasoning fear of the water. He would not wear a bathing suit. Current in the Nazi inner circle at the time was a wartime story told by fellow soldiers who shared the same wash house to the effect that Hitler's "genital organs were almost freakishly underdeveloped" (Hanfstaengl, 1957, p. 137).

Anxiety about Hitler's disorderly work habits persisted among the Nazis. One had written to him before the *Putsch* about the "anarchy" in allocating his time. After 1925, some worried that their leader spent his time in Munich largely in a café with "a bunch of illiterates," inadequate for responsibility when he came to power. Hitler still deliberately permitted his party to drift and its members to quarrel. Hess was then promoting the personality cult, urging *Der Fuehrer* as Hitler's title.

Examples of Hitler's quick switches of position and attitude are abundant. Whereas he contended that he hammered away at the same themes, his principles immutable and his character iron, examination of his speeches shows his ready shifts. "Rebel!" he would instruct one day, "Obey!" the next. In 1925 he supported Ludendorff for president, then rejoiced when Ludendorff was ignominiously defeated. In January he castigated Rosenberg as incompetent, disloyal, and criminal; in April he made Rosenberg editor of the Nazi daily paper. This capacity to shift equipped Hitler as the supreme opportunist. As an actor changes roles, he became a different character before different groups. Nor did he have scruples about altering newspaper reports of his speeches which were to be published as a collection in a book. The same capacity made Hitler the supreme propagandist. He did not dominate millions of minds only through powerful repetition, much as he liked to believe this; rather, he swayed with them. The confusions and contradictions in complex situations did not trouble Hitler; he made no effort to sift facts or reconcile them. Instead, he was able to use any themes he found in the feelings of his hearers to serve his drive to power.

In 1925 and 1926 the National Socialist Hitler brought himself to support the restoration of expropriated property to the princes. His ever more obvious tendency to favor capitalists and members of the nobility troubled some old Nazis, notably the socialist Gregor Strasser, who had built up a vigorous Nazi program in the North with Joseph Goebbels and Heinrich Himmler as his secretaries. In 1926 Goebbels, backing Strasser's socialist position, demanded Hitler's resignation. But Hitler's leadership by this time was seen as above question. He could sweep others along despite his reversals. After a four-hour confrontation, Gregor Strasser capitulated to him, and Goebbels abandoned forever both Strasser and the socialist position. Although he called the ideas with which Hitler demolished all opposition absurd and contradictory, Goebbels was soon making rousing speeches for Hitler. By the summer of 1926 he had adopted and developed Hitler's propaganda ideas and was staging huge mass "Party Days" for him.

When the sales of the second edition of *Mein Kampf* plunged in 1927, Hitler wrote another huge book, *Hitler's Secret Book* (1961), but it was published only long after his death. The solemnity with which he regarded it and himself shapes the first words: "Politics is history in the making." He elaborated his notions: might makes right; the struggle for *Lebensraum* is the basis of fitness for survival; the Jew is the inferior racial enemy bent on the corruption of superiors. He chose a vocabulary of poisoning, disease, corruption: "liquid manure," "abscesses," "purulent infection centers," "racial maggots." The national official who signed the 1918 surrender he called "the bastard son of a servant girl and a Jewish employer," suggesting to some commentators a nagging preoccupation with the paternity of his own father. The aim of the Jew is the conquest of the world, he wrote, and his own struggle against the Jew is one on behalf of the world, not Germany alone. That so extreme a book did not appear in his lifetime can be called another example of Hitler's luck. Toland (1976) believed that Hitler himself forbade its publication, and Waite (1977), that Hitler's publishers refused to bring it out.

A story emerged in 1971 that Hitler sought psychiatric help soon after he finished this book. John Toland (1976) wrote that fear of cancer sent Hitler to a Munich psychiatrist. No other trace has appeared of his having sought help with his numerous phobias or other psychological symptoms. In any case, it is of more than passing interest that the book's timing coincides with that of concealed affairs with women, especially with his niece, Geli Rabaul. Indeed, the relationship is probably not coincidental at all, as the discussion in Chapter XIII indicates.

His first sustained involvement with a woman dates from 1926. Hitler was thirty-seven when he met a pretty blonde sixteen-year-old, Maria Reiter, called Mimi, with whom he started a flirtation (Domarus, 1965, p. 2220). The nature of the relationship that followed was not made explicit. Hitler broke off with her in 1928, and she tried to hang herself. In subsequent years they saw one another on at least two occasions. Describing one of these, the historian Waite quoted a German newspaperman's tape-recorded interview of Mimi: "I let him do whatever he wanted with me" (Waite, 1977, p. 225).

At the time he was beginning his affair with Mimi, which was hidden from most of his associates, Hitler was spending much time in the *Berghof*, now rented by him, where he had installed his half-sister with her two young daughters. One was the seventeen-year-old Geli, whom he was finding attractive. This was also the period when he was sometimes seen with Henrietta Hoffmann, the pretty fifteen-year-old blonde daughter of his photographer, as well as at sex and drinking parties at Hoffman's house. Henny later remembered that Hitler had beaten his own hand furiously with his ever-present whip because she had refused him a goodnight kiss. His relations with these young women in the late 1920s ran concurrently with a new involvement, that with an eighteen-year-old named Eva Braun.

In this period, Hitler's now-consummate skill in politics, his ruthlessness, the impact of his oratory, and his overwhelming appeal to some personalities were displayed. He made an alliance with the leaders of the

Right, took Rightist funds, then simply insisted on using them as he wished. He kept the Leftist elements among the Nazis and used them as an implied threat to the Right. His appeal to the working class was what first earned him the protection of the powerful army. Now he was using both that appeal and its opposite, and industrialists backed him despite all the contradictions. The tough head of the coal syndicate, famed for his economic buccaneering, became a Hitler devotee after being "overwhelmed" by his oratory at a rally. Hitler made a sensation in 1928 with a favorite figure of speech: "heads would roll" when he came to power, a phrase with a literal meaning to him, as would be appreciated only years later (Hanfstaengl, 1957, p. 153). On one occasion he glorified man's brutality as essential to human accomplishment. On another, he asserted that the contradictions of the old Nazi platform did not matter, since the New Testament is full of contradictions that did not prevent the spread of Christianity.

By 1929, Hitler began to demand much more from the Party coffers. He bought the superbly sited mountain house he had rented at Berchtesgaden, and soon transformed it into his luxurious *Berghof*. In Munich he created for himself an extravagant apartment, the very home of his adolescent dreams, and there employed the landlady from his old poor rooms and her mother as well, on his household staff of twelve. He invited Geli, then twenty-one, to share the Munich luxury. In late 1929 Geli moved into Hitler's apartment, where he took over her young life. A month later, in October, 1929, Hitler began to devote attention to Eva Braun, giving her candy and flowers. But while his devotion to Geli was increasingly obvious to his inner circle, his interest in Eva was hidden.

With a huge Nazi treasury and another world economic crisis to exploit, Hitler moved toward the power he sought. But he attended to none of the Party's detail, rarely deigning even to make a note on any matter. Sometimes praised for the Nazis' systematic preparation for power, he in fact fought against planning. He feared it, preferring to stress street fighting and the propaganda at which he excelled. He invented a Party ritual based on his belief in the political power of blood: touching the bloody flags of the 1923 March. His personal leadership, intensely emotional, was by 1930 in full flower. The Party press contained statements of outright deification, and the masses looked to him personally for salvation. To assure loyalty from the Nazi soldiery he took over direct command of the SA in 1930 and exacted from each storm-trooper a personal oath to himself. Lying freely, he testified in court in 1930 that he always required the SA to act lawfully and always maintained "a veto on violence"; privately he encouraged its extreme license.

In the frantic series of parliamentary campaigns beginning in 1930, Hitler still let the Party run without organization, timetables, or realistic arrangements, still brooked no differences, still alternated between energy and lethargy. Sometimes he withdrew completely, and even his secretaries could not get in touch with him. Sometimes he rushed over Germany making four or more speeches a day, all vague as to program but clear in their assertion that Hitler was Germany's only savior. Only a few artists and entertainers mocked and caricatured him as absurd. He expressed personal pleasure in his nation's social agony, a pleasure reminiscent of his exaltation in the agonies of war. In a 1930 speech "world power or doom" was his only message, the same message he would voice on the last day of his life. As bloody street fighting erupted he was exhilarated. He proclaimed "liberation," not votes, as his intention; his frank themes were "blood, authority of personality, and a fighting spirit." In May, 1930, Hitler expelled the socialist-leaning Otto Strasser and had the SA throw out any Nazis who agreed with him. Many Left-tending members, including Otto's brother Gregor, shifted to follow Hitler, as he screamed, "Every one of my words is historic!" He had Heinrich Himmler develop a new special personal bodyguard that later became the SS (the *Schutzstaffel*).

The necessity to have the now huge SA force of 100,000 directed by a chief absolutely loyal to him drove Hitler in 1931 to turn again to Ernst Roehm, the old Nazi pioneer, to take charge of all the Nazi forces. In the Berlin SA an outright rebellion resulted from Hitler's conflicting orders. He had it put down by SS troops, then personally toured Berlin, successfully pleading tearfully that the men trust him. Hitler's increasing reliance on the SS rather than the SA was evident. But he again used his hold over the individuals in both groups to hold them together with mystical words: "I am the SA and the SS and you are the members of the SA and the SS as I am within you in the SA and the SS" (Toland, 1976, p. 250).

Serious personal matters disturbed his campaigning in 1931. William Patrick Hitler, Alois, Jr.'s son, and his mother, began to sell information about Hitler to American newspapers. Hitler summoned them to Munich and in the presence of both Alois, Jr., and his sister Angela raged at them, declaring that "these people must not know who I am. They must not know where I came from and from what family." He handed over the equivalent of $2,000 in cash for their retraction (*ibid.*, pp. 245–246). Hitler also ordered the party lawyer, Hans Frank, to make a complete confidential investigation into the paternity of Hitler's father, agitated by the notion that the press might become interested in the possibility that he had a Jewish ancestor. He railed at "a disgusting blackmail plot" connected with "one of his most loathsome relatives." Frank's report concluded "regretfully" that the Jewish grandfather possibility could not be dismissed because of payments from a Jewish family to his grandmother for fourteen years following Hitler's father's birth. Hitler challenged his lawyer's deduction. He knew about such payments, he said: his grandfather had because of extreme poverty used a falsehood as a basis for blackmailing the Jewish family. He said that he knew this directly from both his father and his grandmother. In fact his grandmother had died decades before Hitler's birth (Toland, 1976, pp. 246–247).

Another threat to Hitler's political rise from the personal sphere was the death in his Munich apartment in September, 1931 of his niece Geli Rabaul as a result of a pistol shot. Otto Strasser, stating that she had confided in him, described her misery, which was rooted in Hitler's demands that she accede to his perverse sexual wishes (Langer, 1942–1943, p. 919). She could not bring herself to do, Strasser quoted her as saying, "what he wants me to do." Ludecke (1937) wrote that a physician who examined the body reported that she had died a virgin. If true, genital intercourse was not the dreaded "what he wants me to do" that Hitler wanted to exact. Hanfstaengl, although on the scene and in close touch with participants, could establish few solid facts about the death. However, he was told by a Hitler crony of a "farewell letter" to Geli that Hitler had shown to him, illustrated with a pornographic drawing Hanfstaengl could describe only as symbolizing impotence (1957, p. 167). This was not the only sexual drawing that Hitler somehow made known to others.

When he learned of Geli's death, Hitler reportedly screamed and behaved like a man distraught. He threatened to give up politics and said he would not appear in public anymore. But within a few shocked days after Geli's burial in Vienna Hitler again accelerated his frantic national campaigning. As he did after the World War I defeat and after the failed *Putsch*, he emerged quickly from an episode of depression. For the next few years, however, Hitler enacted a cultlike ritual in Geli's memory, as he had done in memory of his mother. He would make sudden night visits to Geli's grave with her favorite chrysanthemums; he maintained her room as a shrine daily adorned with fresh flowers, commissioned a bust, and had paintings of her installed beside those of his mother in all his bedrooms. For a few years his solitary Christmas Eves, previously dedicated to his mother, were passed in the room where Geli had died.

With Geli dead, Hitler permitted young Eva Braun an expanded role in his life, but only very slowly and, until 1935, covertly. Hitler's affair with Eva was not exclusive of others, and her uncertainty as to her standing was chronic. The nature of his conspicuous attentions to

Winifred Williams Wagner, the English-born widow of
the composer's son Siegfried, is not documented. In
1932, about nine months after Geli's death, Eva shot
herself in the chest, the first of two attempts at suicide.
Only the physician's assurance that it was a near thing
persuaded him that it was not a ploy, and he then became
more interested in her.

Before the elections of 1932, Hitler used superhuman
energy to storm every German state by train, car, and
the still-novel airplane. Yet he had almost no real contact
with people, not even with his associates, who felt they
were touring with a performer. He did not permit them
to be colleagues on a team and kept them away from any
important people, storing information only in his own
memory. He remained a lone wolf, now even harsher,
often jealous, more distant from his senior associates,
and contemptuous of them.

With his Nazis the strongest party, Hitler was closing
in on power; the chancellorship could be his by decree
of the aged President Hindenburg. The army's chief politician, General Kurt von Schleicher, was willing to make
use of Hitler because of his demonstrated popular appeal.
Army associates of Goering and Roehm arranged Hitler's
first meeting with President Hindenburg, but Hitler
failed to charm The Old Gentleman. Hindenburg continued to despise him, as he had done before; Hitler
continued to refuse to be Vice-Chancellor. He would
accept only the sole power, an extremely risky "all or
nothing" insistence. In one August conference in 1932
he furiously demanded, in addition to the chancellorship,
a free hand to "mow down" the Marxists, "three days of
freedom of the streets for the SA," a "Saint Bartholo-

mew's Night" with "5000 dead." Schleicher, shaken, doubted Hitler's sanity (Heiden, 1944, p. 482) but was not, as the event proved, sufficiently warned to protect his country or his own life. President Hindenburg's curt refusal shamed and shook Hitler.

Hitler pushed on with more elections and negotiations. Schleicher naively offered Gregor Strasser the vice-chancellorship Hitler had scorned; Strasser twice refused. Hitler, incoherent with fury at the very offer, nonetheless made a frenzied three-hour-long charge that Strasser wanted to destroy him. The old friend, in fact his thrall, resigned immediately from his Parliament seat and rushed out of the country. In a party meeting Hitler raved that he would kill himself if the party fell apart but also spoke of having Gregor Strasser killed, something he did two years later. With one of his major displays of sobbing, he exacted emotional new pledges of personal loyalty. No Nazi leader followed Strasser.

Hitler always believed what was never to be true, that he would be swept by votes into the complete power he wanted. Although the peak Nazi vote was 37 percent, Hitler ignored the count with feats of pseudo-logic in 1932. He told American journalists that since 51 percent gives total power, his 37 percent entitled him to 75 percent immediately, and that his votes were moreover, worth double, being from the best German material. He asserted his right to complete control and in the same breath denied that he demanded absolute power. H. V. Kaltenborn wrote, "he did not appear to have his own mental and physical processes under sufficient control to be able to harness them to a specific goal . . . what

we underestimated was the appeal of the irrational"
(Kaltenborn, 1950, pp. 185–189).

In 1932 Hitler was so confident of power that he was
already at work on his own monuments; Goebbels noted
on February 3 that Hitler had a project all worked out
for a spectacular rebuilding of Berlin. Hitler indeed finally wore down the resistance of the President and his
advisers to letting him have complete authority. The
economic misery that paralyzed other politicians did not
faze him. And he had never relinquished his threat to
those manipulators who thought to use him: the armed
might of his followers. Adolf Hitler took the oath as Chancellor of Germany January 30, 1933, forty-three years
old, in almost uncontrollable excitement as he bowed
low over the President's hand. With him to the heights
he chose to take not old comrades but useful sponsors:
Hermann Goering, who through high army associations
had helped him open the last door, and Wilhelm Frick,
assistant to that sympathetic and crucially important police chief of Bavaria back in 1923.

CHAPTER VII

Power Wielder
(1933–1945)

Hitler objected to the very title "Chancellor," with its implication of being an aide to some higher authority (1953, p. 310). The offers of a vice-chancellorship he had found unthinkable. Solemnly he told Magda Goebbels, "Now the world must realize why I couldn't be Vice-Chancellor. How long my Party members did not understand me!" (Toland, 1976, p. 293). Magda, although she chose to die with him, once said that "in a sense Hitler is simply not human, unreachable" (Fest, 1974, p. 523). But once in office, Hitler at first appeared less strained. His superb memory and grasp of detail im-

111

pressed officials and diplomats. His choice of clothes improved; he relinquished his dog whip. In 1933 he was often seen as charming, genial, sometimes even relaxed. Yet in 1933 the Chancellor bit his nails and evidenced jealousy, still closed to new information, still arrogant about his rigid preconceptions. He now compared himself favorably with Bismarck, and on the constant excursions by car which he still required, he limited his driver's speed with the words, "How terrible if something had happened to me" (Speer, 1970, p. 36). He continued to keep his relationship with Eva Braun as closely guarded as ever. Old Munich comrades were avoided by the new Chancellor, and he was ungracious to those he regarded as unimportant: he was, for example, almost rude to a young architect, Albert Speer, who had been summoned about a small job.

But this handsome ambitious professional soon won Hitler's personal favor, important commissions, and, finally, high position. Speer put his training at the service of Hitler's passion for mega-constructions and became part of his daily life. In a work life almost as secret as his sex life, Hitler devoted uncounted hours to giant projects which Speer drew up for him. Hitler may have partially exempted Speer from his dislike of the fortunate and educated, but when he was being tried for World War II crimes, Speer said the last word on Adolf Hitler's capacity for friendship: "If Hitler had had friends, I would have been his friend" (Norden, 1971, p. 86). After decades of reflection, Speer realized that the likable qualities he had found in Hitler were only superficial, a judgment supported by close observations set down in his memoirs of Hitler's acts and words.

Speer vividly recorded Hitler's duplicity, how readily
he adjusted his behavior to different situations. As Chancellor he used his new polished manners and his old
charm to receive the world's famous, usually voicing
moderate views; few refused to believe in the appealing
face he presented. Those in places both high and low
also succumbed to his new promises, accepted his audacious installation of Nazi control, and affirmed his belief that his Reich would last a thousand years. Old
campaign promises in the framework of socialism were
simply ignored. Private property was not to be abolished;
rather, it belonged to the superior, just as strength and
intelligence did. He kept only his pledge to the aristo-
cratic establishment to make no economic innovations,
displaying his contempt for most old followers. Old comrades not acceptable to the establishment were simply
passed over in appointments. He forbade any reform
moves by Nazis and used violence against all liberals.
His self-confidence and audacity again contagious, he
ignited faith in his person that overcame all contradictions. When he, long known for his emphasis upon family
life, shouted that "we shall take the children away from
you and educate them to be what is necessary," millions
accepted the paradox, as he did himself.

Declaiming his first lofty public proclamation, Hitler
shook with agitation. He pledged to foster Christianity
and family, eliminate class struggle, honor traditions,
restore the economy, reconcile foreign nations, and re-
vive the spirit of unity. But two days later, to the commanding generals of the army, he unveiled the full extent
of his real intentions. He promised to overturn the Versailles Treaty and conquer new living space in the East

with "ruthless Germanization" and thus bring prosperity. On his anti-Jewish intentions alone he preserved his more characteristic secrecy. In blaming the depression on lack of living space, he ignored economic fact, as he had done before. He expressed only one fear: that France would attack him first "if she possessed statesmen," clearly equating statesmanship with aggression (Fest, 1974, pp. 389–390). This speech to stiff, cool officers, which he called one of his most difficult, was a masterpiece of calculation of motives. The officers, keepers of the public peace, were content that he would not make Roehm's SA part of the army and willing to look away while his stormtroopers terrorized Hitler's few remaining active enemies.

Hitler's lifelong refusal to address material realities, even his own self-support, is striking. In the 1933 economic crisis he did not address economics. His aim was loftier: the creation of a New German Man by special Nazi breeding and education. He declared that a follower could instantly become "one of the chosen" simply by proclaiming allegiance to him.

Hitler is credited as the first to use the political processes of democracy to create totalitarianism, but he also used controlled terror, alternately loosening and checking the reins on the SA to keep the appearance of legality. He said he regretted having to rein in his urge to violence, blaming the German people for being too attached to legality and himself for not pushing bloody surprise operations that would have succeeded in 1923. Thus he was wildly delighted when a fire destroyed the Reichstag building, his longed-for excuse for arresting the entire Left. A future Gestapo chief was witness to his "utterly uncontrolled" behavior at the scene. Red faced, he screamed that now there could be no mercy because "the German people" (*sic*) would not put up with leniency. Having his pretext to defeat the last vestiges of resistance to his dictatorship in the cabinet, he politely greeted each Cabinet Minister by rank the next day and then seized almost all the powers of the other Cabinet Ministers for himself. He said, however, that he could not act against the judiciary, the foreign office, or the army while The Old Gentleman was still alive. Hindenburg's presence not only had him keeping regular daytime hours for the first and only time in his life, but moderating his public utterances as well.

At the same time, he was using force extensively. Hitler's first two months cost more than five hundred deaths, including those of many old associates. Concentration camps, no longer secret, had swept away about a hundred thousand. Hitler replied to complaints about such force with praise for the "restraint" with which the SA was acting, considering his absolute right to "exterminate" Marxism. At the same time that he made such pronouncements, he told the SA and SS to hold back, for the sake of his image as a moderate man and the maintainer of public order.

Image making was as ever Hitler's main concern. Nazi propagandists developed a massive campaign to humanize him, which that first year included a book of beguiling photographs by Hoffmann (1935), *Hitler wie Ihn Keiner Kennt* (The Hitler Nobody Knows), all casual poses of the new Chancellor often smiling, receiving the adoration of children. Later Goebbels staged giant festivals on Hitler's birthdays, as well as the annual Nazi Party rallies.

Leni Riefenstahl, an actress, dancer, and cinema director, was also a major image maker for him. She received
almost unlimited support and privileges from Hitler for
her film work and was a frequent guest at the chancellery.

Hitler in the 1930s and until his death had the devotion
and services of one persistent woman, Eva Braun, although he concealed her for two-thirds of their fifteen-
year relationship. The most patient scrutiny can find little
that is not trifling in Eva Braun, beyond small kindnesses
and her final refusal to preserve her life when she joined
Hitler to die, courageous but still largely occupied with
her hair style and manicure. Eva's very triviality seems
part of what made Hitler comfortable with her. Like his
chosen cronies, Eva possessed no troubling distinction.
He often described the ideal woman as an adoring and
undemanding doll (Speer, 1970, pp. 92–93). Speer remembered Eva as part of the *Berghof* furnishings, and
Hanfstaengl flatly called her no mate for the Fuehrer but
only a domestic adjunct. For five years Eva was hidden
in a back street little frequented and only scantily funded
by Hitler. But then and later Eva showed a stubborn
persistence in pursuit of marriage to him, a stubbornness
recalling how his mother Klara endured humiliation to
marry Alois Hitler.

In 1933, because the new Chancellor still needed the
bourgeois parties, Hitler's propaganda stressed tradition
and Christian morality under the guise of a seductive
Nazi slogan, "The National Awakening." This campaign
climaxed in his appearance at the Potsdam Garrison
Church as the star of a ceremony designed to connect
him with the lofty pre-Weimar heritage. A production
orchestrated down to the last "spontaneous" offering of

flowers by a child, the occasion nonetheless deeply moved both participants and viewers and sent an extraordinary ripple through foreign observers and the entire public. Hitler's speech there called the old political process "impotent." He expressed yearning for redemption and a new German life to replace wretchedness, growing, perhaps, out of art. He could count on the Germans to share his estimate of what he called the power of art. German nationalism of the nineteenth century celebrated Germany's special gifts of music, poetry, and art. The Germans' high regard for the artist remained so strong an influence that even the Nazis were affected by it. Hitler not only thought of himself to the end as a sidetracked artist: almost all of the few words of admiration he ever uttered were for artists, including the poet Eckhart and his two architects, Troost and Speer. Even the rough and tough Goering was an art robber and collector, and Goebbels had written a novel.

Not fully expressed in the Potsdam speech was Hitler's disposition to link power and force, but he would soon hint that to him power meant force, using catch phrases from Nietzsche, including *Wille zur Macht*. Two days after the uplifting formal church ceremony, he changed into a brown shirt and marched with the SS into the Reichstag, to get by threat of civil war his *carte blanche* Enabling Act, the destruction of the German Constitution. In a matter of only months he had achieved the dictatorship that Mussolini had needed seven years to obtain, and he marveled, "Who would have thought so miserable a collapse possible?" (Fest, 1974, p. 415). Taking over a nation, he settled a petty account as well: he took away from Otto Strasser his Wurzburg University doctorate.

In the Chancellery Hitler created the orderly-room atmosphere he found essential. The undistinguished, even dubious, quality of most of those he selected as personal associates has often been remarked. Also striking is the mediocrity of many to whom he gave the highest responsibility, some of whom had failed in the arts, like himself. Speer decided that Hitler was comfortable only with those from backgrounds like his own, and further, that because they were controllable he also liked men with imperfections, such as immorality or a trace of Jewish ancestry (Speer, 1970, pp. 121–122). The German Army historian Schramm, assigned to Hitler's headquarters, stated that Hitler could indeed quickly judge one thing: whether a man would succumb to his personal impact, which to almost all was "almost physically tangible . . . like a magnetic field" (Schramm, 1971, pp. 32–35). The historian illuminated a comment of one of Hitler's doctors, namely, that Hitler was loyal to *some* old comrades, namely those absolutely in his thrall. Others he avoided or eliminated.

A court soon developed around the new Chancellor's meals. He held forth daily for a large audience of top Nazis at luncheons three hours long. Cabinet ministers did not appear at these, nor at Hitler's insistence, did high army officers, who might look down on Hitler's crew. The simple menu was ordained by his poor digestion, a necessity made into a virtue with extensive publicity. He contended that he could not bear to eat better than his chauffeur. In fact, preparation of his vegetables, eggs, and elaborate sweets was, like his enormous ward-

robe of simple clothes, a costly matter. For late suppers
Hitler assembled a group of perhaps eight. For years
Hitler refused to relieve the mediocrity with any distinguished guests. He made his preference for undistinguished company into the legend of another virtue,
egalitarianism. Every night he avidly watched movies for
three or four hours. He talked for days about *King Kong*,
the movie about the huge berserk animal that was his
all-time favorite. He also had pornographic films made
for him.

The Chancellor used his status to express his sexual
interests both directly and indirectly. While visiting the
Academy of Art, he would interrupt the classes for long
chats with the young nude models. His tastes in art, now
indulged on a grand scale, were conspicuous for untrans-
muted sexuality, e.g., what Speer in his memoirs (1970)
called an unusually sensuous bronze in the Chancellery
drawing room. In the *Berghof*, nudes painted for nudity's
sake filled an entire room, and Hitler also revealed his
longstanding fascination with the suggestive nudes of the
Munich painter Stuck, representing Sin, Temptation,
and Evil. More directly, Chancellor Hitler's resources
for procuring sexual partners were greater than ever,
and his reported choices were the very young. He would
urge young girls to tell him in great detail about their
first and subsequent sex experiences. His response
would be to talk with mounting excitement about his
importance in history. Years later, in his wartime table-
talk he still emphasized the importance of a young sex
partner. Holding forth for a mistress rather than a wife
for the "exceptional man" because marriage creates
rights and claims to attention, Hitler added that there

is nothing finer than to be able to educate a young thing into one's own ways.

As to the work of governing a nation: after the ailing President Hindenburg ceased to occupy a nearby office, Hitler abandoned his attempt to follow a conventional schedule and again reversed night and day, to the obvious detriment of administration. He bragged about how he escaped bureaucratic detail. In government as in politics, his policy was to foster an administrative jungle with chronic tensions among his aides, who often learned first about drastic steps in the newspapers.

Applying his "Big Lie" technique world wide, Hitler in his infamous Peace Speech in 1933 (Domarus, 1965, p. 277) accepted Franklin Roosevelt's plea for disarmament, promised respect for his neighbors, and eschewed the "Germanization" so recently promised to his generals. With this welcome Big Lie he achieved an international influence on public opinion.

Although he furiously denied "atrocity stories," he had already begun to proceed against Jews with a large-scale boycott against Jewish businesses. When the boycott was seriously opposed, Hitler claimed that he had made his point and desisted. But he predicted "with absolute certainty" that in centuries to come his name would be honored everywhere "as [that of] the man who once and for all exterminated the Jewish pest from the world" (Toland, 1976, p. 310). He explicitly recognized the tactical value of anti-Semitism, saying that if there were no Jew he would have to be invented to provide a visible enemy. Yet the quality of what he said and wrote evidenced an emotion beyond tactics in his "redeeming formula" that the crimes of Jews explain all the world's ills. To a proposal for immigration of German Jews financed by Americans and endorsed by his Foreign Minister and Reichsbank President, Hitler replied sharply that he needed the Jews "as hostages" (Hanfstaengl, 1957, pp. 210–211). As his pressures on Jews increased, he was always capable of making a few capricious personal exceptions. The Jewish violinist he admired was allowed to emigrate with his fortune, and a cook he wanted was declared a non-Jew.

In his first year in office, he formally announced that "Reich Chancellor Hitler still belongs to the Catholic Church and has no intention of leaving it" (Heiden, 1944, pp. 632–633). The Church had recently impressed him with the overwhelming public response it achieved to a display of a certain sacred relic. From the Pope he obtained a blessing, a Vatican Concordat, and an order that German bishops swear allegiance to his regime. At the time Hitler was telling his patroness Winifred Wagner that soon he would not have to bother with the Cabinet and could dissolve the monasteries and seize their wealth.

Overwhelming popular support for Hitler in 1933 is sometimes explained as a result of his understanding of the yearning to belong. Adolf, the loner, presented for every age and interest a Nazi group in which to serve and, as he repeatedly said, to sacrifice. The Nazis celebrated the undoubted joy of action and work, of fulfilling a function, even the simplest. These concrete experiences had more appeal than abstractions of autonomy and liberty. And with his constant cornerstone-laying ceremonies for new projects all over the nation and his speeches full of military metaphors, Hitler created an atmosphere of happy mobilization against the old despair and ennui. Repeatedly referring to "gigantic" plans, he hid the fact that he was improvising, with no real program except for war preparations that could not be avowed. Slogans and proclamations kept all parts of society inspired, his words alone ever magic. His own epigram was "Great liars are also great wizards" (Fest, 1974, p. 433).

Because he needed unquestioning support from the SA, should the former Kaiser attempt a threatened restoration, Hitler belatedly elevated Ernst Roehm to his Cabinet and on New Year's Day, 1934, wrote this old political protector and comrade an effusive letter of gratitude and praise. That summer Hitler had Roehm killed, and with him at least two hundred others, in a savage action called the "Blood Purge." The violent reversal came after six months of indecision, contradiction, and conflict in Hitler. On the one hand, Roehm kept pressing for a role within the regular army for his SA, as well as for promised social changes urged also by many within and outside the SA. On the other hand, the Vice Chancellor, Papen, speaking for the Army and the aristocracy, opposed any moves toward the political Left and eventually challenged Hitler publicly to put down ths SA's "Marxism." Hitler, citing the fear that Roehm was plotting a *Putsch* against him, launched a coordinated blood bath of which Roehm was the primary victim. That Roehm intended an SA *Putsch* against Hitler is now regarded as a fiction. However, the violent deaths which Hitler ordered and unleashed not only solved his differences with Roehm's policies and embarrassment about Roehm's behavior. They also settled many accounts, removed many possible threats, and won Hitler the capitulation of the High Command and control over the German public at a new level.

In the extension of Hitler's control over the nation by means of murder, many who had crossed him during his rise were felled. Those included the former Chancellor von Schleicher and his wife; Gregor Strasser, knowledgable about Geli's relations with Hitler; the aged Gustav von Kahr, victor over Hitler's 1923 *Putsch*; Father Bernhard Stempfle, early Hitler collaborator who became involved in blackmail over Geli; and two close colleagues of the Vice Chancellor who had provoked Hindenburg's threat to take the government from Hitler. Papen himself, protected by his intimacy with the President, lived on to serve Hitler. Hitler's hatred of former Chancellor von Schleicher may have had long roots. Von Schleicher, in World War I a captain in the regiment in which Hitler was a soldier, was in a position to know the contents of records of Hitler's physical examinations, as well as the details of his prized Iron Cross and two alleged charges of pederasty.

The success of the violence was astonishing. The British historian Trevor-Roper rated the blood-drenched episode as more significant than the Enabling Act that made Hitler dictator. The Blood Bath's very enormity condoned it, giving him a superhuman dimension as the embodiment of a historical necessity. The contemporary commentator Heiden believed that it awakened a belief in the necessity of evil. President Hindenburg congratulated Hitler. Even the churches did not challenge the acts of violence. Hitler, after being uncharacteristically silent in public for ten days, gave a long speech of self-justification (Fest, 1973, pp. 468–469). After hours of rambling, he became aggressive and declared to the Reichstag that he had chosen the "ruthless and bloody blows" because he was personally "the supreme judge of the German people." The Nazi press dwelled upon every detail of the "discovery" of SA homosexuals and his order for the "ruthless" extermination of "this pestilential tumor" that defiled his pure movement, contradicting his recent tolerant statements, both private and public.

Hitler, however, could extract from President Hindenburg neither a dramatic deathbed farewell nor a mandate. In the hours just before the death Hitler did extract from the Cabinet a new law combining his Chancellorship with the Presidency. This coup made him at last both Chief of State and Commander of the Armed Forces. He had ready at hand an unprecedented oath, not to the Constitution and the President, as tradition required, but one of "unconditional obedience *to Adolf Hitler.*" Before nightfall he received the personal pledge from every German under arms, including the members of the High Command.

His affair with Eva Braun was continuing at this time. The quality of their sex relations is strongly implied in what Eva said and wrote. In late 1934, she complained that she felt imprisoned. She confided to the Nazi labor leader's wife, her friend since schooldays: "As far as his manhood is concerned, I got absolutely nothing from him." About his treatment of her in 1935, history has a brief diary from her hand, from early February through May. Its twenty-two handwritten pages, now in the American National Archives, are authenticated by her sister Ilse and by a close family friend. The entries show the twenty-three-year-old's immaturity, limited intellect, and emotional shallowness, as well as her attachment and her desperate insecurity because of Hitler's erratic visits and messages. On March 11, she noted, "He is only using me for very definite purposes." During this time she complained of his insensitivity in passing her money in an envelope, after sitting beside her on a public occasion for hours without once speaking to her. The 1935 diary ends with Eva's second attempt at suicide, which was aborted when she was found by her sister. This second brush with death was again followed by a change in Hitler's treatment of her; he then gave her a house and some luxuries, but no open acknowledgment.

Although abnormality in Hitler's sexual demands is strongly suggested by Eva Braun's comments and those of other partners, direct evidence is scanty. The available accounts are those collected by the OSS (Langer, 1972, p. 134). A film actress described Hitler as requiring her to expose her genitalia to Hitler's gaze and then to urinate on him (Chapter II). Shortly after this episode, the actress committed suicide. It is striking that of seven women known to have been intimate with Hitler, three committed suicide and three made serious attempts to do so (Waite, 1977, pp. 237–243).

Hitler's valet has described his daily rituals. Not until about noon would Hitler reach outside his door for newspapers and important messages. He bathed and shaved himself; the valet was not permitted into his room until he was fully clothed. After a full hour the valet served milk, rusks, peppermint or chamomile tea, perhaps cheese and an apple. Sometimes Hitler summoned him for a strange little game: the valet tied his necktie while Hitler counted to ten. Evenings at the Chancellery had developed a reputation such that decent women would not appear. Speer hinted at a scandal, which was detailed to American Intelligence, about evenings involving film actresses selected by Goebbels to be brought to the Chancellery. After the parties, Speer said, Hitler would "rave a bit about the women . . . more about their figures than their other charms," conveying in his "schoolboy" tone the feeling that his wishes were unattainable. Around 1935, Hitler abruptly cancelled the Chancellery parties (Speer, 1970, pp. 129–130).

At the *Berghof*, where Eva Braun appeared only with the cronies, his day was lazier: a long lunch at 2 p.m., followed perhaps by a walk. For his evenings he required all the newest movies. On the mountain he became increasingly dilatory, even in preparing speeches. As always, he banned serious topics at meals and sought amusement in harsh jests displaying his general contempt. He never told off-color stories but in the absence of women knocked the churches. Always, he made fun of foreign statesmen and taunted his associates. Exploiting his pleasure in destroying others' self-respect, Goebbels and Bormann would tell him as malicious jokes their versions of party events, counting on his reluctance to change his mind to prevent any effect of reports he might hear later. Despite his distrustfulness and his mastery of deceit, he did not, Speer remembered, see through a complex gambit of clever moves.

As Hitler swept from victory to victory in the mid-thirties, he personally proclaimed his 1935 laws "For the

Protection of German Blood and German Honor." Called the "Nuremberg Laws," they forbade marriage or sexual relations between Germans and Jews and the hiring by Jews of female German servants under forty-five years old and deprived Jews of citizenship and the right to fly the German flag. Yet a puzzling requirement of Hitler's inhibited the police: only men were to be punished. Women, even Jewish women, were not to be jailed, Hitler insisted (Hilberg, 1973, p. 107). He expressed the idea of "ghettoizing [Jews] in zoo-like places" where Germans could look on "as one watches wild beasts," and at a secret meeting on the Nuremberg Laws he startled and baffled a participant by seeming incoherent when he suddenly said he needed four years to be ready for war (Dawidowicz, 1976, pp. 122–123, 214).

After the success of his very risky move of sending troops into the Rhineland in 1936, Hitler had Wagner recordings played for him to relax his enormous tensions. *Parsifal* suggested to him that his own "religion" was one "without pretenses of humility . . . one can serve God only in the garb of the hero." *Gotterdammerung* recalled to him that after first hearing that opera he became "madly excited . . . over a few yammering Yids I had to pass" (Fest, 1974, p. 499).

Now sure that nations like people were manipulable, Hitler boasted that an exact calculation of all human weaknesses underlay his ideas, assuring them a certainty of success virtually "mathematical" (Speer, 1970, p. 122). He pursued his most extreme goals: to create a New German Man and to destroy the Jews. In secret Nazi leadership meetings he stressed that he was zealously advancing step by step toward their destruction. He once said of the Jews, ". . . 'I will destroy you! . . . maneuver you into the corner that you cannot fight back, and then you get the blow right in the heart' " (Dawidowicz, 1976, pp. 124–125). About his other aim he was more open; he set up an entirely new education system, beginning with "Adolf Hitler Schools" and providing "Order Castles" for higher education. Nazi leaders avoided sending their children to these new institutions, Speer recalled.

During 1936 Hitler installed Eva in the remodeled *Berghof*, to the displeasure of his half-sister, Angela, who consequently left her housekeeping job there. Eva had no role when he entertained important guests, including the Nazi leaders; on such occasions Hitler simply confined her to her apartment. But although Hitler ignored her feelings, often voicing disparagement of women in her presence, he also fretted conspicuously over her safety. As Eva became more visible, some of the Nazi wives resented her—Magda Goebbels most markedly. Hitler always accepted Frau Goebbels' adulation, which she expressed by personally cooking vegetarian dishes for him when he again became suspicious of poison.

By the mid-thirties, Hitler's passion for building was being fully expressed openly in the construction of roads, defense structures, public edifices, and palatial homes and offices for Nazi leaders and for himself. He drew up the sketches for a huge, ostentatious new Chancellery and a redoubt of staggering splendor at Berchtesgaden. There with only minor use of Hitler's funds, a new Hitler operative, Martin Bormann, used the costliest materials and technology to push around the mountain and exploit the Alpine panorama. The redoubt's spectacular glass-walled "tea-house" soon lost its charm for Hitler, but he used it to impress visitors.

In all public construction, giantism was the theme. For Nuremberg he ordained a complex of 6.5 square miles to be ready in 1945, with a stadium four times the size of any extant. The structure was to be among the largest in history, three times the size of the pyramid of Cheops, with its cost concealed from his Finance Minister. The activity, Speer believed, reflected Hitler's talent for camouflage and masked his war preparations. But at the 1937 ceremony for Nuremberg, Hitler publicly revealed his emotional investment in the mammoth construction when he exclaimed to the architect, "This is the greatest day of your life!" In 1939 Hitler explained to construction workers, "Why always the biggest? I do this to restore to each individual German his self-respect. . . . I want to say to the individual: We are not inferior; on the contrary, we are the complete equals of every other nation" (Speer, 1970, pp. 69, 107).

The Chancellor did not use his power to realize those ideas for improved housing for workers attributed to young Hitler by Kubizek. Speer noted that the Chancellor was soon found to be "indifferent to the social dimension" and that "his passion for building for eternity left him without a spark of interest in traffic arrangements, residential areas, and parks." Hitler enthusiastically agreed to a proposal by Speer that his buildings use only expensive special materials that would after millennia retain their glory even in a ruined state. After 1936 Hitler secretly advanced a gigantic project of self-aggrandizement, a new capitol for his future Greater German Empire. This "Germania" was revealed only long after his death by Speer. For his Germania "he proposed to destroy and replace the middle of Berlin." After his triumph in the Rhineland, he handed Speer two cards preserved more than a decade, his own sketches for its main structures. From that day forward, the Chancellor himself worked almost daily at those plans, keeping Speer at his side far into the morning hours, both in Berlin and at the *Berghof.* The most imposing building was to be Hitler's palace, called by Speer "the very expression of tyranny" and self-idolatry, seventy times the size of the Chancellery just completed, with a dining room for a thousand and a quarter-mile of hallway from the steel front door to his office. This grandeur, he explained to his circle, was necessary for his successors, not for him. Along a three-mile "Street of Splendor" nearly four hundred feet wide were to be the Great Hall, six times the size of St. Peter's in Rome, a Triumphal Arch higher than a forty-story building, and an "Adolf Hitler Platz" for assemblies of one million. Planning all of this relaxed Hitler so conspicuously that an associate called Speer "Hitler's unrequited love" (Speer, 1970, p. 133).

The dimensions upon which Hitler insisted were in the end self-defeating, Speer realized, since those of Germania would reduce the human figure of any orator to "optical zero." The other requirements of Hitler's "architectural megalomania," as Speer finally termed it, were over-elaborate imperial motifs rooted in the gilded styles of the Vienna of his youth. Paul Troost, Hitler's first official architect, was an austere neoclassicist who died soon after his appointment. Never troubled by contradictions, Hitler praised Troost extravagantly and displayed toward him "a kind of reverence," making Troost one of the few men—all famous and most in the arts—for whom Hitler professed some brief respect. But he soon abandoned Troost's principles (Speer, 1970, pp. 40–41).

When he began to give his major projects to the twenty-eight-year-old Speer, Hitler showed a pattern thereafter fixed: in all matters he chose young and pliant specialists to execute his decisions, rather than experienced experts who might inform and enrich them. In relation to his numerous architects Hitler "usually behaved with restraint and civility" (Speer, 1970, p. 79), a contrast to his manner in political conferences. To Speer he once gave some rare public praise. Hitler's own drawings of buildings improved enough by 1938 to win Speer's admiration. But the architect thought that Hitler avoided the serious in government by playing at architecture. He did credit Hitler with "allowing a problem to mature" while occupying himself with trivia. The opinion of Oswald Spengler, expressed in 1936, was that Hitler could not "really work," a flaw which alone would bring him down (Waite, 1977, p. 222).

Although he was by 1937 at a pinnacle of world recognition, inconsistencies persisted in him. Contemporary impressions of him with Mussolini were unfavorable to Hitler, who appeared disorganized. Carl Jung saw Hitler as robot-like in comparison to the Duce (Toland, 1976, p. 419). Yet the Duce was now impressed with the German Dictator. Hitler was feeling, in his own words, "as fresh as a foal in the meadow," ready to move toward his dream of empire (*ibid.*, p. 420). For all this, he talked of a short life and referred often to his own death. In a secret meeting with the military where with a dazzling display of memory for military detail he revealed his specific plans to fight in East Europe, he made this aim his "last will and testament." He added that "if he were still living" his unalterable resolve was to solve Germany's problem of space at the latest by 1943–45 (*ibid.*, pp. 420–422).

When vestiges of independence among some cautious generals in the High Command angered him early in 1938, Hitler seized fortuitous circumstances for another brutal purge. He removed his own devoted advocate, General von Blomberg, upon the excuse that his recent bride had been a prostitute photographed in pornographic pictures. The logical successor, a man resistant to Hitler's ideas, was removed on charges of homosexuality, later disproved. Hitler's behavior is described by an adjutant present as that of a "broken-hearted man," pacing and exclaiming, "If a German field marshal marries a whore then everything in the world is possible!" (*ibid.*, pp. 426–431). Another account agrees that he was wildly agitated and says that he insisted the man in the pornographic picture must be a Jew. Here Hitler ended any of his lingering uneasiness with generals; he not only took command himself but also abolished the War Ministry. When the second general was later exonerated of charges of homosexuality Hitler made no restitution.

Hitler's triumphant takeover of Austria in 1939 involved one of his often-remarked-on performances of intimidation, that over Austria's Prime Minister. Hitler boasted that he staged a tirade hours long in the presence of Austrian Nazis and German generals, bluffing that he was about to issue attack orders. Speer (1970, p. 97) believed that most Hitler outbursts were staged, and that his self-control was usually strong.

When he moved into Austria he begged for Mussolini's acquiescence. His extreme gratitude for it included an extravagant pledge "to stick by" Mussolini. That he kept this pledge among so many broken ones suggests the personal meaning to him of the seizure of the land of his birth. His frenzied welcomes as he passed through his birthplace and through Linz made him weep. But his intimates could not discern much of his emotion as he visited his parents' graves and talked briefly with three people who had known him. He telephoned Eva Braun to come to be present, secretly, for his triumph in Vienna. During his visit to Linz he developed stomach cramps that lasted three days. At news that his predrafted *Anschluss* had been accepted, he wept again, saying ". . . Yes, a good political action saves blood" (Bullock, 1964, p. 434), then cursed his general when mechanical breakdown delayed his triumphal march into Vienna. The roommate he had abandoned thirty years before sought him out on this visit. August Kubizek recounted how Hitler, although he used the formal *Sie* in their hourlong conversation, promptly ordered education in art and music for Kubizek's sons, invited him to the Bayreuth Festival, and suggested that his postcard mementoes be part of the official Nazi biography then in preparation (Kubizek, 1955, pp. 277, 280–281).

Hitler wrote out a personal will and testament in his own hand, bequeathing his considerable personal fortune in a most impersonal way. No person, but the Nazi Party, would receive all his funds, real estate, and personal property, from works of art to memorabilia. The only person singled out as the recipient of memorabilia was Geli's mother, who was to receive the contents of her room. Personal documents were to be disposed of by Julius Schaub, his longtime strongarm man, who was granted a singular description, "my old friend," along with a tiny Party annuity and ten thousand marks in a lump sum. The Party was to pay out the measures of his personal thanks: identical twelve-thousand-mark annuities, roughly the salary of a manager of a small office, to "Fraulein Eva Braun," "my sister (sic) Angela," and "my sister Paula"; one hundred and fifty marks a year to "my housekeeper, Frau Winter," a hundred to "my valet, Krause." Lump sums of sixty thousand marks went to "my step-brother (sic) Alois Hitler" (actually his half brother), thirty thousand marks to Paula to distribute among "my relatives in Spital," and three thousand each to "my valets, Linge and Junge." Less precisely, he instructed the Party to make "generous provisions" for two adjutants and for the couple in charge of meals at his headquarters (Maser, 1974, pp. 147–157).

The tiny proportion of his enormous assets that he assigned to human beings is striking. Also striking is that he ranked Eva Braun precisely with Angela and Paula. His allotment of a sum equal to the annual salary of the Chancellor of Germany to his prosperous and detested half brother recalls earlier payments to assure his silence about their connection. No political colleague outside the palace guard received even a token of remembrance—not Goebbels, not Hess, not the indispensable Bormann. All beneficiaries, with the possible exception of the headquarters food manager, were people privy to unpublished facts about Hitler's personal life.

For a state visit to Rome, Hitler had five hundred elaborate uniforms designed for his entourage, specifically, he stated, to set off his own simple attire. He was then infuriated to be outdone in stagecraft by royal etiquette; the king also humiliated and enraged him by saying that he injected drugs and he demanded a woman to turn down his bed because he could not sleep unless he watched a woman do so. In his reaction Hitler revealed the antipathy toward any king that had long governed his consistent, if sometimes concealed, objection to the German monarchy.

Displaying the Austrian imperial insignia, at Nuremberg in 1938, Hitler inflamed his followers and intimidated the world with "The First Party Rally of *Greater* Germany" (italics added). Speer said that the audacious declaration was typical of Hitler's pleasure in going so far that he could no longer retreat without risking his prestige. When foreigners thanked him for attaining his goal "without making one mother weep," he responded "with a malicious smile," his adjutant said (Toland, 1976, p. 470).

With ever more successes as the years passed, the man was persistently rigid, even in his insistence on observance of empty forms of parliamentary democracy. His assertive manner toward all around him became painful to them in 1938; Hess and Goebbels now evaded his previously coveted invitations. His tyranny over associates' personal lives remained absolute, e.g., his decision that the Goebbels, long deeply estranged, must remain married. His fits of rage when crossed, always common, became more marked, and his tirades sometimes extended to a half-hour. He now sometimes became so violent that his purpose was no longer served, and he would check himself suddenly. The episodes left him sweating and visibly exhausted. His insomnia became more severe; after his favorite young chauffeur had died in an accident in 1936, trouble sleeping and a sharp buzzing in the ears developed, so that his doctors prescribed mild sleeping pills. Later came reports that he required young men to keep him company at night because of extreme anxiety. One described scenes of shaking, shrieking, gasping, and sweating, and an episode when he screamed as though hallucinating, "He! He! he's been here!" with a meaningless stream of figures and broken "un-German" word formations (Langer, 1972, p. 132).

In the climactic year 1938, he was more than ever concerned with his health; not yet fifty, he called himself an old man. Despite chronic stomach and chest pains, intestinal gas, and eczema, he persisted in self-directed diets and adamantly refused the physical examination urged constantly by cohorts and doctors alike. Even in the safe secrecy of a military hospital, he contended, the Leader could not afford to be less than perfectly well and strong. Yet he did not reject examination of his throat and permitted removal of a benign node. He accepted the unproved methods of a skin and venereal-disease specialist, Theodor Morell—the administration of the new anti-bacterials, the injection of vitamins, minerals, and hormones, some from bulls' testicles, and the withdrawal of blood by leeches or a syringe—and installed Morell in his inner circle.

Throughout the international crises he made in late 1938, he created so convincing a public appearance of peaceful aims that a group of alarmed generals who plotted to remove him could not continue their plan. But Hitler's deep bellicose feelings erupted as he watched maneuvers and told his adjutants that war was the "father" (*sic*) of everything, and that every generation must experience war once, recalling his 1914 relish of combat (Toland, 1976, p. 470). Hitler was at the same time convinced that he was threatened and "surrounded." He told his Foreign Minister, "There is no international morality left, everybody snatches whatever booty he can" (*ibid.*, pp. 476–477). Although he declared that "The thought of striking was always in me" (Fest, 1974, p. 574), at first he succeeded without striking. He uttered the Big Lie that the Czech concession was his last territorial demand.

Some statesmen dealing with him were, to his great advantage, frightened by their impressions of his psychological state. Others rejected estimates that he was mad or close to madness. He made conflicting impressions upon different people witnessing the same behavior in him. Chamberlain was sure Hitler was deeply pleased with the Munich Pact; the interpreter judged him somehow reluctant about the wording; his valet called him exultant over having forced the elderly Chamberlain to come to him and accept a "noseful," his adjutant believed Hitler actually liked Chamberlain and was not considering "any dangerous steps" (Toland, 1976, pp. 472, 480, 493). To William Shirer, an American journalist on the scene, Hitler seemed on the verge of a nervous breakdown, his eyes deeply shadowed, his walk marred by a ticlike jerking of his right shoulder and left knee (1960,

p. 391). The French Ambassador to Berlin, André François-Poncet, summarized Hitler in these words:

> I knew him to be changeable, dissimulating, contradictory, and uncertain. The same man . . . who across a tea table expressed reasonable opinions on European politics, was capable of the wildest frenzies, the most savage exaltation, and the most delirious ambitions. These were the days when, bending over a map of the world, he upset nations and continents, geography and history, like some demiurge in his madness. At other times he dreamed of being the hero of an eternal peace within whose framework he would raise the loftiest of monuments [1949, p. 286].

His actual military situation at the end of 1938, as many German generals saw, was such that Hitler would have lost the real war in days. But his risk taking and lying continued to be effective. In 1939, Hitler browbeat the ailing Czech President into capitulation, as he himself bragged. He rushed out of the confrontation and demanded kisses from two secretaries, crying out, "It is the greatest triumph of my life! I shall go down in history as the greatest German!" (Speer, 1970, pp. 115–116; Toland, 1976, pp. 515–517). After the Czech takeover he realized that he had revealed too much of his innermost nature and ordered the press to postpone any further use of the term "Greater" German Empire. When the English offered Poland military support, Hitler, not trusting his own turbulent feelings, recorded his public remarks so they could be edited before being heard. He secretly ordered an attack on Poland for five months later, confident that the West would not act. Hitler now conspicuously preferred to discuss plans with young adjutants from each military branch rather than with the less admiring generals.

Against all counsel for peace, Hitler displayed a great self-assurance in 1939, even when faced with a rare public silence as he passed through Berlin streets. He made stunning use of the complex attitudes of other nations and his ability to think the unthinkable when in a complete reversal, he made his pact with his *bête noire*, the Soviet Union. But a description of Hitler's "terrible temper" and "weird fantasies" comes from an unofficial peacemaker, Goering's Swedish friend, Birger Dahlerus, who attempted to reconcile him with England. In the interview, Hitler, after listening to Dahlerus for a while, became "a completely abnormal person," repeating, "I shall build U-Boats, build U-Boats, U-Boats," then "shrieked as though to a throng, 'I shall build airplanes, build airplanes, airplanes, airplanes, airplanes, and I shall annihilate my enemies' " (Shirer, 1960, pp. 571–572). Similar behavior—screaming repetition and flailing of arms at the suggestion that England might fight—was described by his own Foreign Office State Secretary (Wykes, 1971, pp. 90–91).

When Hitler started World War II with staged "attacks by Poles," he used a Big Lie and brought to bear two of his oldest principles: violence makes the best headlines, and blame should be shifted to the adversary. The speech declaring war on Poland was almost unique in that he did not once mention Jews, yet later he mistakenly referred four times to its date as the day he threatened the Jews with destruction for causing war. What he did say was: "Whoever fights with poison will be fought back with poison gas" (Domarus, 1965, p. 315). In his mind, his war and his annihilation of Jews had become the same.

Hitler appeared stunned when England and France declared war on him. His circle noted sudden attacks of anxiety. Believing the West feeble, he simply denied that real war had come and held back his forces to let "the whole business . . . evaporate" (Speer, 1970, pp. 164–165). He refused to use any information about his enemies' activities and began to play at architecture again. Some of his notions, based on contemptuous underestimation of his opponents, contradicted others. He called England Enemy Number One, yet clung to hope of an arrangement with her; he wanted war, yet delayed the necessary final preparations. Aware that Germany was materially unprepared, he acted as though the strength of his will would make the difference. His self-estimate permitted him to believe that he could swiftly take over the resources of successive victims and on their material base sweep on country by country. But *Blitzkrieg* as an economic policy proved unrealistic without an unbroken series of total victories.

Hitler refused, moreover, to require from his unenthusiastic public the disciplines of modern war. He mobilized only in his own fashion. With his bias against science he ignored the importance of young scientists and for three years allowed them to be drafted while protecting performing artists by tearing up their draft records. His hatred of Jews figured in Germany's lag in nuclear physics, a field he associated with them. Although he called the war a life-and-death struggle, for years he insisted that neither staff nor material be diverted from his personal building program—either re-construction of public buildings or secret work on his dream capitol. Hitler at war was in Goebbels's view an enlargement of himself. He still considered propaganda paramount and clung to its details; he personally chose the musical fanfares for victories announced on the radio and edited newsreels. For the sake of his own image, he abruptly refused a costly new headquarters and ordered further outlays for a simple one.

After the quick victory over Poland, Hitler secretly made SS Commander Heinrich Himmler the Reich Commissioner of German Folkdom, with orders to initiate Hitler's long-formulated campaign against the Jews there, out of the public spotlight. Hitler valued and praised Himmler's willingness to serve him without question and to use reprehensible methods and create accomplices, although he said he did not like such policemen. Conquering Poland permitted Hitler, through Himmler, to enact fantasies about selective breeding toward a new master race, again secretly, in a program named *Lebenborn*. This "Fountain of Life" had a staff of seven hundred to run human stud farms and genetic experiments, and to sterilize or kill people found undesirable.

Hitler escaped what was or appeared to be an assassination attempt and again asserted his unique mission, declaring to the generals that "the fate of the Reich depends only upon me" (Toland, 1976, p. 595). After a plot by military men opposed to him then evaporated, he told the generals that he could violate the neutrality of Belgium and Holland because "nobody will question it when we have won" (Fest, 1974, p. 627).

In the successful Norway gamble, he set up his own Supreme Command alongside the traditional command structure, institutionalizing his distrust and also creating his favorite divide-and-rule situation. Hysterical outbursts that gave voice to impossible demands became prominent. He diverted his master engineer from war work to draw up a fantastic project for a gigantic recreation center in the Norwegian fjords, to be connected to German roads by huge bridges.

The cost to him of conquering France in six weeks was a daily crisis of nerves, the frequent cause being the alarm he felt at his own successes. As he seized three helpless neutral nations, he is reported to have forbidden his troops to take any loot. Hitler abruptly halted his armor's advance against the British forces within sight of the channel port of Dunkirk. Already extremely anxious, he welcomed Goering's assurances that the entrapped British could be liquidated from the air, preferring a victory by the Nazi-associated Luftwaffe to one by the regular army. With his denigration of others, he could not conceive of the voluntary heroism of the Dunkirk rescue of three hundred thousand Britons in an armada of small boats. After France fell he was puzzled by Britain's determined refusal to accommodate him and stop fighting, just as later he thought his bombing of London would surely bring revolution there.

When the French capitulated, Hitler "was literally shaken by frantic exuberance" (Toland, 1976, p. 614). At the surrender ceremony he staged, he used his whole body to express defiance and contempt and "triumphant hate" (Shirer, 1960, pp. 742–743). Yet at the time of the ceasefire, Hitler, according to separate accounts, mentioned the great responsibility he felt and sat slumped, with bowed head, in the jubilant company. Visiting conquered Paris unannounced for just three early-morning hours, he was photographed at the Eiffel Tower, his expression strained and hands characteristically clasped over his crotch. During a long stop at Napoleon's tomb he spoke of his own, to be built in Munich. He decided against a victory parade, saying "I am not in the mood," another contrast with his recent elation. He shocked Speer when he said, "I have often wondered whether we would not have to destroy Paris," and added that his new Berlin would overshadow it (Speer, 1970, pp. 172–173).

Now hailed as a master military technologist, Hitler claimed total credit for the victory over France. In a rare acknowledgment, he did remark privately that he had learned from Charles de Gaulle's book on motorized warfare. At this point, sometimes seen as his zenith, he also remarked that a campaign against Russia would be like child's play by comparison. But soon his adjutant noted, "Fuehrer is obviously depressed" (Fest, 1974, p. 641). Although he said once that terror bombing among London civilians was to be a last resort, soon he expressed the willingness to destroy London with a new incendiary bomb.

In the midst of diplomatic victories came three failures: to gain control of Gibraltar by drawing in Franco Spain, to induce the French to be allies, and to control Italy. He expected Franco to capitulate, like so many other statesmen, to his invincible personal force, but Franco used Hitler's own psychological tricks, stood firm, and outwitted him. When Hitler suddenly learned that the

Italians secretly planned to attack Greece without him, he was beside himself but swallowed his fury and said flatly that he did not want to cross Mussolini. Even when the Italians failed in Albania and North Africa, he did not deny Mussolini support and was astonishingly calm about the Duce's demands upon him. In late 1943 he staged a daring rescue of the fallen Duce and forced him to continue to try to lead the Italians (Toland, 1976, pp. 773–776).

When he decided to "settle accounts with Russia as soon as fair weather permitted," Hitler remembered only his victories. He said he was the only mortal who had achieved a "superhuman state," that his nature was "more God-like than human"; further, he claimed that he was the first of a new race of supermen, "bound by none of the conventions of human morality" and "above the law." In this mood that all things were possible to him, he ordered preparations for a huge drive to take India (Toland, 1976, pp. 646–651). He stopped thinking through the next possible steps his adversaries might take; he refused to be informed or persuaded. Often impatiently, he would make his old claim to divine guidance, but now stated it as a reassurance: "Providence has arranged all this" (Fest, 1974, p. 646).

Convulsive rage led him into his fateful mistake in attacking Yugoslavia. When a government overthrow there frustrated his original plan simply to march through on his way to Russia, with froth on his lips he ordered "Operation Punishment" to smash that country. The cost would be a month of warm weather, fatal to his intended attack on Russia. Rage and hate marked his preparation of the military when it did come. Declaring to his officers that he alone could stop the Bolsheviks, he shouted that the only problem was dealing with prisoners and non-combatants, which must be done, "not in a knightly fashion" but with "unprecedented merciless and unrelenting harshness." Russian civil officers were to be liquidated, since German soldiers, he decided, were not bound by the Hague Convention (Fest, 1974, p. 680).

By 1940 Hitler, despite the war, spent more time at the *Berghof*, and Eva was at last acknowledged as its mistress. Hitler was observed after 1940 to use the *Du* to her, but his diminutives were not ones usual among lovers, being rather words that are unusual between adults such as neuter expressions, quite sexless and part of baby talk (Waite, 1977, p. 229).

Hitler was visiting at the *Berghof* when told that his Deputy Fuehrer Rudolf Hess, who long had been neglected and avoided, had flown off alone toward Scotland. He was heard to cry out like an animal and to exclaim, "If only he would drown! Then he would vanish without a trace, and we could work out some harmless explanation at our leisure" (Speer, 1970, pp. 174–175). He announced on the radio that Hess had gone mad, a charge as puzzling to the leaders as to the public. Passing over the logical successor, he appointed as deputy his current tool, Martin Bormann. Hitler first began to speak of Hess to the leaders softly and sadly, but shifted to anger and called him "insane," a "deserter," a "traitor." He hid from them his fear that Hess would reveal Hitler's then-imminent move, the turn against Russia, still secret from the inner circle. Hitler arrested Hess's brother and staff, but not his wife, nor would he permit Bormann to confiscate her home. By 1944, when he was hanging plotters,

Hitler would speak of hanging Hess, too, as a traitor (Toland, 1976, p. 665), only to shift again in 1945 just before his suicide, then calling Hess the sole pure idealist whom the Nazi program had made indelible in history (Fest, 1970, p. 196).

Three longstanding themes were conspicuous when Hitler struck at Russia. One was self-justification, the note also sounded in the final chapter of *Mein Kampf*, "The Right of Emergency Self-Defense," where he wrote of "holding under poison gas twelve or fifteen thousand Jews." Indoctrination pamphlets for the German soldier charged him to be "an avenger of all bestialities inflicted on the German people" and stressed "the necessity of a severe but just atonement [*sic*] on Jewish subhumanity" (Dawidowicz, 1975, pp. 166–167). He sent justifications to Mussolini, and even to the Kremlin. He now saw the war in cosmic terms, a struggle between pure blood and inferior, between the all-good and the all-bad. Two other lifelong themes were his contagious self-confidence and his propensity for risktaking. He said he had only to kick the door "and the whole rotten structure will come crashing down" (Toland, 1976, p. 675). The night before the assault, however, he spoke of "pushing open a door into a dark room never seen before, without knowing what lies there" (Fest, 1974, p. 647).

The management of the realities of life was increasingly taken over for him by Bormann, who soon provided a new outlet for his oral outpourings to replace the old release of oratory. Bormann arranged to record Hitler's words as he held forth at the ever-longer meals in the East Prussia headquarters. An official took notes and dictated a draft to be edited by Bormann. The volume produced from Bormann's collection, the most extensive extant, *Hitler's Secret Conversations*, covers the monologues from July, 1941, through November, 1944. In his introduction Trevor-Roper called this sample of the content of Hitler's mind "the intellectual *detritus* of centuries." He judged its cast to be "mean, mechanical, inhuman," and noted its major capacity, a "terrible simplification." The German historian Schramm stressed the persistence of expressions from Hitler's nineteenth-century youth, observing that his notions of history, biology, and medicine were as outmoded as his language (Schramm, 1971, p. 20). Despite his announcement of 1933 that he remained a Roman Catholic, he spoke often of a deadly reckoning with the Church and said ominously that after the war he would "solve the religious problem"; he called Christianity "an invention of sick brains" (1953, pp. 117–118). He did not, however, support ideas for a Nazi religion.

One pronouncement from the childless Hitler was this: "If I want to believe in a divine commandment, it can only be this: preserve the species" (Schramm, 1971, p. 91). An unconnected sentence placed just before a statement of the uses of conquest declared, "It's a man's nature to act through his descendants. . . . for my part, I must say that when I meet children, I think of them as if they were my own. They all belong to me" (Hitler, 1953, p. 14).

The SS Commandant at Auschwitz testified at the War Crimes trial that Himmler gave him a rare explicit justification for the Fuehrer's order in 1941 that the extermination program be undertaken: it would have to be done then or the Jews would later exterminate the German people. He explained that the Fuehrer expected to leak the truth a little at a time and thus gain complicity and consent. In the early thirties Hitler had urged on Nazi leaders "a technique of depopulation," as always with a justification: "If I send the flower of German youth into . . . the coming war, should I not also have the right to eliminate millions of an inferior race that multiplies like vermin?" (Fest, 1974, pp. 679–680).

When he prematurely declared that he had defeated the Russians, Hitler's crudity of language and brutal ideas were recorded by generals and statesmen: "No pig will ever eject me from here"; the "people" were "reduced to chopped meat"; he would "starve out" Moscow and Leningrad to make an "ethnic catastrophe," would raze both and create a gigantic reservoir on the spot to wipe out the memory of Moscow; he would turn down any offers of surrender that might be offered to spare the cities as Paris had been spared (Fest, 1974, pp. 651–652, 806). When the Russian winter came and the Russian forces suddenly counterattacked, Hitler still painted his world visions, delayed orders to make repairs essential to any retreat, and simply denied the complete change on the Russian front. In the "Night and Fog Decree," he ordained that all persons "endangering German security" were to be killed immediately, to "vanish" without a trace, their fates never to be revealed to their families. People, like the city of Moscow, were to be obliterated.

Hitler's inability to delegate had become even more marked; his generals were humiliated by the distrust that underlay it. His interference now reached down the line to individual military positions, to which he telephoned orders. He finally took over personally as army commander, although he was already directing two levels of command above that one. He ordered removals and transfers of generals not holding the line, and even the execution of one of them. Signs of his deterioration mounted. An official of the Propaganda Ministry recalled considering Hitler "mad" by 1942 and the Nazi Youth Leader felt him to be "slightly insane" then. The noon conference was more than ever an ordeal to the generals because of his ravings, although he still used his extraordinary memory for detail to exercise control in periods of brilliant lucidity. Speer reported that Hitler still listened to reason in regard to some matters in 1942 but now abjured the new technical developments he had once welcomed and was fearful even of a new landing device on his own plane. Still, his old faith in the efficacy of his wishes continued to serve him; extreme demands upon industry were often met, although initially refused as impossible. The recorded table-talk of this year is that of the conqueror convinced he was speaking for history, seeking to impress hearers with the quality of his thought. Yet he was already expressing willingness to let the German people disappear unless it stood up for its own survival. Describing the need for extreme penalties in wartime, he suddenly asserted that "unnatural offenders," i.e., sexual perverts, "generally turn into homicidal maniacs" and called for the strongest punishment for them no matter how young (Hitler, 1953, pp. 210, 408–409).

Hitler's usual administrative tangle resulted in a fatal mystery when Dr. Todt, respected and important chief of all arms and munitions, was rudely attacked by Goering and decided to resign. Dr. Todt, a man uniquely resistant to Hitler's magnetism over the years, left a long conference with Hitler in his headquarters depressed and silent. His departing plane crashed and killed him. To general astonishment, Hitler that afternoon tersely commanded Speer, who escaped being on the death plane only because Hitler kept him up most of the night, to take over. In tears, Hitler could scarcely continue the eulogy at Todt's funeral, but when Speer began to suc- ceed in Todt's job, Hitler said that Providence had both caused the crash and spared Speer so as to bring Hitler an increase in arms production (Speer, 1970, pp. 191–193, 197–198). Yet he told an elderly patroness that he was "now deprived of the only two human beings among all those around me to whom I have been truly and inwardly attached: Dr. Todt is dead and Hess has flown away from me!" (Toland, 1976, p. 666). Alas for the devoted Eva Braun, he thus acknowledged only a remote man who could rarely be induced to sit at his table and a man he could not bear to converse with, denounced as crazy, and wished dead.

Hitler continued to revile and insult generals who dared argue for strategic retreats, at least once with clenched fists and foam at his lips. In August, 1942, when a large and highly placed secret ring of German oppo- nents was caught plotting, he had them all savagely ex- ecuted. He broke off any association with his generals, refusing even to shake hands. For months he dined in his bunker alone with a new Alsatian dog given him by Bormann, while he took over still another personal com- mand, this time of the forces in the South.

When Stalingrad again held and he furiously cashiered

his Chief of the General Staff, Hitler made explicit his pervasive distrust with these words: ". . . you will never discover my thought and intention until I am giving my orders. . . . you will never learn what I am thinking and those who boast most loudly that they know my thought, to such people I lie even more" (Waite, 1977, p. 217). The general later wrote that Hitler's use of intuition instead of logic was one of "many proofs" that feminine characteristics were dominant in him. Hitler's belief in his superhuman abilities, long fed by the adulation of associates, now overwhelmed some of them altogether; one general became, in Hitler's own words, as loyal as a dog. His real dog, Goebbels said, was closer to him than any human being.

Traveling in 1942, Hitler chose not to show himself to the people in his habitual way but ordered the shades drawn in the face of ragged and wounded soldiers on passing trains. Thereafter he had shades drawn even in his isolated headquarters.

He could not be deflected from his dream of making the Slavs helots for a hundred million German migrants, nor from fanciful programs to permit extra wives for German heroes. In the West, he still intended a hegemony based on German subjugation, as he had sketched in his unpublished book of 1928, the same New Germany he had mapped in 1940, reaching the English Channel and including part of France, to be ruled by a vast network of garrisons. From the Atlantic to the Steppes, great towers would memorialize the German dead. He would breed his new superman. His great postwar settling of accounts with the Churches would require hanging the Pope. Although details of this vision were not publicly known, the wives of Cabinet Ministers in Berlin were discussing rumors that Hitler had "become insane." A famous surgeon reported him broken and quoted his disjointed mutterings that ten enemies must die for each German and that he "must go to India" (Toland, 1976, pp. 723–724).

At news of the victorious winter offensive by the Russians, he refused to heed his highest officers or the pleas of Mussolini. He denied the disaster, the turning point of his war, and began to plan new campaigns. "Surrender is forbidden" was his last order to the Germans defeated at Stalingrad. Hitler, his physical deterioration accelerating, lived two years and four months before he staged his suicide, ordering punishment for the Germans for permitting the defeat. Within a narrowing daily discipline he had worked harder than ever before, directing his giant war machine until its loss was undeniable even by him. His swift aging, with changes in posture and gait, depression, and massive medication, has been described in detail by Toland, Fest, and others and has occasioned much conjecture.

In 1945, with defeat inevitable, Eva Braun insisted that she be flown to join Hitler in his bunker headquarters under Berlin. She refused to leave the bunker when she could, and Hitler surprised the staff when he kissed her. Still, when her sister's husband was shown to be about to desert the embattled bunker, Hitler had him shot despite Eva's tears. Hitler in the last bloody drama he staged gave Eva her dearest wish. Calling his thirty-three-year-old mistress "the girl" who after years of loyal friendship had joined him of her own free will, Adolf Hitler in a written personal testament declared that she "at her own request goes to her death with me as my wife" (Toland, 1976, p. 883). A wedding, almost ludicrously meeting all formalities with his usual legalistic precision, took place hours before the violent deaths he ordained for them both. Speer sensed Hitler's cynicism in this act (Speer, 1970, p. 93). Adolf Hitler clung, rigidly as always, to his hatreds, his manipulations, and his glorious self-estimate. His hatreds dominated his last public testament, which excoriated the Jews (1973, p. 374).

THE LIFE AND THE DIAGNOSIS

CHAPTER VIII

The Life and the Diagnosis Compared

Having first examined the typical behavior, thinking, and feeling now diagnosed as making up a narcissistic personality with paranoid features functioning on a borderline personality level, and having reviewed the life record of Adolf Hitler, we can compare the features characteristic of that syndrome with those of Hitler. Facts to support the diagnosis here offered were, in hindsight, almost unmistakable by the time Adolf Hitler approached

157

puberty. During his adolescence, data rapidly accumulated. His adult life continued in the same pattern.

The early indications of the disorder cast doubt on the attempts of some authors to attribute Hitler's aberrant behavior largely to a postencephalitic state. Recktenwald (1963) speculated that Adolf contracted encephalitis from his brother, Edmund, who is said to have died of measles—considered an unlikely cause of death for a six-year-old in good health. But Stolk (1968) believed that there are no convincing arguments to support Recktenwald's theory, an opinion in which Walters (1975) apparently concurred. Nevertheless, both Stolk and Walters also speculated that Hitler may have been exposed to epidemic encephalitis—during the period 1916–1918, in their view. No data are available that confirm an episode of acute encephalitis. It is true that certain of Hitler's symptoms a few years before his death can be regarded as meeting major diagnostic criteria of postencephalitic disease. It is, for example, well established that toward the end of his life, Hitler had a left-sided limb tremor suggesting parkinsonism, a late manifestation of encephalitis. In light of all the uncertainties surrounding the question, however, what could in fairness be said is that if Hitler did indeed suffer from a postencephalitic state, it might account to some extent for the extreme and exaggerated manifestations of his narcissistic-borderline disorder.

The possibility that his psychopathological state in early youth was merely a manifestation of common adolescent conflicts does not withstand examination. First, whereas aspects of ordinary adolescent conflicts may resemble features of this syndrome, they do not fit it so totally as do the features of Hitler's adolescent personality, revealed unintentionally by his admirer, Kubizek. Since adolescence is a transition phase, many of its signs of psychological flux can be interpreted as a search for an identity different from the child's but not yet stabilized. Hitler's failure to achieve an ego identity during this period of his life is not at all unusual. But two characteristics separate Hitler's adolescence from that of less disturbed individuals. In him the failure to achieve an ego identity during this phase was accompanied by a severe deficiency in the capacity to move toward real or lasting interdependence with any other person, and by total incapacity even to speak to a young woman. In the usual course of development, these primary tasks of adolescence move forward in short advances, alternating with progress in the capacity for intimacy. Advances in ego identity support the achievement of that capacity. But in Hitler the capacity was so inhibited that in late adolescence he abruptly gave up even the nonreciprocal, exploitive relationship he had temporarily found possible with August Kubizek. Second, and even more telling, almost all the personality traits that were significant in Hitler's adolescence persisted until his death, many becoming even more pronounced. Scrutinizing the voluminous testimony on the rest of his life without slighting any report that does not fit the hypothesis, one finds dominant in Hitler's life the features of the diagnosis.

GENERAL ANXIETY

A strong signal of the borderline personality, usually evident on first examination, is a marked, nonspecific anxiety. Although a few observers reported seeing Hitler in a relaxed state, he was most often in a state of tense and restless anxiety, lifelong. Many close-up photographs revealed a tense, anxious man, even when their evident purpose was to show a determined, serious leader. Kubizek described a very high-strung youth, constantly pacing restlessly to release his enormous tension. Adolf's short flights to the countryside, from which he was eager to return, bespoke a similar purpose of decompression. The high-pitched rageful harangues characteristic of him throughout his life left him emotionally spent, associates noted, that is, with his anxious tensions at least temporarily dissipated. In his youth these methods of dealing with his anxiety proved inadequate and on two occasions he fled from Linz to Vienna, probably in efforts to cope with it more effectively. Chronic restless anxiety would account in part for the puzzle of the satisfaction Hitler manifested in remaining a mere message carrier during World War I. For the rest of his life he restlessly moved around any city where he lived and impulsively traveled over all Germany, even using the airplane despite his fear of flying.

Hitler's own revelation of the intense anxiety which disturbed his sleep was his statement in the recorded table-talk: "Speaking for myself, it is the nights which I find are a torment; I know that I shall never reach the ripe old age of the ordinary citizen." He made more direct statements about his anxiety to the Gauleiter of Hamburg. He gave as reasons for his changed living habits in the mid-1930s his states of extreme excitement, outbreaks of perspiration, and trembling of limbs. He also mentioned stomach cramps, which he was sure presaged the advent of cancer (Toland, 1976, p. 277). The fear of cancer was only one of many phobias that plagued Hitler, described below among his many neurotic symptoms. Another was his fear of being shaved by his personal barber because he could not bear to have anyone with a razor operate close to his throat (Bezymenski, 1968, p. 10). The anxiety involved in such morbid fears is evident.

The frequent excited and often protracted talk, his lifelong habit, was a means of discharging anxious tensions and aggression rather than of communicating ideas. Evidence for this is the regularity of impulsive verbal outbursts throughout his life. The startling scenes he created at inappropriate times and to the astonishment of his hearers were only occasionally useful to him; yet after he had attained power he deliberately exploited such outbursts.

POOR IMPULSE CONTROL

The burden of these explosions was anxious rage, directed at an audience of one or of many. In these incidents he screamed at the top of his voice and pounded a table or a wall, all the while spewing out a stream of vulgar abuse. He could be neither reasoned with nor interrupted. Sometimes he would suddenly stop and sneak embarrassed glances at the witnesses, as though to see whether his behavior had elicited the derisive reactions he half expected. After the impulsive eruption, he would correct the disarray that resulted from his antics and resume talking in normal tones.

Poor control of other impulses was also obvious. His sudden and ludicrous gestures and declarations of passion for certain women, including the wives of his close colleagues, bespoke faulty control of libidinal impulses. Hitler never ceased his impulsive behavior, nor did he limit it to the personal or the inconsequential. By 1942 the Chief of the Army General Staff observed that Hitler's disastrous military decisions "were the product of a violent nature following its momentary impulses" (Trevor-Roper, 1953, p. xii).

EGO WEAKNESS

The impulsive temper tantrum, obviously childlike, regressive, and the kind of behavior at other times unacceptable to Hitler, was evidence of another feature, namely, an ego weakness. It indicated an intolerance for a quantum of anxiety in excess of the amount habitually experienced. The tantrums often came at times when he felt special anxiety because of frustration of strong wishes, those he had been sure of having fulfilled. As Hitler himself admitted, when his soldiers marched into the Rhineland he could reasonably expect that the French would attack, and before he could be sure that they would not, he was consumed by an anxiety so severe that he could not, he confessed, endure another such strain for ten years (Toland, 1976, p. 388).

ANGER, HATE, AND CRUELTY

Among the traits for which Adolf Hitler is known even to the most uninformed are the furious aggression and destructive hate he so clearly expressed as a national leader, the 1934 Blood Purge being an early example. His half brother said he was "quick to anger from childhood on." In adolescence he proclaimed a long list of hatreds, exempting only his mother and Kubizek. Yet that adoring satellite reported that his hero, in speaking of his mother, repeatedly used the harsh expression "settling accounts" and persisted in behavior he knew caused her anxiety and anguish. Kubizek could not hide how frequently he was himself the object of Adolf's rageful anger, scorn, and derogation. Later, when World War I took Hitler to the front, the fighting and killing gave him conspicuous contentment. There his furious angers were not only expressed but also sanctioned, and he often recalled how happy he was as a soldier. When he finally assumed the presidency Hitler is reported to have said, "Externally, I end the revolution. But internally it goes on, just as we store up our hate and think of the day on which we shall cast off the mask, and stand revealed as those we are and eternally shall remain" (Rauschning, 1940, p. 175). Perhaps lack of courage permitted him only rarely to express his rage in personal violence. When he did attack, as when he assaulted a monarchist political opponent and was jailed for it, he was always surrounded by his strongarm men.

Early in his life Hitler found the Jews to hate and to harm. But he also expressed hatred of the Americans, Czechs, Poles, Russians, and all other "non-Aryans," whom he considered fit only to be slaves of Germans. His oratory aimed to stir audiences to envy, rage, and hate, all of which ultimately was to prepare them emotionally for battle and wars of annihilation. One of Hitler's

basic beliefs was that "He who wants to live should
fight. . . ." He repeatedly asserted that peace and sta-
bility are debilitating, and only conflict and war good.
For him, fighting dominated the national scene as well;
his idea of politics was battle with no quarter given.
When Hitler spoke of conflict and war he used these
terms in a literal rather than a symbolic sense (Hanfstaengl, 1957, p. 153). Abstract conceptualizing was rare
with him, great pragmatist that he was. This concrete
mode of thinking characterized his racial anti-Semitism
as well.

He excused his drive to destroy all Jews as a wish to
protect the whole world and the Germans in particular.
But not all Germans were spared his venomous ire.
Among Germans he despised the clergy, the intellec-
tuals, the educated, the officer class, Marxists, members
of the labor unions, judges, teachers, economists, and
even artists whose creativity did not conform to his tastes.
All the rest of the Germans joined the company of the
Hitler-damned when they failed to provide him with the
military victories he demanded. At the end of his life he
declared that the Germans deserved their defeat and
suffering and just before his suicide ordered a scorched-
earth policy which could have destroyed Germany had
it been carried out. Albert Speer observed: ". . . long
before the end I knew that Hitler was not destroying to
build, he was building to destroy" (O'Donnell, 1969).
Indeed, aggression and destructiveness can be seen as
the core of all his strivings for power and its brutal use,
both domestically and for conquest and genocide that
reached beyond the boundaries of Germany.

Hitler's destructive cruelty determined even the

games that he enjoyed, those that embarrassed or hurt others. His idea of a practical joke on a member of his entourage was to terrorize him with fear that he was out of favor. To a large extent the extreme reaction he could expect in a follower was due to the fact that Hitler's most devastating invective was used upon helpless Party members who had fallen from grace. A favorite amusement of his last years was repeated viewing of a horrifying film he had made of the execution of the generals who had conspired against him in the plot of July 20, 1944. He ordered that piano wire be used to strangle each one and that pressure be periodically released in order to intensify his death agonies (Norden, 1971, p. 193). He once declared, "brutality is respected. Brutality and physical strength . . . They [the people] want someone to frighten them and make them shudderingly submissive" (Rauschning, 1940, p. 83).

GRANDIOSITY AND OMNIPOTENCE

Situations sure to stir Hitler's rage and often terrible retribution were those that intended to diminish his grandiosity. He could tolerate no doubt of his infallibility in any area: his knowledge, his strength, his intuition, his judgments. Witness the fates of his questioners, Gregor Strasser and Ernst Roehm. The surpassing cruelty of his punishment of the generals after the 1944 assassination plot he may have rationalized on the ground of the enormity of their crime: a threat to the life of so exalted a being as himself.

MEGALOMANIC SELF-IMAGE

His megalomanic self-image was as pervasively demonstrated as his hatred. Hitler set himself up as the un-
questioned, infallible, and omniscient leader of the
Germans. His extravagant opinion of himself appeared
early in the record of his life. Adolf before age seven was
described by his half brother as "imperious," a child who
thought it his due always to have his way. His teachers
observed that he "demanded of his fellow-pupils their
unqualified subservience, fancying himself in the role of
leader." When his peers rebelled, he chose younger,
more readily dominated, playmates. One of his excuses
to Kubizek for his all-encompassing hatred of others was
their failure to appreciate his superior qualities. Adolf
in adolescence rejected all schooling because he thought
no one had anything to teach him. Later, in the Vienna
shelters, he fancied himself an authority on almost all
subjects. He clung throughout life to the notion that he
was an artist, a calling then highly respected among
Germans.

The intensity of his hatred of the officer class, which
appeared early and grew ever stronger, is probably expl-
icable as rageful resentment that so magnificent a person
as he saw himself had to accept its help in his political
beginnings and even to fear its disapproval far into his
Chancellorship, until he had at last brought the military
establishment under his personal domination.

As Chancellor in his after-dinner monologues he pontificated on every imaginable subject: architecture, the
arts, science, philosophy, history, politics, crime. He
based his political and military confidence on claims to

omniscience, the idea that he was chosen and endowed by Providence with incomparable and infallible intuition, intelligence, and ability. On one occasion he remarked to the Party Secretary, "mark my word, Bormann, . . . I'm going to become a religious figure. Already Arabs and Moroccans are mingling my name with their prayers" (1953, p. 167). Discussing his "metamorphosis-to-super-man" idea, Hitler said "[National Socialism] is more even than a religion: it is the will to create mankind anew" (Rauschning, 1940, p. 246). National Socialism, of course, was Hitler himself to himself.

Hitler repeatedly likened himself to Jesus, as when, trying to gain the attention of a woman who excited him, he brandished his whip and shouted, ". . . in driving out the Jews I remind myself of Jesus in the temple," and when he declared, "Just like Christ, I have a duty to my people . . ." (Waite, 1977, p. 27). Shortly after coming to power he admonished an audience that should he not fulfill his duty, ". . . you should then crucify me" (Domarus, 1965, p. 214). Even his early patron and bard, Eckart, commented in 1923, ". . . something has gone completely wrong with Adolf . . . with that damned whip of his . . . shouting 'I must enter Berlin like Christ in the temple' " (Hanfstaengl, 1957, p. 83). Hermann Rauschning's conclusion was accurate: "Hitler's God is Hitler himself" (1940, p. 143).

Closely related were fantasies of omnipotence. He often indicated that his "will" could accomplish what others thought impossible, and thus would brook no contradiction from lesser souls. The absolute power he in fact obtained served then to reinforce his idea that his will was magical. When he made his first big speech at the end of his trial for the aborted *Putsch* of 1923, he explicitly declared that an ordained leader like himself is never compelled to seize power as lesser men are, but rather *wills* it.

RISK TAKING

His fantasies of omnipotence as well as his needs to be exhibitionistic and to deny his weaknesses were all related to Hitler's uncontrollable drive to take risks. This drive figured large in his successes, both domestic and foreign, when he overcame all opposition by thinking the unthinkable and risking it—for example, invading the Rhineland or making his pact with the Soviets. This drive was supported by the fantasy that he was under the special protection and guidance of Providence. But even when he had some doubts about that fantasy, the compulsion to gamble was irresistible. "You know, I am like a wanderer who must cross an abyss on the edge of a knife. But I must, I just must cross," he once confessed (Waite, 1977, p. 393).

HUNGER FOR PRAISE

One might expect that a person with so exalted an opinion of himself would have no need for praise and admiration from others. But quite the contrary was true of Hitler, as it is of all narcissistic personalities. From childhood on, he demanded that his idea of his pre-eminence be recognized, appreciated, and admired. Adolf was able to tolerate some limited closeness to Kubizek largely because of Kubizek's outright and boundless adulation of him. Such limited intimacy as he developed with Eva Braun had as one of its bases a similar abject adulation. This need for admiration became more manifest as he became more powerful. He boastfully laid claim to all kinds of superior qualities, inviting admiration and praise when he was in need of it. Eventually, surrounded by a fawning retinue, Hitler absorbed it all as his due, no matter how nauseatingly exaggerated. As he always expected, the Chancellor's observations were received as the products of a brilliant genius by those around him, although in actuality they were marked by platitudes, inaccuracies, and inanity.

He was also, of course, not at all above praising himself. An interesting manifestation of indirect self-admiration occurred early in his life in his ideas about the "Stefanie" with whom he said he fell in love. Beyond her attractive appearance, Adolf knew nothing whatever about her until he sent Kubizek to investigate. Thereafter he had no interest in the facts garnered unless they confirmed his preconceived notions. Adolf surrounded her "with grandiose thoughts and ideas . . . to such an extent as to make her the female image of himself" (Kubizek, 1955, p. 68). It was with this image of himself that Adolf fell in love. Decades later, when he ordered his soldiers into the Rhineland in 1936 and the French did not retaliate, Hitler, relieved of almost overwhelming anxiety, said grandly, "Yes, the world belongs to the courageous," and "You can serve God only as a hero" (Toland, 1976, p. 388). When one of his secretaries asked him why he had not married, he answered that he did not want to be a father because "the children of a genius have a hard time in this world." Even the devoted secretary was disturbed by the smugness of his self-praise (Gun, 1968a, p. 169).

HYPOCHONDRIA

Hitler never lost a fearful preoccupation with his body and its functions: his lungs, his digestion, his blood, his "nerves," his general health. He claimed that in adolescence he was often ill with lung ailments, although Dr. Bloch, his physician at the time, could recall neither their traces nor any organic basis for lung trouble. This may have been the beginning of his later hypochondriacal complaints, which were legion. In a rare personal note to an acquaintance of his Vienna years addressed as "Franzl," Hitler wrote in 1911 that after "a small stomach colic" he was trying to cure himself by a diet of fruit and vegetables since "physicians are all idiots." However, he found it "simply ridiculous" to speak of a nervous ailment in his case since otherwise he was the healthiest of persons (Von Müllern-Schönhausen, n.d., pp. 195–197). Apparently a physician had told Hitler that his gastrointestinal complaints were what today would be called psychogenic, something his grandiosity could not tolerate.

Descriptions of him in his Vienna derelict days indicate real physical weakness. As late as 1913, when the Austrian Army caught up with him, he was found "too weak" to serve. But once in the German Army in World War I, he withstood the rigors of the front without any report of physical weakness.

His digestive-tract complaints, however, returned in later life. The Chancellor embraced vegetarianism in an elaborate and costly form and pontificated on its virtues, but could not forego liver dumplings. He maintained special vegetarian cooks, one so important to him that he "Aryanized" her family when she proved to be a Jew under his laws. His food habits were bizarre; he consumed prodigious quantities of sugar in all forms, even dumping it in fine white wine. He came finally to rely upon a doctor often described as a quack and his remedies, taking dangerous medicines in increasing quantities to the end of his life.

Despite all this concentration upon his body, he adamantly refused to subject himself to a complete physical examination. Nor would he try to improve his physique by exercise or sport. Instead, he chose the theatrical device of costuming to make his person distinctive and memorable when he displayed himself. Successively he affected the fine clothes of a dandy, the trench coat, the unusual mustache, the Bavarian country costume, and finally the military uniform.

NEUROTIC SYMPTOMS

Some of Hitler's many other neurotic symptoms probably explain why he was called an hysteric by some commentators and an obsessive-compulsive neurotic by others. Certainly he manifested hysterical symptoms: the hysterical blindness diagnosed during his army days, and fuguelike states described by Kubizek and later by others who observed him as the Fuehrer. He was a compulsive hand-washer and had compulsive bedtime rituals. Finally, he had many phobias in addition to fear of cancer, including fear of large bodies of water, of small boats, of horses, of infected blood, and of premature death from cancer or a heart disease. But, as described in Chapter II, the syndrome postulated includes a complex of neurotic symptoms, especially phobias.

An interesting example of how he exploited even his phobias in the interest of his intolerance of opposition occurred when his Foreign Minister, while arguing against Hitler's plan to invade Russia, lost his temper and shouted his opposition. Hitler suddenly sank into a chair, clutched his chest, and declared he thought he was going to have a heart attack. Victorious, he told the Minister that he must never again oppose him in that manner (Toland, 1976, p. 678).

EXHIBITIONISM AND VOYEURISM

One of the ways Hitler tried to gratify his need for admiration was exhibitionism. In adolescence he promenaded in the finery of a dandy, quite inappropriate for an unemployed lower middle-class youth entirely supported by a widowed mother. As an adult of some prominence, he once was moved to strut ostentatiously before a buxom Brunhilde of Berchtesgaden, to attract her admiring attention. To another woman the rising politician boastfully demonstrated how very long he could keep his arm extended in a Nazi salute. He enjoyed exhibiting himself as an orator before thousands. He gave great attention to the stagecraft of political meetings in which he starred. Often he staged his entrance in a hall or arena by walking alone down a long aisle through the cheering crowd, followed by his entourage. He had his pictures distributed all over the land by the thousands; in some of them he appeared in knight's armor on a horse, an animal of which he was actually deathly afraid. He was so sensitive about his appearance and so concerned about his weight and his clothes that he had himself photographed in new outfits to study their effect before appearing in them in public. One valet reported that he would often examine himself in a mirror and ask whether he looked the part of a Fuehrer (Waite, 1977, p. 45).

Voyeurism, the other side of the coin, was also conspicuous. After he acquainted himself with the red-light district of Vienna, he took the weary Kubizek on a tour, and not once but twice in one evening. Hanfstaengl reported his pornographic drawings of his niece Geli. His passion for the cinema included pornographic films, some specially made for him. He enjoyed protracted conversations with the nude models of the Art Museum. His obsession with the big buttocks of women farmworkers bent over their tasks in the fields led Roehm to say that such was his sex life. The extreme perversion reported of him was that he required close scrutiny of female genitals, and of urination and defecation, to reach satisfaction.

CONTROL AND MANIPULATION

The child Adolf's incessant demand to have his own way was an early manifestation of his need to control and have things as he wanted them. When his preadolescent peers no longer cared for his leadership, Adolf's need was so great that he sought out younger boys who did submit. He obviously controlled and manipulated Kubizek. Adolf concentrated his efforts on his adoring mother and Kubizek when his schoolmates and his relatives rejected his efforts. When Kubizek achieved some success and autonomy and seemed to be slipping from his complete control, Adolf suddenly and cruelly withdrew from him altogether.

Later, after his histrionic talents flowered with political success, his effect upon certain followers became extreme, serving to bring them into complete submission to his control and manipulation. With Ludecke, who wrote that he gave Hitler his soul, the manipulation lasted about fifteen years. Goebbels, at first his enemy, soon wrote that he loved him (Fest, 1973, p. 245) and submitted to Hitler's control for an even longer time, that is, until his death. Hitler's insistence that he be accepted and obeyed as absolute dictator, first of the Nazi Party and then of the nation, frankly shows the drive to control and manipulate on the grandest scale.

Sometimes he used money to manipulate people. When he needed a loyal housekeeper in his Alpine retreat, he installed his impoverished half sister, on whose discretion he could count. When he needed silence from his half brother's wife and son, he bought it with money and the furious insistence that they lie about their connection to him. He greatly enriched political associates who were acquainted with his private life, notably the photographer Heinrich Hoffman, whom he made culture czar of all Germany. Even in his will, his bequests went to those whose discretion he wanted, like his banished former adjutant, and the relatives he otherwise ignored.

His insistence upon absolute control of all matters important to him led him to take personal charge of function after function in the armed forces. Here again, as when his childish control faltered, when the control over the outcome of battles fought by his armies in Russia eluded him and he suffered successive defeats, he withdrew more and more in remote and isolated headquarters until the end was undeniable. Losing all control in defeat, he controlled his own death by suicide.

DEMANDINGNESS

As the uniquely superior individual he believed himself to be, Hitler showed throughout life that he felt entitled to the gratification of all his wishes. As his power grew, so did the ruthlessness with which he asserted his needs. The child demanded his own way; the adolescent expected to be supported in elegant style by his widowed mother; he took as his due Kubizek's admiration and submissive companionship. The young man exploited fellow-derelict Hanisch. The rising politician began to demand absolute submission to his will by the Nazi Party in all matters. That he felt completely justified is shown by the fact that he so coolly eliminated, sometimes literally by death, those who had helped him but no longer served. At no time did Hitler question his right to be supported and indulged by the German people in the luxuries and interests that took his fancy, while concealing aspects incongruent with the image of asceticism and self-denial he wished to convey.

ENVY

All his life Hitler used derision and contempt to deal with his pronounced inclination to jealousy and envy. His youthful jealousy of young officers brought forth a torrent of denigrating names for his "competitors." When he envied the young men relaxing in the Linz café, he abused them contemptuously. When Kubizek succeeded in music, Adolf could not contain sarcastically derisive remarks. When he was a dictator, the successes of Churchill and Roosevelt elicited brutal outpourings. The Chancellor used his well-known talents in mimicry and histrionics to ridicule some of his most devoted supporters (Speer, 1970, pp. 123–124; Langer, 1972, pp. 85–86). Even Goering's lusty enjoyment of life often earned his envious dislike. Sometimes denigration poured from him out of sheer rage: his excoriations of his desperately embattled generals were boundlessly venomous as he approached inevitable defeat in World War II.

APPARENT KINDNESS (CONTRIVED, AMBIVALENT, AND WITHOUT WARMTH)

Toward very few people, and only briefly, did Hitler show positive attitudes. Usually his kind words had an obvious purpose: to show he was a precocious Nationalist by praising a history teacher, to show he had some early contact with a renowned artist by mentioning the kindness of Dr. Roller of the Vienna Opera. Dr. Bloch earned notes and cards of gratitude after he cared for Adolf's mother, but not enough regard to protect him from penury when as a Jew he had to flee Austria. The influential Munich poet Eckart, who was his patron, received a verbal toast in *Mein Kampf* but was neglected just before he died. Rudolf Hess was an early devotee who was treated in a complex way by Hitler. Hess was barred from personal association for years but retained in high office until he made his independent flight to seek peace with England. Then he was totally beyond the pale and at one point threatened with hanging; yet at the very end of his life Hitler remembered him with a kind word. Dr. Fritz Todt was valued as Hitler's major technician of construction engineering and science, held in high regard until his death in a plane crash after leaving Hitler's headquarters. Soon Hitler said God had arranged for him to have a better technician. Albert Speer, who shared and served Hitler's building fantasies daily for years, was once praised by Hitler orally and in writing, but said of himself that even he was not Hitler's friend, since Hitler had none.

A figure closely associated in his feelings with his mother was his half sister, Angela. To some extent Angela actually played the role of mother to the younger Adolf in his early boyhood. Although she lived in abject poverty as a widow in Vienna during his rise to prominence, he, knowing few women he would care to acquaint with his private life or have close to him, turned to her to run his elaborate *Berghof* for him. Angela did not break with him over his attentions to her daughter Geli, even at her death. But when she disapproved of Eva Braun or when other differences with her developed, she departed his household with so little apparent feeling about it on his part that he did not attend her subsequent wedding. Still, he made her the beneficiary of a modest annuity in his 1938 will, as he did his sister Paula.

Certain friendly acts can be found in his history. For the Popp family with whom he roomed in Munich before the war, he provided a stipend in 1935. He sent small gifts to the senior Mrs. Kubizek, and Kubizek said that he provided funds for the musical and artistic education of his sons. The limited and impersonal nature of these few gestures reveals that Hitler may have realized that he was indebted to these people for kindnesses to him. As often happens with such individuals, Hitler, having no warmth to offer, repaid their kindnesses with niggardly sums of money. Thus, in return for the warmth and friendship he received, he played the role of the grateful financial benefactor and kept their favorable regard as well. This pattern is possible, given the characteristic identity diffusion which imparts the chameleonlike quality to the ego identity of the borderline personality. When the situation called for some gesture of gratitude, Hitler, the angry aggressor, could become for the moment the gracious benefactor, albeit in a thoroughly painless way, since it deprived him essentially of nothing.

Propaganda stories and pictures portrayed the dictator as a kindly, gentle man who loved children and dogs. His reputed love of dogs did not, however, prevent him from beating one mercilessly in order to appear masculine before a young girl. Although he was reported to behave affectionately toward children, Hitler had little or nothing to say in his writings or his interminable monologues about their attributes or his alleged love of them. His occasional play with Hanfstaengl's little son was at the level of play-acting the child himself. Speer's children did not respond to Hitler's overtures.

Besides his hostility and its paranoid projection and his need to devalue everyone, Hitler harbored another reason for not developing warm, friendly relationships: he had no capacity for sustained empathy, consideration, or reciprocal concern for another human being. Only the most trifling public displays of charity or sentiment, usually conspicuous acts that cost him personally very little, are to be found. Hitler, an excellent propagandist and public relations man, had a keen eye for the gesture to impress the masses and promote their admiration and often staged photographs with such ends in view. In *Mein Kampf* he discussed in considerable detail how crowds of people can be influenced in their thinking and behavior. The timing and staging of his speeches at mass meetings attest to his successful application of the strategies he propounded. The narcissistic-borderline personality's façade of great kindness and charm had great value in his propaganda program, and he exploited it to the full.

His only long connection with a woman was his grudging relationship with the personally limited, subservient, and much younger Eva Braun. They were apart during much of its fifteen-year duration. Her diary attests that he had no empathy for the pain he caused her by his long periods of neglect and his attentions to others. The position in his entourage to which he relegated her for years was humiliating, and his gifts were not princely, as Speer reported (1970, p. 93). He refused marriage to her until the hour of his suicide, then built a grisly wedding ceremony into the image of himself that would pass on into history, the project with which he was concerned until his last moments—an image that Speer called cynical.

LACK OF ENJOYMENT

Even as a youth Hitler did not enjoy life. As an adolescent, he was very inhibited in that he never relaxed or raised a little harmless hell. He eschewed alcohol as firmly as he avoided girls, and there is no slightest suggestion that he ever raised his voice in songs of fellowship, even in the Munich beer cellars where his political rantings were heard.

His sole pleasure was the transport produced in him by the grandiloquent music of Wagner. That these anthems served him as the accompaniment and reinforcement of his fantasies of grandeur is a possible explanation of why this composer was so exclusive a favorite throughout his life. As a politician and head of state, Hitler did acquire luxurious possessions, including works of art. But he seemed to react most to the erotically stimulating realistic paintings and statues of nudes and stallions. Socially, he was rarely at ease, did not dance, seldom relaxed his pomposity even at his own table. Rather he built his image there as well.

Finally in the last years, when he had his very words recorded for posterity by stenographers, the monologues reveal how humorless and rigid Hitler was. Early on Kubizek had observed that his friend lacked the ability to pass things over with a smile. Later, those around him observed that humor was foreign to him except when it was at the expense or the misfortune of others. In his personal habits, in his speech, and in his writing he showed inability to change. His memoirs in *Mein Kampf*, like his conversations, constantly referred back to views formed in his Vienna years. Some who tried to counter what Hitler himself called his unshakable obstinacy found that their efforts were in vain and sometimes counterproductive. Toward the end, when it was suggested to him that some things might have been done differently, he exclaimed, "But don't you see *I can not* [*sic*] change!" (Dietrich, 1955, p. 216).

Even his elation over successes and victories was short-lived. Thus he had ever to strive for new victories to feed his grandiosity, his chief source of satisfaction. Between 1939 and 1942 Hitler bemoaned his life as that of an unwilling warlord, a great artist deprived of the joys of creativity. Of course, no one forced Hitler to become a dictator, to involve the world in war; in fact, he proudly proclaimed that he willed it. These complaints can be seen as reflections of his recurrent feeling of emptiness and boredom.

All narcissistic personalities must devaluate others because to acknowledge that one has received anything from another tends to diminish one's grandiose self-image and to stir up envy. Hitler's constant denigration of others kept his social life without warmth or depth or richness—in short, empty and boring. Extreme boredom was certainly the feeling conveyed to Speer and all who

participated in their Fuehrer's dreary attempts to fill his
waking hours. If great achievements could have made
him happy, he should have been by 1942 the happiest
of men, for in the areas of his choice, power and war,
his achievement was enormous. Yet he was, as he declared himself, the most miserable of men.

LOW SELF-ESTIMATES

Despite his propensity for boastful claims of superiority in everything, and confidence in the omnipotence
of his word, his record contains expressions of embarrassment, self-criticism, inferiority, insecurity, and shame
from youth on. These are the feelings—and so often the
complaints—first presented by patients of the narcissistic-borderline category. Grandiose and omnipotent trends
are also often uncovered behind these inferiority feelings. Hitler's record includes several direct, expressions
of shame and unworthiness, e.g., his calling himself a
"shithead" while comparing himself to Frederick the
Great (Schramm, 1965, p. 171). Since one usually does
not add to one's shame by proclaiming it, direct admis-
sions of this feeling are predictably few; and yet some
obvious deductions from his statements and behavior are
possible.

Kubizek called young Adolf "shy and reticent" and
described Adolf's efforts to make up for the "utter insignificance of his own existence," thus hinting at the shame
this insignificant existence cause his self-proud friend.
Shame played a part in Adolf's unwillingness to introduce
himself to "Stefanie" and her mother. Again, Kubizek

noted Adolf's self-criticism, his self-torment, his giving himself orders. At musical evenings in the homes of cultivated Viennese, the otherwise voluble Adolf was ill at ease and silent. Finally, his shame prevented him from ever admitting that he had failed to gain admission to the Academy of Art until he felt goaded into an impulsive confession.

The derelict period was so humiliating to him that years later he could never allude to it. When Hitler was twenty-five years old, Heiden (1944, p. 75) wrote, he felt himself to be nothing in the presence of men. Indeed, when he became the Party leader and his influence grew fast, he was still described as having the demeanor of an obsequious waiter. And as the omnipotent Dictator of Germany he confessed deep shame about using his final school certificate as toilet paper. The Chancellor was constantly fearful that he would appear ridiculous or commit a *faux pas*. Before he ventured on a political appearance in a new suit or headgear, he had himself photographed to study its effect. In addition to asking his valet whether he looked the part of the Fuehrer, he would check with Hess the manner of speech he should use on different occasions. His anxieties lest he appear ridiculous, weak, vulnerable, incompetent, or in any way inferior are indications of this endless battle with shame. His most direct statements of shame and self-abasement came in relations with women. This urge was so great that the presence of others did not prevent him from repulsive groveling before a woman when trying to interest her. The rising politician would tell a lady that he was unworthy to sit near her or kiss her hand but hoped she would look on him with favor. In the course of an

episode of sexual perversion during his chancellorship,
one woman reported that after all kinds of self-accusations he said that he was unworthy of being in the same
room with her.

Hitler's efforts to deny his shame and to avoid situations that would make him feel ashamed pervade much
of what he said, wrote, and did, for reasons explored in
Chapter XII. He inveighed against anything he considered indicative of weakness, inferiority, or defeat. Himself far from his tall, blonde, trim, lithe, tough, ideal
German male, he allied himself with the tough image.
He who feared to swim or sit in a boat or on a horse
boasted of racial, political, and military superiority, su-
perlative courage, and physical excellence. In writing
and speeches he denied his awareness of humiliating
weakness with boasts of his "granite hardness," brutality,
mercilessness, and unchangeability, all of which he
equated with masculinity. Hardness, brutality, mercilessness, and stubborn perseveration also marked his
acts.

Had Hitler died before setting in motion World War
II, he might well have been remembered as a great figure
in German history, the man who freed Germany from
the burdens of Versailles, the creator of Greater Germany and of a community of German people. But Adolf
Hitler could not stop his strivings for ever greater conquests. Since his shame and feelings of weakness, inadequacy, and inferiority were results of deep-seated
psychic conflicts as well as of his inferior physique, the
painful feelings could not be relieved completely by unconscious denial, by boasts, or even by astonishing successes. Although these may have given Hitler some

temporary relief, the mental conflicts were not eliminated and the drives continued, to his undoing.

To put his situation slightly differently, no matter what his rationalization for the conquest of other countries, an unconscious psychological motive was to deny his inferiority feelings, especially his image of himself as a man. Many of his decisions are more understandable if this motive is seen to have been dominant. The relentless persistence of his unconscious self-estimate of inferiority could not be permanently countered by real successes. Nevertheless, like others in this psychological trap, Hitler tried repeatedly to demonstrate by victories and successes that he was not an inferior but a uniquely superior man. Since realities do not touch the underlying unconscious conflicts, they are of no lasting help. Unaware of this fact, as is anyone with this pathologic formation, Hitler persisted in the pursuit of ever greater conquests until he overreached and suffered total defeat. Another aspect of his final accelerating headlong drive was the confluence of psychological factors in him which resulted, as many observers of his last years judged, in his often being out of touch with reality. Included was the paranoid element so conspicuous in his lifelong suspiciousness and the near-predelusional ideas of his own godlike qualities.

CONTRADICTIONS

Hitler's many contradictions have been baffling. He boasted of being the greatest German, the leader of the greatest race; he confidently planned to write the "Mon-

umental History of Humanity." Yet his favorite literature
was the collection of Karl May Wild West Stories, and
his favorite films were *King Kong* and Disney's *Snow
White and the Seven Dwarfs*. While hiding himself from
public gaze when victories ceased and deriding the courage of some of his World War II generals, he continued
to proclaim his own surpassing courage. Yet in World
War I he was, in fact, awarded the Iron Cross. Always
he was full of fears: of impending death; of illness, especially of cancer and gastrointestinal and blood diseases;
of dirt; of horses; of large bodies of water. Repeatedly
referring to himself as humane and truthful, he also
boasted of being a cruel, unmerciful barbarian, admitted
to lying, and promoted the art of the Big Lie. Hitler took
pleasure in quoting a line from Nietzsche: "Thou goes
to women? Do not forget thy whip!" Yet in public his
approach to a woman was to fawn and grovel, or to play
the part of the little child, and in private, he demeaned
himself utterly in seeking sexual gratification. He claimed
a constructive urge to rebuild cities and edifices for the
nation. Yet Speer, who knew most about this obsession
with architecture, recognized it as such and judged finally that Hitler was not destroying old structures in
order to build but was building to destroy. After twenty
years of reflection in prison, Speer was still baffled by
the paradoxes of Hitler's personality. He wrote that Hitler was "cruel, unjust, unapproachable, cold, capricious,
self-pitying, and vulgar" (1976, p. 426). But, he added,
Hitler "was also the exact opposite of almost all of these
things" (1976, p. 426).

SPLITTING AND REVERSALS

These contradictions were possible in him because he used the defensive maneuvers of the narcissistic-border-line personality, especially the combination of primitive denial and splitting, in several ways. One of the most significant was his lifelong consignment of others into "all-good" and "all-bad" categories. During his adolescence almost everybody belonged to the "all-bad" group: adults, including especially teachers and anyone who advised him to learn some way of livelihood; students; soldiers; girls. In effect Adolf said to Kubizek, "The only all-good ones are me and thee, and I'm not always sure about thee."

Later, at least temporarily the all-good embraced the Germans and indeed all Aryans, whereas others were all-bad. Among his more specific split categories were those in the arts; all-good were German composers, especially Wagner, and realistic painters and sculptors. Dictators (except, perhaps, Franco) belonged to the all-good, including even Stalin most of the time. His attitude toward Mussolini bespoke primitive idealization. Still, the possibility always existed that any individual or group could be shifted suddenly from one category to the other. Toward the end of his life the Germans themselves became all-bad because they failed to give him the glorious military victories he felt rightfully his.

An abrupt reversal of conceptualization and feelings from one extreme to the other often occurred in relation to individuals. Examples of this important aspect of the syndrome bear repeating. Kubizek, a temporary exception to the all-bad rest of the world, was suddenly shifted

by Hitler in 1908 to the category of those with whom he
would have nothing to do. Decades later, in the 1930's,
Hitler responded to Kubizek as though he had never
been excluded from the all-good. In the 1920's his ov-
eridealized mentor Eckart was suddenly dropped from
favor. In 1934 Hitler physically destroyed Roehm, his
formerly indispensable and indulged cohort. Shortly before his suicide Hitler consigned to oblivion a group of
his chief lieutenants, including even Goering and Himmler. Only Goebbels, willing to die beside him, escaped his obloquy.

Hitler, the virulent anti-Semite, could not only sus-
pend his raging hatred of Jews at times but could even
accept being the beneficiary of the kind helpfulness of
a number of them. To Dr. Bloch young Hitler wrote that
he was "eternally grateful." In his derelict days he became sufficiently intimate with a Jew to tour Vienna and
take a room with him for a week. The Viennese art dealers who befriended him and regularly bought his me-
diocre watercolors were all Jews. The Iron Cross, First
Class, so highly prized and invaluable in politics, he
received only through the persistent efforts of his regiment's adjutant, a Jew. When a question was raised about
the propriety of having a Jewish cook, Fraulein Kunde,
prepare the Chancellor's special meals, his only response
was to turn furiously to Bormann and say, "Aryanize the
Kunde family." Whereas he may have appreciated these
benefits from Jews at the moment he received them,
when he needed relief from inferiority feelings and other
sources of anxiety, he had no difficulty in projecting them
onto "The Jew" (i.e., all Jews) with the help of the splitting defense available to the borderline personality.

Splitting was also evident in his alternately expressing opposite sides of an issue, with denial of, and without concern about, the contradictions in the ideas and feelings involved. Hitler professed to be an honest and straightforward man who would, for example, abide by treaties "blindly and faithfully." But he also saw himself as a clever dissimulator who could fool people into believing anything, as the man who was, he said, "the greatest actor in Europe." Playing this role, he confided that "treaties will be honored only as long as they are useful . . . treaties exist for the purpose of being broken at the most convenient moment" (Rauschning, 1940, p. 110; Domarus, 1965, p. 1423). His stunning establishment of his Russian alliance and its later betrayal represent an example.

These extreme swings between Hitler's contradictory self-concepts are also expressions of opposite sides of characterological conflicts. In repeated speeches, particularly between 1933 and 1936, Hitler affirmed his love of peace, his lack of interest in revenge, his rejection of an imperialistic policy of conquests abroad: "Germany makes no demands and presents no claims against other nations." But in August, 1939, when a Swedish emissary suggested that the British, after their long experience with his broken word, might not believe his promises with regard to Poland, Hitler was horrified at the thought. He stopped pacing, turned in hurt surprise and cried, "Idiots! Have I ever in my entire life told a lie?" (Waite, 1977, p. 35). Since defenses sometimes break down, at least temporarily, Hitler was able to answer that question himself in the extraordinarily revealing beginning of a speech in September, 1943, that broke a long silence after the catastrophe of Stalingrad: "Freed from the heavy burden of expectation weighing on us for a long time, I now consider that the moment has come again to address myself to the German people without having to resort to lies, either to myself or to the public" (Domarus, 1965, p. 2035).

Hitler often boasted that his ideas and beliefs never changed, that they were immutable as iron or granite. Certainly he was extremely fixed in habits and even tastes, such as that for Wild-West stories. "Unteachable, unreasonable, and unapproachable" was one associate's description. He vaunted these deficiencies as great virtues. However, with the help of the splitting mechanism, his belief in his own constancy and unchangeability never interfered with convenient reversals of attitudes, as when in 1925 he was blithely able to espouse restoring property to the nobility despite a contrary cardinal point in his own Nazi platform.

Finally, splitting was revealed in Hitler's demonstrated lack of impulse control. In certain areas he repeatedly displayed explosions of primitive impulses such as violent rages, conduct acceptable to him during the episode, although not always when it was over. And yet, to the surprise of observers who came to expect such outbursts, he sometimes controlled himself quite well. When frustrated by truly important political or military defeats, he usually kept his self-control, showing that lack of control was not pervasive but selective. Sometimes he in fact exploited his reputation for explosions, as when he browbeat the aged Czech President.

PRIMITIVE DENIAL

The extreme of primitive denial found in the narcissistic-borderline syndrome occurred repeatedly. As a youth, Adolf indulged in periods of self-criticism, but Kubizek gave no evidence that he lost his grand opinions of himself for more than the moment. His subsequent glorious self-estimates were not tempered by the memory of his feelings of low self-esteem, nor were his "torments" of self-abasement mitigated by the elevated ones. They were separate, not integrated in the normal way, a developmental failure that marks the pathologic formation characteristic of the syndrome.

Adolf's drive to play fighting games was almost insatiable well into adolescence. Yet we are told that as a youth he was utterly averse to anything that related to war or soldiers. Absorption in books on military subjects started early and never ceased. His pleasure as a man and head of state in playing the mighty warlord needs no elaboration. Yet while preparing attacks and invasions Hitler often protested that he was peaceful and humane. He would at times glory in his brutality and at other times say specifically that he was not a brutal man. He demanded and exercised absolute power and allegiance to his own person but proclaimed that he was no dictator and would never be one. In April, 1942, the man who ordained the 1934 Blood Purge of hundreds declared at his dinner table that in the Nazi political struggles he had never allowed assassination (Hitler, 1953, p. 317). He could speak with apparent utter sincerity on both sides of an issue because adoption of a given view never interfered with later espousal of its opposite.

Unbelievably, Hitler could order a second front in the East in World War II without even forgetting his former dread of such a situation or the reasons for it, because of splitting and denial in combination. When he suffered military defeats on that front, he flatly denied them and punished as both traitors and liars the officers who dared to try to report them. As the Russians moved into the center of Berlin toward the end, Hitler talked alternately about triumph and disaster. On April 27, 1945, in his last operational conference, he spoke of a great victory because Russian strength was being dissipated in house-to-house fighting. Then he announced that he would rest a bit and was not to be awakened unless a tank was standing in front of his bedroom (Toland, 1976, pp. 876–877). Splitting and denial can explain the coexistence or swift alternation of opposite emotional states in Hitler, an occurrence central to the longstanding puzzle of his personality.

PROJECTION AND PARANOIA

Most frequently, Hitler sought to mitigate episodes of intense anxiety, agitation, anger, and shame with the mechanisms of projection and projective identification. From early youth on he blamed others as a way of coping with painful feelings of shame and inadequacy. Adolf was spoiled by his doting mother, as he confirmed in *Mein Kampf*, but he explained his inability to get along with his Linz classmates by claiming that it was they who were spoiled. Although not earning a penny to support himself or help his widowed mother while she bought him such luxuries as elegant clothes and a piano, he accused young men in a café of being idle parasites. "[Adolf] wallowed deeper and deeper in self-criticism. Yet it only needed the slightest touch . . . for his self-accusations to become an accusation against the times, against the whole world . . ." (Kubizek, 1955, p. 155).

No matter how unreasonable or even irrational Hitler's hostilities, he had rationalizations and excuses for them which usually were quite transparent projections. In Vienna the inconsiderate, angry, and hostile Adolf, hating practically all around him, "saw injustice, hate and enmity" wherever he looked, Kubizek noted. Later decisions on which the lives of millions hinged were sometimes made on the basis of projection. The final precipitation of World War II relates to both denial of reality and projection in Hitler. Knowing that he was at the moment bluffing, Hitler would not believe that England and France would protect Poland, although he had clear warning. "England is bluffing," he is reported to have said, "and so am I" (Toland, 1976, p. 569). Among the many reasons he attacked Russia in 1941 was his conviction, against all evidence, that his ally, Stalin, was about to launch an attack on him, a likely projection of his intention to invade Russia. Toward the end of the war, when his generals brought unmistakable news of Nazi defeat, Hitler insisted that the reports were lies and the reporters cowards trying to force him to authorize retreats. Instead he furiously ordered his officers to take suicidal stands. Convinced that he was being betrayed and traduced, he told his personal pilot that his tombstone should read: "He was the victim of his generals!" (Toland, 1976, p. 888).

Projection largely shaped Hitler's intense anti-Semitism, as discussed in detail below in Chapter XIII. The historian Alan Bullock wrote as directly as might a psychoanalyst of the personal fantasy involved in Adolf Hitler's anti-Semitism, and of its obsessional quality. Bullock stated that to read the sexually obscene pages about the Jews in *Mein Kampf*, where Hitler "does not bring forth one fact to support his wild assertions, is to enter the world of the insane" (1964, p. 40). Practically all the qualities Hitler attributed to the Jew as grounds for his contempt and hatred are projections and projective identifications that declare that it is not he but the Jew who is ugly, weak, diseased, fearful of death, incestuous, eager to conquer the world. The more he projected aggressive impulses onto the Jews, the more fearful he became of them, and in turn the more he hated them. Thus a ceaseless spiral of projected aggression toward, and hatred of, the Jews developed, so that his hatred was not assuaged by the reality of his extermination of six million of them. The end of his hate-loaded last political testament "above all" calls upon followers "to implacably oppose the universal poisoner of all races, international Jewry" (Maser, 1973, p. 375).

Hitler's paranoia was not limited to his ideas about Jews. His recorded *Tischgespraeche*, published in English as *Hitler's Secret Conversations*, reveals that he also feared the evil intentions of priests, Freemasons, Jehovah's Witnesses, liberals, journalists, artists, cigarette smokers, academics, meateaters, poets, skiers, French, English, and Americans. Imperial Germany he believed was ruined and latter-day Germany threatened by rapacious enemies intending its annihilation. Young Adolf pointed out injustice, hate, and enmity wherever he looked. Once, choking with his catalogue of hates, he vented his fury against mankind in general, who did not understand or appreciate him "and by whom he was persecuted," and at the same time he railed wildly against "tripwires . . . cunningly laid . . . for the sole purpose of ruining his career" (Kubizek, 1955, p. 176). Paranoid thinking persisted and became more intense until the end. Throughout life Hitler saw the world filled with evil threatening momentarily to undo him. Wherever he lived, he believed that he was surrounded by numerous seen and unseen enemies—witness his refusal to eat in his Munich rooms in 1924 because the house was owned by a Jew, and he believed that he could be poisoned through the walls (Hanfstaengl, 1957, p. 66). Like most dictators, he feared assassination, but Hitler's fears were unusually intense, wide ranging, and extreme.

POOR RELATIONSHIPS

Hitler's closest associates noted that after many years they never really knew him. The youth shared with his adorer Kubizek some of his fantasies but not his feeling about his rejection by the Vienna Academy of Art until the truth escaped him in a fit of rage. Though he became financially dependent on his fellow derelict Hanisch, he was never emotionally involved with him. Hitler showed no friendly feelings for the man who helped him when he was all but completely exhausted from undernourishment and neglect, and later set him up financially. The outcome revealed that Hitler distrusted this benefactor, hated him, and deliberately hurt him.

The nearest Hitler came to a sustained acceptance of anyone was when he sometimes temporarily idealized a person from whose help, protection, or reflected glory he wanted to benefit, with Kubizek the earliest example. Adolf was displeased that Kubizek did poorly in school, although he himself had no use for anything connected with schooling. Though he had not yet earned a single penny, he insisted that Kubizek earn his half of the money for their all-powerful lottery ticket. His idealization of "Stefanie" was as his own mirror image. Later in life, Dietrich Eckart, General Ludendorff, Rudolf Hess, and Ernst Roehm were each idealized similarly for a time. All were eventually denigrated; some were dropped unceremoniously, and Roehm was assassinated.

The pattern of human relationships in the Vienna home for homeless men, providing some human contact with undemanding and usually limited people, with anonymity and a controllable distance, was one that suited Hitler. He sought that undemanding casualness as his daily pattern, found it again in the trenches, created it in his café rounds during his climb, and preserved it in his meals and evenings with orderlies and chauffeurs even as Chancellor.

Although surrounded after age thirty-four by many cohorts, he had no friends or confidants among his aides, not even Goebbels. By the time he was Chancellor, no one in Nazi Germany called him by his first name, and only a very few did so in the early days. He continued to fear and mistrust his most ardent supporters long after he had consolidated total political power and established the principle that he alone held all authority in the Reich. No one knew the whole of any of his plans, and he bragged of lying to preserve this secrecy. He refused to adjudicate serious policy disputes between chief henchmen, preferring their rivalry and separation lest any one man, however devoted, acquire too much information and thus some power.

Hitler considered women fickle and untrustworthy, ready to betray a man at any moment; his own inconstancy was described as almost pathological. He explicitly considered the masses very much like women, and therefore not to be trusted but rather to be feared. This fear of women might have been at the root of Hitler's otherwise puzzling failure to deprive German women of consumer goods and luxuries in wartime, or to mobilize their labor promptly.

The self-centeredness, demandingness, arrogance, raging anger, suspiciousness, and denigration of others that make good relations with people impossible were evident from his youth, as his halfbrother, co-boarders, fellow students and teachers, his roommate Kubizek, and his fellow derelicts all attest. Comrades in arms during World War I and most others who knew him before he entered politics are unanimous too: his tendency was to shun contact with others. One factor was his intense envy of those who seemed to have what he did not, or who seemed to enjoy their lives.

When the Chancellor felt disappointed or betrayed by associates or generals, he sometimes appeared to be depressed, but he showed by subsequent behavior that what he really felt was anger. He harbored vengeful feelings upon which he acted in extreme forms, as in the

murders of Father Stemple, General Schleicher and his
wife as well, Roehm, and Gregor Strasser, among many.
He took revenge in petty forms, as when he revoked the
university doctorate of Otto Strasser after his escape.
Hitler's insistence in the Russian campaign that his generals either stand their ground or attack in the face of
certain death, so inexplicable on the basis of any military
principle, could contain an element of revenge for their
failure to achieve victory for him.

A QUESTION OF CONSCIENCE

With all of Hitler's demonstrated propensity for seeing
so many others as all-bad, for projecting his hate and its
consequences, for all his lack of empathy or sympathy,
there still remains the question: how could any human
conscience allow him to be aggressive and cruel on such
a scale, carrying out such indescribable destruction of
human lives? It will be recalled that the superego, part
of which corresponds to conscience, was described by
Freud as a precipitate of the ego. Like those of most
narcissistic-borderlines, Hitler's ego was defective in
several functions. His superego was thus also inevitably
underdeveloped and flawed, as described in Chapter
XII. Although he repeatedly prepared excuses in advance to justify his public acts, this effort was largely to
meet the anticipated criticism of others, and not that of
his own conscience—an aspect of public relations.

APPARENT DEPRESSIONS

With a poorly developed conscience, being so self-centered, unempathetic, and prone to projective identification, Hitler was unlikely to experience genuine depression any more than warm, mutually dependent emotional relations with anyone. Despite his complaints of unhappiness, he separated himself from longstanding associations with little apparent feeling beyond angry charges that the individuals had failed to serve him as he wished.

The two occasions when deep depression appeared to afflict him briefly occurred when he was deprived of important sources of gratification: first his doting mother and later Geli, the young niece he desired. After each death he seemed to be overwhelmed with feelings of hopelessness and helplessness. Dr. Bloch, who as a physician was familiar with the grief of survivors, remembered young Hitler's extreme unhappiness many years later. Yet within two months Adolf was able to move to Vienna and pursue, in fantasy, his self-ordained life of intellectual pursuits. Years later, the death of Geli seemed for a matter of days to have disorganized Hitler so severely that those immediately around him feared that he might commit suicide. However, very soon he was compaigning again. In the narcissistic-borderline, the reaction to the loss of a significant source of gratification is due to the temporary breakdown of the fantasies of omnipotence, a massive blow which the weak ego cannot easily sustain.

SEXUAL PERVERSION

Sexual deviations are among the presumptive diagnostic elements of the borderline personality. Reports
of sexual perversion appeared during two decades of
Hitler's life and from a number of sources, detailed by
Langer and Waite, among others. The implications of
these reports are examined in Chapter XI.

PSYCHOANALYTIC
SPECULATIONS

CHAPTER IX

Reflections on His Personality Development

Although the facts of Hitler's life fit the postulated diagnosis, all the complexities of a human being cannot be reduced to a syndrome. One must still consider the extraordinary dimensions of his personal pathological features and their impact upon a nation he seized. As a social phenomenon, the total explanation for Germany's response is beyond the scope of this study. But the extremes of Hitler's pathologic traits are less astonishing when one considers the number of malign elements that converged on him. While none is in itself necessarily pathogenic, and certainly not extremely so, clinical experience teaches that each is potentially adverse. When several malign elements coexist, they operate synergistically to make the potential actual, and by mutual reinforcement they make psychopathologic conditions more severe. Such influences that converged on Adolf Hitler included the following: possible constitutional aggressivity and monorchidism; established infant frailty; established maternal overconcern and indulgence; established confusing and contradictory paternal example; probable paternal harshness; established psychologically damaging timing of family events, including births, deaths, and household moves; and possible postencephalitic state.

His family's heritage included inbreeding, common in the remote regions. Such inbreeding could account for the intensification of constitutional features, such as extreme aggressive drives.

Hitler's frailty as an infant was an unfavorable reality. That he was a sickly baby gave potential for more serious consequences than might at first appear. We know that to the infant the source of all pain is outside himself, and that the mother, being most frequently present, becomes for him the source of his distress. The mother is at first the only important representative of the outside world. If the baby is in pain, she, that "other," has brought it. If the pain or distress is frequent or unmitigated, all "others" in time may become representatives of a hostile and dangerous outside world to be feared and hated.

We know definitely that Hitler's mother was overprotective and overindulgent. The effect is doubly damaging: it increases the child's narcissism while diminishing his real sense of self-confidence. His stern, impatient, and restless father probably contributed to his son's sense of the world as erratic and threatening. The death of his father removed male guidance of any kind when Adolf was an adolescent.

Another deleterious fact is that every move of the family, every birth and death, even the absences of his father, occurred at a most unfavorable point in the son's psychological development.

Still, this child became the man whose phenomenal impact on Germany and the world must be understood. What endowments and what factors made his rise possible? To a considerable extent it was just his pathologic traits that represented a major element in enabling him to secure the power over others that, in turn, made it possible for him to use certain of his personal endowments effectively. First among these, he was an unsurpassed orator and had remarkable gifts for acting and stagecraft, as discussed in Chapter XIV. Second, his intelligence was of a kind especially adapted to politics. Its most conspicuous element was a prodigious memory for details, especially in relation to subjects that were emotionally meaningful to him, such as war and fighting. In his thinking, one finds little if any abstraction or subtlety. He scanned pragmatically for ideas and facts that would serve him and clung to them. His use of LeBon's ideas about the masses is an example of literalness. This concreteness was an asset in making propaganda, especially in his graphic and theatrical devices and in his personal myth-making as well. Witness the flood of pictures of him with children, with their message: the Chancellor is loving, lovable, and human.

To pursue a more complete understanding of the man, some speculations are suggested, based on clues found in the known facts already surveyed, as well as on the application of clinical data.

In the parents of patients with the proposed diagnosis, psychiatrists usually find severe disturbance in self-regard. The mother or father may use the child's special abilities to gratify the parents' needs, which often are exhibitionistic. The child can be treated as an extension of a parent; he is sometimes punished for a parent's moral conflict. Otto Kernberg observed that chronically cold people with covert but intense aggression are numerous among the parents of narcissistic-borderline personalities (1967, p. 59). The mother frequently shows a need to possess and control those close to her. She gives contradictory or confused emotional messages to her child. Often she withdraws into herself in periods of depression. She usually is a woman who functions well on the surface but conceals a measure of indifference, a non-verbalized spiteful aggression. In this emotional climate, a child develops intense oral frustrations, resentment, and aggression, and in the need to defend against those painful feelings the basis is laid for extreme envy and hatred (Kernberg, 1970, p. 59). Specific data to confirm all these influences are insufficient in Hitler's case. But many elements fit the personalities of Alois and Klara Hitler as described by neighbors and friends. The same sources give facts and impressions indicating that the other elements were at least possibly present in them.

The evidence regarding the father is conflicting, probably reflecting contradictions in his character as much as the fact that the observations are by different individuals and from different times in his life. Much that is recalled shows that Alois had marked disturbances in his narcissistic equilibrium. He presented the picture of an upright, conscientious, and industrious man at his work; in general, he was liberal, tolerant, convivial. Yet he was excessively dignified and even pompous toward others and in his attitude about his position. He was not so conscientious when it suited him, as in his treatment of women, and when he requested a Papal dispensation *gratis,* although far from poor. His exhibitionism was clear in the way he wore his uniform and in the form of address he demanded. He displayed his own exaggerated self-estimate, letting it be known that he considered himself far above the level of most people around him. His selfishness was unmistakable. In his life there appeared no sacrifice to any person, idea, or ideal. And even beyond absence of sacrifice there was little if any trace of emotional support of another human being—not of his wives, and certainly not of his growing children. When his eldest son at fourteen fled the home or was banished, Alois disinherited him. This father showed less than the ordinary caring and consideration for women or children, beyond financial support of the home. Even in his happier relations with men, his wishes dominated, as when he cajoled a junior colleague to come and drink with him instead of studying. Hitler's father was described as always appearing to play some role. Confusing and contradictory messages from him could not have been lost on the son.

One can infer the father's emotional make-up from his

life. He was endowed with a strong sexual drive and a strong aggressive drive. His forcefulness and industriousness were displayed in his career rise as well as in the energetic pursuit of his hobby and pleasures. Some said that he could be physically aggressive to those weaker than himself, although this is denied by others. Hitler's father was intelligent, beyond his family and his competition. His standards of conscience were flexible. He was self-centered, self-reliant, self-willed, and self-congratulatory. He gave very little to others.

Adolf certainly did not emulate his father's industriousness, his capacity to enjoy wine, women, and song, nor his devotion to the Austro-Hungarian Empire. Nevertheless, his father seems to have been a model for other characteristics, major and minor: outbursts of aggression, authoritarianism, exhibitionism, easy acceptance of conflicting ideas and behavior, low opinion of women, and the overly elaborate observance of social forms. Adolf's uneasy relationship with his father can be seen in his subsequent temporary submission to obvious father substitutes, upon each of whom he would later turn: Rudolf Hanisch in Vienna, Dietrich Eckart in Munich, President von Hindenburg in Berlin.

Everything we know about development of personality stresses the pervasive effect of a mother on her child. The way she behaves, or the child fantasies her to behave, bears more than does the father's behavior upon developing character, beginning when the infant blames the mother for pain, whatever its source. That Adolf's mother suffered a series of miseries is evident. She was treated sympathetically by the two observers closest to her in time and place. Both August Kubizek, who visited in her home occasionally over a period of more than two years just before her death, and Franz Jetzinger, the archivist and biographer who consulted many who recalled her vividly, describe Hitler's mother as a victim. If patience under repeated indignities, disappointments, and afflictions is the criterion for admiration, Klara Poelzl Hitler certainly earned it. But more than respect for fortitude in sorrows is needed to comprehend her as a person and as a mother. The bare outline of events in her forty-seven years bespeaks a personality more complex than that of a submissive sufferer and near-saint.

Her life story presents the perfect picture of the "wretched woman" characterized by Kubizek. She had the briefest economic protection from her father, no emotional support from the man who after humiliating years finally married her and fathered her children, no success in saving her first two babies, no reasonable response to her wishes from her surviving son. Although she was never estranged from her relatives, her endearing qualities did not assure their protection when as a very young girl she was being pushed from pillar to post. Before he married her, Alois Hitler took her in and out of his home according to his needs and convenience. After they were married, he demanded of her an unusual degree of respect and compliance with his demands. As a husband he was described by a close, faithful friend as "awfully rough" with her, and as one who "hardly ever spoke a word to her at home," so that she "had nothing to smile about" (Jetzinger, 1958, p. 51).

During the five years of life remaining to her after she was widowed, Klara's loneliness, sad demeanor, and, particularly, helplessness to direct her son Adolf toward any constructive planning for himself or the family were remarked by all. Kubizek commented that Klara's home had few if any visitors between the years 1905 and 1907 when he called there for Adolf. He writes that she "never complained" but nevertheless told him what a hard time she had had when she was young, and specifically that her hopes and dreams as a young girl were not fulfilled in her marriage.

Others who knew Hitler's mother give strong hints of the personality of this unhappy human being. First mentioned in all accounts is her devotion to "spotless" cleanliness—of her home as well as of her children and stepchildren—an emphasis indicating the unusual degree of the trait; it must have been remarkable, given the place and time. She was seen as an excellent manager of family resources, taking pride in their accumulation, and as markedly energetic and conscientious. But there is no trace of any expressive outlet for Klara. There is no indication that she could read or write; correspondence about pension rights, for example, was written for her (Jetzinger, 1958, p. 78). Her husband's colleague remembered her as "very quiet and subdued. She seemed a disappointed woman." Kubizek felt that "she had almost entirely lost her own personality," so all-forgiving did she appear to be (1955, p. 34).

Klara early evinced this apparently all-forgiving nature: she was willing to return to Alois' household to care for him and his two little children after being banished from the home by her rival four years earlier, as described in Chapter III. The almost saintly degree of kindliness here could also suggest that Klara was capable of considerable suppression or denial of feelings; refusal to help might have been a more direct response to the treatment she had received. Klara was a product of an earthy backwoods environment that might make her accept as only natural, behavior by so imposing a man as Alois that a more sophisticated young woman would resent. But no one who knew her even hinted that she was dull or of subnormal intelligence. That she truly felt no hard feelings is indeed highly questionable. Instead, a stubborn persistence despite insult might be read into the series of events.

Klara lived with Alois from the spring of 1884 and became pregnant by him around August of that year, just as her rival Fanni died. Four months later Alois married Klara at last. Her emotions about sexual matters were quite likely to have been complex rather than direct and simple. A devoted and even enthusiastic Roman Catholic, she was certainly instructed as to the sins recognized by the Church. For committing adultery, and for transgressing against the two former wives and then surviving them, it is reasonable to suppose that she felt guilty. The second wife was Klara's friend, contemporary, and victorious rival in love, circumstances that also might produce guilt. The presence of guilt would shed light on Klara's docile acceptance of defeat in exile and her service on behalf of Fanni's children. Almost unavoidable emotions of both guilt and anger and their denial, thus equally likely feelings of sadness, disappointment, helplessness, and relative unworthiness vis-à-vis and all powerful Alois, must have affected the home into which Adolf Hitler was born only a few months after the death of her second child. His weakness at birth hints that her recovery from the physical strain may not have been complete during the pregnancy that brought him into the world.

The intensity with which such a woman later gave her energy to her home and to her sole surviving child can safely be inferred. Laden with humiliation and disappointments, unsupported by her husband in meeting the daily burdens of her child, her stepchildren, and family life, awed by his patriarchal authority, she probably had to repress considerable anger as well as guilt. The still young Klara Hitler, equipped largely with passive obstinacy, could not be expected to put her energy to constructive use in child rearing. How she treated her two stepchildren is not clear. Calling her a typical stepmother who continually set her husband against his oldest boy while wanting everything for her own son Adolf, Alois, Jr., blamed her for having the stepson sent away from home at age fourteen. Some historians state that the boy himself ran away, to his father's great disappointment. An indication that Hitler's mother could be hostile and capable of expressing it is a letter to her stepson which she apparently dictated. In handwriting identified as that of Adolf, the letter answers a plea for help from the youth when he was in danger of being jailed for theft. Harsh indeed, the stepmother's reply includes the "advice" "to go and hang yourself" (Hitler, 1961b, pp. 55–56). The wording and tone, if not the refusal of help, may have come from the half brother, Adolf, but Klara sent the letter over her name.

Some accounts indicate that both of Klara's stepchildren, Alois, Jr., as well as Angela, liked and respected her. Angela demonstrated strong positive feelings toward her stepmother by remaining in intimate touch with her after her own marriage. Angela also cared for her little half sister, Paula, after Klara died in 1907, just as Angela was bearing her own child.

At present, a scrutiny of all that has come to light about Klara permits certain hypotheses about her behavior and its several effects upon her beloved son Adolf, collectively contributing to the intensity of his narcissism, grandiosity, and destructiveness, and also the borderline defense of splitting.

Whether or not Klara suffered a depression in the technical sense, she was a disappointed woman whose prevailing mood was sad and unhappy. Her several reasons for guilt and repressed anger support this estimate, as does her tendency to shun friendships. The effect of a depressed maternal mood on the development of the child has been adumbrated. One possible hypothesis is that Klara unconsciously promoted some of her son's traits as vicarious expressions of her own angry feelings, disappointed hopes, and disturbed self-regard. Such a possibility gains credence because of her continued indulgence of Adolf for many years after the end of any danger that he would die early.

Another hypothesis would explain Hitler's conspicuous lifelong orality. As is known to be universally true, an infant in discomfort perceives his mother as its source; in Hitler, this inevitable perception could have become a source of complications if his mother with her peasant upbringing pushed feeding on the child as a way of strengthening him. Supporting this inference, in addition to a photograph of Adolf as a fat child, is a family recollection that Klara in her continuing oversolicitousness brought milk fresh from the cows to Adolf's bedside even when he was an adolescent. We know that either excessive gratification or excessive deprivation during a phase of development tends to produce a fixation. Evidences of an oral fixation are striking in the adolescent and the adult Hitler: his extraordinary sweet tooth, food fads, greed, demandingness, his pleasure in speech and oratory, and most importantly, his aggressive, abusive, and prolix use of words and language.

Proceeding chronologically to consideration of the second year of Hitler's life, we find another influence of his mother in the probable origins of the splitting defense in Adolf's ego development. The infant's fantasy of omnipotence and expectation that his needs will immediately be fulfilled continue for several months after birth. This follows from the very gradual diminution of the feeling of unity with the mother. During the normal process that leads to the child's feeling himself to be a separate individual, a critical phase around the end of the second year has been identified, the rapprochement crisis (Mahler, Pine, and Bergman, 1975, pp. 95–100, 225–230).

This is a period during which the toddler's gradually increasing awareness of separateness from his mother becomes acute and his fantasies of omnipotence are threatened. We find him struggling to be separate from his mother and at the same time to be united with her and to use her as an extension of himself. These conflicting aims can only result in frustration, which shows in sudden mood swings, whining, general dissatisfaction, and temper tantrums. With adequate handling by the mother, the child overcomes the conflicts of this critical phase and goes on to the next development period. If the mother is not sufficiently available to him or is excessively anxious and solicitous, however, serious consequences result. The crisis in the toddler may remain an unresolved intrapsychic conflict, leading to the defense of splitting and a failure to develop strong ego boundaries. Interference with later oedipal development also results.

Klara was known to be an excessively solicitous, pampering mother. Such a mother almost constantly hovers over her toddler and limits his explorations and excursions away from her out of fear that he will hurt himself or get into dangerous situations. This behavior inhibits the completion of the separation-individuation process. Her child grows up consciously and intellectually capable of distinguishing between himself and others, but because his ego boundaries are still weak, he unconsciously does not clearly distinguish between himself and others. He therefore continues to treat others as though they were extensions of himself. When they behave in a way that he does not expect or in one that does not respond to his wishes, he becomes anxious, frustrated, and enraged. Because he unconsciously sees others as parts of himself to be used to serve his needs, their needs are nonexistent to him, and his attitude toward them is demanding, manipulative, and inconsiderate.

To deal with his intensely ambivalent feelings toward his mother, the child splits his image of her into a "good" mother and a "bad" mother. In order to protect the "good" mother image from his rage, this splitting is perpetuated, and a lasting tendency to see all others as well as himself as either all-good or all-bad ensues.

Also during early childhood, Klara's insistence upon

extreme cleanliness suggests that her management of her son during his anal phase caused fixations. Hitler showed seemingly inconsistent traits that are nonetheless characteristic of anal fixations. The adolescent and the adult Hitler were at times excessively clean, obstinate, and frugal. Yet when his defenses did not operate, as during his derelict days, he was extremely dirty about his person and scatological in imagery and language. Other traits considered anal in psychoanalytic theory would erupt: rage, defiance, marked ambivalence, and sadomasochism.

Still another unfavorable factor, a physical defect and a possible source of concern to his parents, may have been present from birth: the condition of monorchidism. Reports that Hitler had only one testicle are the subject of controversy among biographers and historians. An autopsy report by Russian pathologists was released decades after his death. Having studied the burned body found on the Berlin Chancellery grounds, the pathologists noted: "The genital member is scorched. In the scrotum, which is singed but preserved, only the right testicle was found. The left testicle could not be found either in the scrotum or on the spermatic cord inside the inguinal canal or in the small pelvis" (Bezymenski, 1968, p. 46). One of the Russian pathologists present, queried about the significance of the genital finding, replied that monorchism is a fairly frequent phenomenon, not an interference with normal sex, and as a rule congenital. His remarks indicate that no evidence of surgical removal such as scar tissue in the scrotum or in the groin was found.

Werner Maser argued at length that the body the

Russians found was not Hitler's (Maser, 1973, pp. 478–485). To the contrary, after surveying the mass of evidence and professional opinions including those of American dental experts and the final view of the respected German periodical *Die Zeit*, the American historian Robert G. L. Waite (1977, pp. 150–152) supported the claim that the Russian autopsy was indeed performed on the body of Adolf Hitler. No one who knew Hitler in life asserts that he was monorchid except Joseph Rottenburger, who claims to have been Hitler's masseur from the time of Hindenburg's funeral until the Berlin Olympic games (Brady, 1974). A mocking soldiers' song from World War II proclaiming Hitler's monorchism is still known to American schoolboys. A World-War-I story circulating in Munich in the twenties that Hitler's genitals were "freakishly underdeveloped," reported by Hanfstaengl (1957), has been mentioned.

In a controversy about the facts alleged in a matter of this kind, clinical findings from psychology have a bearing. Much of Hitler's behavior is consonant with his having been monorchid or having genital impairment of some type. Puzzling acts and attitudes are thereby illuminated as well. The psychological effects of monorchism probably started in Hitler's early development. In a group of narcissistic personalities with minor and generally inconspicuous physical anomalies, William Niederland (1965, pp. 532-533) found that modifications of normal ego development usually set in early in life. When the defect was found soon after birth a marked disequilibrium in the relationship between mother and child ensued which hardly ever fully subsided. Some mothers became oversolicitous, seductive, or otherwise defective in their nurturing functions, thus further traumatizing the child.

Because cryptorchism, or undescended testicle, may be considered at least a temporary monorchidism, certainly to the child, the findings of studies of that condition are relevant. Although many boys have grown to manhood without suffering significant untoward psychological effects from cryptorchism or from monorchism, under certain conditions unfavorable to psychological development, the opposite is true. So much psychological damage is seen among boys with one testicle in the scrotum that one group of urologists and pediatricians (Smith, Lattimer, and Masoud, 1973) now recommends very early surgical correction of cryptorchism—between the ages of four and five. Struck by the number of emotional problems and personality disorders found in their patient population, they recommend insertion of a prosthesis if surgical correction is impossible, to spare a monorchid boy these difficulties and protect him from invidious comparison with others.

In one study of cryptorchid boys, Peter Blos (1960) distinguished those who suffer emotional consequences from those who do not: emotional difficulties occur when a disturbed parent-child relationship also exists. In the child's mind, the mother is considered the perpetrator of the body damage. "A castrating possessiveness and the passive aloofness of the father both constitute a matrix of family interaction in which cryptorchism gives rise to typical symptoms" (*ibid.*, p. 398), i.e., hyperactivity, learning difficulties, compulsive toying with physical danger, social inadequacy, chronic indecision, and tendencies to exaggerate, to lie, and to fantasize. Also found were a bisexual sense of identity and symbolic substitution for the absent testicle in concrete objects in the outer world, or the whole body or its parts, such as the eye, breast, or tonsils.

Hitler showed so many of these symptoms that the list becomes almost a personal one for him. Adolf's need to continue playing cowboys-and-Indians and war games after his playmates had become bored with them attest to his youthful hyperactivity; his endless pacing, chronic restlessness, and ceaseless touring bear witness to his adult tensions. At school and later he could not apply himself to learning new subjects or skills. He wrote that his rough play caused his mother anguish. He behaved as though immune from danger in World War I. His social inadequacy persisted throughout life. His chronic indecision was the bane of his lieutenants throughout his career. Exaggerations and flagrant lies stand out in his record. His fantasies of world sovereignty and messianic mission he made explicit again and again.

Hitler's symbolic substitutions for an absent testicle merit detailed consideration. Such substitutions are familiar to psychiatrists. Paul Schilder (1950, p. 123) said that in the adult as well as in the child, body and world are constantly interchanged. Niederland's (1965, p. 532) statement was even more specific. He reported that in his patients with hidden physical defects, either from birth or arising during the first year, development of the body ego was affected virtually from the beginning, resulting in a sometimes distorted body image, *incompleteness of body reality and, via projection, of external reality*.

Hitler seems to have used two psychological strategies:

displacement, a defense he often used, and substitution. He displaced his displeasure with his defective body image onto concrete objects in the outer world, specifically, the various buildings and other structures which he so frequently found faulty wherever he lived. This displacement illuminates his lifelong mania for criticizing and changing, so great in his youth that it fills two chapters in Kubizek's book: "Adolf Rebuilds Linz" and "Adolf Rebuilds Vienna." Speer attested to Chancellor Hitler's plans to rebuild Berlin with the same zeal, here expressed on the scale that only unchecked power made possible (1970, pp. 73–79, 132–143).

Resorting to substitution, Hitler used parts of his body, particularly his eyes, in a manner that made them unconscious symbolic representations of a missing testicle. A number of devotees were particularly struck by Hitler's eyes. "What extraordinary eyes your friend has," Kubizek quoted his own mother as saying; ". . . I can clearly remember that there was more fear than admiration in her tone" (1955, pp. 17–18). Apparently, the youthful Hitler had started to cultivate those "piercing stares" or "piercing glances" which, as a valet later reported, he carefully practiced before a mirror. They may be seen as his way of communicating: "See, I do have two powerful (potent) testicles, and I can penetrate others." His aggressive use of his eyes shows too, in the "stare-you-down" games the Chancellor played at his dinner table. During World War II he was direct and explicit: "Now I have to go and hypnotize Quisling" (Waite, 1977, pp. 7, 375). In his speeches, as described in Chapter XIV, he substituted his whole body for a genital as he harangued and conquered the crowd.

Still another consideration tends to support the like-lihood of Hitler's monorchidism: his conviction of justi-fication by Divine guidance and protection. Freud pointed out that individuals who suffer congenital de-formities or protracted sickliness in childhood often feel that they have renounced enough to be spared further submission to any disagreeable necessity. Some are con-vinced that a special Providence watches over them. In effect, they say that they were punished though guiltless and that they are exceptions and intend to remain so. To illustrate, Freud cited Gloucester in *Richard III*, who argues that since he cannot play the lover because of his deformity, he will be a villain, intriguing and murdering as he pleases. For the physical wrong done him, he claims the right of exemption from the scruples inhibiting others (Freud, 1916, pp. 314–315). The similarity to Hitler's feeling of justification for any behavior is striking. His capacity to think the unthinkable and to do it enabled him to take adversaries by surprise time after time.

Niederland (1965, pp. 523, 529) in his study of nar-cissistic adults with minor physical anomalies found ad-ditional features that also stand out in Hitler's life record: these include a secret fantasy life replete with narcissis-tic-exhibitionistic-aggressive themes, sadomasochistic fantasies, eroticized megalomanic daydreams, conscious or semiconscious aspirations to greatness and immortal-ity; compensatory self-aggrandizement; heightened ag-gressiveness, often accompanied by outbursts of aggression and hate in word and deed; castrative aspects of the defect and its bisexual elaboration; and revenge fantasies. He also stated that the formation of the distorted, per-manently incomplete body image appears particularly intense in male patients in whom inguinal or genital anomalies such as testicular malformations exist. Overly strong bisexual identifications and compensatory narcissistic features such as ideas of being unique, possessing special powers, magical qualities, or the like, as well as intense exhibitionistic strivings and strong anal preoccupation also form part of the clinical picture; psychopathic impulses and behavior are equally noteworthy. These observations could stand as a fairly accurate description of Hitler's personality and behavior throughout his life.

Monorchism thus throws some light on otherwise inexplicable behavior in the exhibitionistic Hitler: refusal to permit a complete physical examination or to allow his valets to see him undressed. The intense castration anxiety this indicates is not surprising in a man who could feel half-castrated in reality. In Hitler's case, monorchism would have converged with the many other factors to produce increasingly severe castration anxiety by reinforcing it over and over again.

Extreme castration anxiety is central in Hitler's personality development. One probable source of castration anxiety goes back, again, to his physically distressed infancy. Recent studies of babies between the ages of fifteen and twenty-four months (Roiphe, 1972) have established that at this age they markedly increase the manipulation of their genitals, including frank masturbatory behavior. Some such very young children have a birth defect or have suffered severe illness, the loss of a parent, or, equally, the experience of depression in the mothering person. Having taken in the differences in anatomy of the sexes, such children develop unmistakable severe reactions indicating that they fear for their genitals. These situations prevent an infant from developing either a consistent concept of his own body or of an "other" good and benign person. The reaction noted in these studies shows clearly that the very young child then fears injury to, or loss of, the genitals—i.e., castration anxiety is created.

The infant Adolf was susceptible to early castration anxiety of this sort on all counts. He was sickly and also probably monorchid, a situation potentially troublesome to both parents. His father was absent so much that he could easily be perceived by the baby as a lost parent. His sad and burdened mother could have experienced periods of true depression; she was certainly very sad. As Adolf grew, other situations developed to augment the early fears into intensified castration anxiety.

Until Adolf was three years old, his father was erratically absent and all too present in the small crowded home. This alternation would further the strong bond between mother and son which her oversolicitousness produced. Then for eighteen months after these first three years, the father stayed home more often. At best the father is regarded as an unwelcome interloper by the boy around three. Very strong negative feelings would be understandable in Adolf when his harsh and impatient father suddenly dominated the scene. Alois Hitler's forceful and uncaring behavior was of a kind to make it particularly difficult for Adolf to identify with his father in the usual way and thus loosen his sexual bonds to his mother. Conflict about father figures and hostility to all authority persisted in Hitler's life.

But his relationship to his mother was greatly com-

plicated and still another source of intense castration
fears. This aspect of Hitler's psychosexual development
is treated in Chapter X.

About his third year, according to evidence in *Mein
Kampf*, Adolf seems to have reacted to experiences which
traumatized him and affected his emotional development: observing the sexual relations of his parents. One
effect was, again, an increase in his castration anxiety.
An elaborate statement by Hitler himself supplies the
data: a passage, very early in *Mein Kampf* (1943, pp.
31–34) disguised as a fantasy, subjected previously to
psychological interpretation (Kurth, 1947). To a psychoanalyst it is unmistakable as either a childhood recollection or a fantasy of a couple engaged in sexual
intercourse, a *primal scene*. The passage in *Mein Kampf*
seems to begin with a series of incidents or fantasies
when Adolf was about three years old; it rambles on to
memories of later years. Adolf was three in April, 1892.
Later that year came the eighteen months of the father's
first long stay with the family. The family probably occupied just one bedroom; witness Adolf's drawing at age
ten of "our bedroom." Hitler presents the following detailed scene:

Now let us imagine the following: In a basement apartment, consisting of two stuffy rooms, dwells a worker's
family of seven. Among the five children there is a boy
of, let us assume, three years. This is the age in which
the first impressions are made on the consciousness of
the child. Talented persons retain traces of memory from
this period down to advanced old age. The very narrow-
ness and overcrowding of the rooms does not lead to

favorable conditions. Quarreling and wrangling would very frequently arise as a result. . . . But if this battle is carried on between the parents themselves, and almost every day in forms which for vulgarity often leaves nothing to be desired, then, if only very gradually, the results of such visual instruction must ultimately become apparent in the children. The character they will inevitably assume if this mutual quarrel takes the form of brutal attacks of the father against the mother, of drunken beatings, is hard for anyone who does not know this milieu to imagine.

At the age of six the pitiable little boy senses things which would make even an adult shudder. Morally infected, undernourished . . . the young "citizen" wanders off to elementary school. . . . All the other things that the little fellow hears at home do not tend to increase his respect for his dear fellow men. Nothing good remains of humanity, no institution remains unassailed; beginning with his teacher and up to the head of the government, whether it is a question of religion or morality as such, of the state or society, it is all the same, everything is reviled in the most obscene terms and dragged into the filth of the basest possible outlook. . . .

The three-year-old child has become a fifteen-year-old despiser of all authority. Thus far, aside from dirt and filth, this young man has seen nothing which might inspire him to any higher enthusiasm. . . .

Now he begins the same life which all along his childhood years he had seen his father living. He hangs around the street corners and bars, coming home God knows when, and for a change now and then he beats the broken-down being which was once his mother, curses God and the world. . . .

And his dear bourgeois fellow men are utterly amazed

at the lack of 'national enthusiasm' in this young 'citizen.' . . .

As though trashy films, yellow press, and such-like dung could furnish the foundations of a knowledge of the greatness of our Fatherland!—quite aside from the early education of the individual.

What I have never suspected before, I quickly and thoroughly learned in those years:

The question of the 'nationalization' of a people is . . . primarily a question of creating healthy social conditions. . . [italics in the original].

On its face this passage describes a brutalizing atmosphere. Whereas some brutality may have been the reality in Adolf's home, certainly filth was not. In part at least, the harshness could be the projection of Hitler's own aggression, and the filth of what he read into the sexual act. It could also be a manifestation of the deprecation of others conspicuous in narcissistic-borderline personalities; here he deprecates both parents and siblings.

Hitler does not pretend that he is describing an observation of strangers; he indicates a fantasy by beginning with the phrase, "Now let us imagine," and he continues with "let us assume." That the fantasy is about himself is inadvertently revealed in the abrupt change of person Hitler employs toward the end of the passage: after using the third person throughout, Hitler suddenly lapses into the first person singular. What he says about himself is that he quickly and thoroughly learned something "in those years." Again, the antecedent to "those years" can only be the childhood years of Hitler himself, since he clearly was describing himself all along. Although Hitler may have used certain notes, *Mein Kampf* was largely dictated aloud, a process certainly conducive to the flow of associations.

Another reason to see the passage as autobiographical is that the isolated youth, Hitler, had no opportunity to observe any mind through the third, sixth, and fifteenth and subsequent years except his own. Moreover, the only living person he really acknowledged as "talented" at this time was himself; even later such acknowledgments of others were extremely rare. Also, Hitler often portrayed his real father as he does the imaginary one, as a sodden brute who beat the boy mercilessly. As to the size of the family mentioned, if Dr. Bloch is mistaken in remembering a fifth child kept hidden, then at the age of three Adolf was one of only four children born to his mother; but by the time he was the six-year-old he speaks of, he was one of five acknowledged children in the family.

In cultures or settings where sexual behavior is not associated with emotional conflicts the child need not be traumatized by witnessing sexual relations. However, such an observation is especially traumatic to a child when the emotional climate around him is one of marked overt aggression. If frequent quarrels or violent incidents occur between the parents or if they are aggressive toward the child, he will misinterpret their coital behavior as an expression of aggressive feelings. The child's reaction to the scene is also influenced by his stage of psychosexual development. A child can, for example, interpret the primal scene as both a fecal attack by the woman and as an anal penetration by the man. Evidence suggests that Alois Hitler was often aggressive toward both Klara and Adolf. The psychoanalysts Walter Langer

(1972, pp. 142–145) and Gertrud Kurth (1947, pp. 28–31) have separately interpreted this passage in *Mein Kampf* as based upon Hitler's memories of sexual scenes witnessed or fantasized beginning around the age of three years.

Psychoanalysts find connections between fantasies about the primal scene and the fantasies of beating many individuals report. A widespread idea uncovered from very early memories regards coitus as an attack, the beating of the female by the male, because of the positions and the misinterpretation of sounds the child may hear. This link of sex to aggression is reflected in the fact that in many languages words and expressions for aggression are closely related to words for coitus, sometimes even the same.

Two terms Hitler uses suggest both his highly personal expression of the link between sex and aggression and its special dirty, i.e., anal, connotations. He speaks of the six-year-old boy who "senses things which would make even an adult shudder." (The German phrase can be translated more freely: ". . . suspects the existence of things which can inspire even an adult with nothing but horror.") Obviously, in either translation, Hitler is not thinking of a literal beating itself. Attacks are openly brutal; for this the little boy does not have to "sense things" or "suspect the existence of things." These mysterious "things" that would horrify an adult he says further have to do with "shudders" of awe and being "morally infected" or "morally poisoned," as the term has also been translated. These might well have, for Hitler, the meaning of some abhorrent or contaminating perversion. Both translations as well as the concept of perversion relate directly to expressions which Hitler repeatedly used in other writings and speeches to describe the behavior of Jews and the dire effects of their sexual relations with Aryans.

During part of Adolf's fifth and sixth years his father was away from the family most of the time, permitting the boy unrestricted rough play with neighborhood children, primarily war games and cowboys-and-Indians. The birth of his little brother when he was about six and in the period of maximum oedipal struggle with his father could be expected to increase the intensity of his feelings. The reader will recall that by age seven many lifelong traits were present: the little boy was remembered as quick to anger and rage, intolerant of opposition, "heartless," and without friends because he "took to no one," "imperious," and getting away with "the craziest notions" because his mother always took his part.

Little other information is recalled about Adolf between the ages of six and eleven except that he did well in the easy Austrian primary school and continued his wild play. In the more exacting Realschule his school achievement suddenly went downhill; the authorities made him discontinue formal education at age sixteen. Yet Adolf was far from stupid; his difficulties had to result from some interference with the effective use of his intelligence. Neighbors and teachers, it will be recalled, did not remember him as a child obviously disturbed, but neither did they think of him as an average youngster. He was thought of as an odd one, just as he would be later in the army. He played only with younger boys; he had poor relations with peers and teachers; he displayed strong aggressive impulses and violent rages. His teacher and adviser at Linz remembered him as "hostile, sullen, willful, arrogant and irascible" (Jetzinger, 1958, p. 68).

Adolf explained his difficulties with his schoolmates by his charge that they were "all spoiled." On his own later admission Adolf himself certainly was spoiled. Here as elsewhere, he attributed to others a characteristic in himself which he did not find acceptable, the first specific report of his later extensive use of the defense of projection. The youth's reaction to his failure to gain acceptance, to say nothing of admiration, was to withdraw and sulk, later also characteristic. "If I can't be the ringleader I won't play," he seemed to say. When he was one of six youngsters boarding together in Linz, he busied himself in solitary reading and drawing, so reserved that he never used the familiar form of address, as they did. His poor relationship with adults shows in his behavior toward his sponsor on his confirmation day and in his insistence to Kubizek that it is better to have nothing to do with adults.

Obviously his difficulty lay in his own personality traits and developing emotional conflicts in adolescence. These conflicts broke out sometimes in episodes marked by an altered sense of reality. Hitler when Chancellor reported to an ear specialist a school memory that the teacher's voice would sometimes seem very loud, while simultaneously his head would grow bigger and bigger and seem to move closer. A Linz professor reported that he heard Adolf hold dialogues with the trees stirring in the wind, another suggestion of disturbance in the perception of reality. Moreover, with the onset of adolescence and the inevitable burgeoning of sexual impulses came strong conflicts in this area, e.g., his violent fear of being kissed by his five-year-old sister, a shameful sexual episode in school, and his drawing of a teacher masturbating. Kubizek's testimony about Adolf's rigid inhibition of masturbation and his strict avoidance of any contact with females is further evidence of the unusual strength of these conflicts.

While direct data to document the development of splitting, oral and anal fixations, or very early castration anxiety are rarely available except in psychoanalytic treatment, the information recorded about Hitler's childhood and youth suggests the existence of the conditions that we know lead to these psychological developments.

A number of influences converging on Hitler are described here which had synergistically deleterious effects on his early development, and thus account for the intensity of many of his pathological traits. The negative aspects of each phenomenon were summarized, with the result being a description of Hitler's known characteristics. Many different phenomena produce a similar outcome, and, remarkably, in Hitler's case a very large number combined to produce intensifications of the same group of traits.

CHAPTER X

The Special Influence of Hitler's Mother

The relations between a male child and the first woman in his life strongly influence his relations with all women and affect his relations with all other persons. In Hitler, complex feelings toward his mother can be seen in his relations to the German nation, and in a most destructive aspect of his political policy and program.

On the evening his mother died, one neighbor reported that Adolf sat a long time in the twilight staring at her dead body and carefully drew her picture. The family physician wrote that Adolf bore for Klara a love that "some regarded as bordering on the pathological."

The doctor did not share that view, but he wrote that he had never seen in a son the intensity of grief displayed by Adolf. All his life Hitler carried his mother's photograph in his pocket, and her portrait hung over his beds in Munich, the Berlin Chancellery, the *Berghof*, and his military headquarters. For some thirty years Hitler would not permit a tree to be lighted on Christmas Eve. Until his niece Geli's death a quarter-century later, he spent the holiday in his own bedroom, taking all his meals there until the evening of December 26. When a valet asked him why, Hitler replied, "My mother died under Christmas-tree lights." After Geli's death this same ritual was transferred to her bedroom in his Munich apartment and performed there until he abandoned it in the late 1930s.

Always making Hitler conform to an ideal, Kubizek chose extreme language on this aspect of Adolf's feelings: "Adolf really loved his mother. I swear to it before God and Man" (1955, p. 36). Having already described how Adolf acted toward his mother, the sensitive Kubizek perhaps perceived that the very facts he presented made the existence of filial love in Adolf puzzling to his readers. Far more than the usual amount of ambivalence shows in the way Klara Hitler's son behaved while she was alive.

The probable early sources of great frustration in Adolf as a result of his mother's overanxious treatment of him have been noted. We know that the child projects the angry and aggressive impulses thus produced in him onto the mother, making her a dangerous figure to him. Child-development theory holds that in an effort to protect himself against the resulting fear of her, the child may experience genital strivings far too early in life. But this self-protective effort fails, because those strivings to reach the mother sexually are corrupted by precisely the aggression against which they are meant to protect. Thus when the premature genital strivings are directed toward the mother, the usual fears of the rival father are reinforced by those even earlier fears of the frustrating mother. The deaths of so many of his siblings, combined with his monorchism, might have given Adolf additional reasons to dread his mother and even hate her: she produced defective children, most of whom died, and he was produced with a most troubling defect. In such a situation an image of his mother as not only castrating but also deadly dangerous evolves. When this anxiety is augmented by the oedipal fears surrounding the father, the result is a person with especially intense castration anxiety, much of which derives from an image of his mother as a sexually dangerous figure. What we know of Adolf's early childhood fits with this highly unfavorable psychological situation.

Witnessing the parents' sexual intercourse, when traumatic, adds to hostility toward the mother. Though the event is seen by the child as an assault by the father, he also sees it as a passive acceptance of the assault by the mother. She thereby "betrays" the young observer whose love object she is. If the fantasies Adolf experienced about his parents' sex relations were evocations of beating fantasies or memories of beatings, again he would have felt betrayed by his mother. As he tells one incident at least, his mother stood behind a closed door, listening without intervening while her son was being beaten by his father (Zoller, 1949, p. 46).

Hitler admitted that his behavior as a boy caused his
mother "bitter anguish" but had nothing to say about
any regrets or efforts on his part to make up to her for
that pain. In his adolescence after she was widowed he
made no move to lighten the financial burden of his
support. He did not try to relieve either her anxiety
about his future or the pain she felt about his going to
Vienna when she was gravely ill. In a rare complaint,
she said Adolf behaved as though he were "alone in the
world" (Kubizek, 1955, p. 114). Hitler's mentions of his
mother in his writings were bare and conventional, almost skimpy; in *Mein Kampf* he stated that she was
devoted to her children, and that she made him "a
mother's darling" and provided him with a "downy bed."
Not much more than that: no description, no quotations,
few if any individual recollections. We know that his
father, however, was cited often, from the time of Adolf's
derelict harangues to his table-talk as Chancellor.

Hitler's disappointments in, and fears of, his
mother—especially his very intense castration anxiety
—appeared in many reported actions. Intense castration
anxiety was at the root of the adolescent's extreme ap-
prehension about a wake-up kiss from his five-year-old
sister (P. Hitler, 1959) and his consistent shunning of
females throughout his adolescence and early manhood.
Extreme castration anxiety also accounted for the fact
that throughout life, he regarded women as inferior
beings and yet at the same time dangerous entrappers
of men and thought wives to be impediments to warriors.
Yet evidence is substantial that he feared loss of the
political support of women. He did not deprive German
women of consumer goods during the war; he did not

mobilize the labor of women as promptly as other nations did. Most strangely, his drastic anti-Jewish laws punished only men, not women. Even Jewish women were not punished for "miscegenation" (Hilberg, 1973, p. 107).

A particularly telling indication during adulthood of his extreme castration anxiety is found in Hitler's intense interest in decapitation. To decapitate, as Freud (1922, p. 273) pointed out, symbolically, is to castrate. The long list of Hitler's preoccupations with decapitation and disembodied heads included his promise that when he took power "heads will roll in the sand" (Waite, 1971b, p. 237). Whenever he flipped a coin, heads did not win. He designed the Nazi emblems, and his personal SS wore the Death's Head as its insignia. The first thing he would do on landing in England, he said, was to see the place where Henry VIII chopped off the heads of his wives. A favorite doodle, both as boy and as man, was to draw severed human heads. On the certificate for a promissory note issued by the Nazi Party in the mid-twenties which Hitler designed, an idealized German warrior holds in his right hand a sword dripping blood and in his left the blonde hair of a woman by which her severed head is suspended. The legend below reads, "Warrior of the Truth, Behead the Lie." Hitler was fascinated with the Medusa, a favorite painting being the Medusa by Franz von Stuck. When he first saw it reproduced in a book, he exclaimed to Hanfstaengl, "Those eyes are the eyes of my mother!" (Waite, 1971b, p. 238). His statement recalls Freud's interpretation (1922, p. 273) of the terror inspired by Medusa as a terror of castration, linked to avoiding sight of the female genitals, surrounded by hair, "essentially those of the mother."

Only as Hitler began to rise in prominence and power was he able to tolerate association with some older women, most of them of rich families who contributed money to his cause. He was able to identify them as good, giving mothers, a role the patronesses accepted, petting him and calling him by nicknames as one would a child. In time he began to approach women much younger than himself, publicly playing with them, *ad nauseam*, the exaggerated games of the ardent child wooer. Privately he used some of these young girls to practice his perversion, which is considered in Chapter XI. The extreme form of sexual perversion involving women that Hitler engaged in becomes possible for a person with a borderline disorder precisely because the perversion itself is one of its characteristic defensive maneuvers. (To be able to approach younger women, Hitler called on other defenses as well, as detailed in Chapter XI.)

Another consequence of intense castration anxiety appears in evidence that Hitler unconsciously accepted the idea that he was indeed castrated. These are the direct and indirect revelations of his passive feminine inclinations. His mincing walk, the feminine use of his delicate hands, and the way he carried himself often made observers suspect him of being a homosexual, an idea encouraged by his long and close association with homosexuals. He frequented parties at the home of his photographer which were gatherings of homosexuals of both sexes; Hess and Roehm were widely considered homosexuals; and many of the inner circle in the early Nazi Party were known as such.

That Adolf Hitler was drawn to men is at least possible. His youthful intimacy with August Kubizek, however exclusive on Hitler's part, and however charged with tender feelings on Kubizek's part, might be regarded as a mere adolescent phase. But Hitler often took very young men into his entourage and showed them special favor. His devoted follower, Baldur von Schirach, who became his national Youth Leader, was one of them and reputed to be a homosexual. Another handsome young cohort, whose connection to him was sufficiently meaningful for Hitler to have his portrait painted posthumously and hung beside his mother's at the Berghof, was Julius Schreck, his chauffeur. Schreck was among those chosen to be at Hitler's side in the highly emotional and bloody mission of killing Ernst Roehm in 1934.

Consciously, however, Hitler seems to have fought the very idea of homosexuality, and in the absence of any report it is unlikely that Hitler practiced homosexuality. His ruthless behavior and his boasts of an iron will, icy cruelty, and barbaric brutality, qualities which he associated directly with masculinity, were denials of his marked feminine tendencies and impaired masculinity. And further, defective genitals would preclude comparing them to those of another man to the detriment of his glorious self-image.

For all his negative feelings, an identification with his mother reinforced Hitler's feminine tendencies, an identification with many roots. The universal infant identification with the mother seems in Hitler not to have been transcended in the normal way by a shift to adequate identification with the father. Simply as a woman, she would appear to him at times as castrated, and because he remained fixed in the early identification with her, he would apply the idea of being castrated to himself. When he was a late adolescent and she developed a breast disease, another element was added to the identification: she became anatomically and sexually defective, just as he was defective in the genitals, according to the weight of evidence. With the added influence of primal-scene trauma and beating fantasies to reinforce identification with his mother, apparently Hitler unconsciously accepted female identification. The story of his drawing his dead mother's face, while ostensibly an expression of regret for the loss of so much gratification or an effort to retain some aspect of its source, may have been an expression of his identification with her. This drawing, for all its implied emotional value to him, was not one Hitler is known to have preserved or mentioned, a possible indication of the complexity of his feelings about it.

In his writings and speeches, Hitler identified his mother and her terminal disease, with Germany, "the suffering motherland," as he called it, contrary to the usual German designation of "Fatherland" (Langer, 1943 and 1972; Koenigsberg, 1975; Waite, 1977). Moreover, he equated her illness with Germany's real and imagined political and other difficulties. Indeed, he spoke of Germany's troubles in biological terms. We have seen how many of Hitler's political ideas were externalizations of his fantasies and inner conflicts. Kubizek noted the process once *in statu nascendi* when Adolf was wallowing deeper and deeper in self-criticism and suddenly his self-accusations became accusations of the times and the world. It is not surprising, therefore, that the identification of Klara with Germany is one of the unconscious roots of Hitler's ideology and accounts for some of the intensity with which he clung to it.

Part of his belief that his mission was to save Germany from ruin can be regarded as stimulated by the "rescue fantasy" frequently encountered in boys, a fantasy of rescuing the mother from the degradation of her "unfaithfulness to the son with the father." That Hitler equated himself with Germany is based not only on his identification with his mother (= Germany) but also on many direct statements to that effect. Here again his megalomania was fed from more than one source, and his sense of anointed mission was formed as a result of his seeing himself directly and indirectly threatened. In this urge to rescue Germany he unconsciously rescued not only his mother but also himself.

In sum, Hitler's conscious reaction to his mother included both recognition of her as a source of great indulgence and gratification and resistance to her unwelcome wishes that he behave realistically and with responsibility for himself. Yet she aroused both strong unconscious identification and much unconscious fear. Both feelings tend to interfere with normal sexual behavior with women. In fact, there is still no real evidence that normal sexual behavior was ever possible for Adolf Hitler. Although surviving relatives of Eva Braun have recently attempted to make a case for normality in her fifteen-year relationship to Hitler, her own statements belie it. His identification of his mother with Germany and therefore also of Germany with himself is one of the factors

that made for the furious intensity of feeling associated
with his political idea, inflaming his passion to rescue
Germany from political moral disease.

CHAPTER XI

Implications of the Perversion

Secretive about all things, Hitler compartmentalized everything. Until his last five years, he kept his sexual activity in what Hanfstaengl (1957) called that dark corner of his life. The nature of Hitler's sexual expression was camouflaged in his lifetime, and to some biographers the later contradictory reports are baffling. But the picture is consistent in tone: Adolf Hitler's sexual life seems to have been neither happy nor healthy.

The question of possible homosexuality in Hitler is often raised. From the derelict years in Vienna came reports of extreme misogyny but not clear indications of homosexuality. Information from the World War I period includes the persistence of intense woman-hating as well as some items of sexual aberration. The latter include allegations of a court-martial conviction of pederasty with an officer and a similar, untried, charge in Munich. The first known homosexual important in Hitler's life was an officer who served in his regiment during World War I, Rudolf Hess, known among homosexuals as "Fraulein Anna." One of Hitler's valets labeled the two "most intimate" (Langer, 1942–1943, p. 894). Another noted their special and rare relationship, finding it strange that Hitler would run to "mein Rudi," as he called Hess, like a child to his mother, with a sketch he had done or a present he liked. The only other man with whom Hitler for a time shared the intimacy of the informal *Du* was also a homosexual, Ernst Roehm. In fact, although Hitler was well aware of Roehm's homosexuality for a long time, it was that sexual orientation which Hitler later gave as one pretext for the assassination of this follower.

Other suggestions and hints of homosexual feelings are on record. Hitler commissioned a painting of his young chauffeur who had been killed in 1936 and had it installed in the Berghof, as his mother's was. He frequently visited parties at Heinrich Hoffmann's home, a meeting place for homosexuals of both sexes, at which there was little inhibition in sexual activities of all kinds. Finally, there were his frequent boasts as to his cruelty, brutality, and hardness, which he considered very masculine and which were intended to contradict any ideas about his femininity. A similar purpose, that of denying any homosexual leanings, probably motivated the extremes of his public acts against homosexuality. His new government promptly moved harshly against all sexual deviation as well as against sex crime. Nine times as many cases involving homosexuality were prosecuted during 1936–39 as during 1931–34. He set up a special SS section to destroy "enemies of the state," explicitly including in their number homosexuals, and as late as 1942 he set death as the penalty for homosexuality within the SS.

All this notwithstanding, the prevailing opinion is that Hitler was probably not a practicing homosexual.

The German journalist, Konrad Heiden, who was close to the Nazi scene, observed before 1943 that Hitler had a penchant for using and abusing people in politics and even in what he called love. Nevertheless, he maintained that Hitler was not a sadist, but rather the most extreme of masochists. Hitler's sadism, of which he often boasted, was obvious, but his masochism, not as blatant, was equally unmistakable. Both a valet and his personal pilot wrote of the importance to Hitler of his whip, a traditional symbol of sadism. He carried it with him for many years and at times used it on himself. During an early Berchtesgaden visit the blonde Junoesque wife of his pension host so inflamed Hitler that he gasped and whistled in his breath, sucked his fingers, and strode back and forth before her, beating his thigh with his whip as he declaimed about the moral depravity of the Berlin Jews and his wish to flail them like Jesus driving the money changers from the temple. When the fifteen-year-old daughter of Heinrich Hoffmann refused him a good-night kiss, Hitler beat his hand with his whip.

Film actresses, often supplied by Goebbels, were regularly present at late-night parties at the Chancellery at which "no decent woman" would appear. A German film director told American Intelligence that he helped sup-

ply Hitler with starlets for the night, one of them Renate
Mueller, who described an explicit example of Hitler's
sadomasochism. She told her director about a shattering
experience with Hitler when she came to spend the night
as his sex partner. First she described torture methods,
both medieval and Gestapo, in great detail. Then, after
they undressed, Hitler lay on the floor and groveled
around, accusing himself and begging to be kicked. Finally, as the scene became intolerable to her, she
acceded and her kicks excited him more and more.

Renate Mueller committed suicide by flinging herself
from the window of a Berlin hotel. Frau Inge Ley, wife
of Hitler's Labor Front Leader, also killed herself after
an affair with Hitler. In all, known suicide attempts by
women connected with Hitler total seven. Hoffmann,
usually so devoted to Hitler's image, told of Hitler's affair
with a young married woman who tried to hang herself
in a Munich hotel after a strange encounter with Hitler.

The masochistic aspects of such experiences are obvious, but the sadistic ones are no less evident. Aside
from the introductory description of torture methods,
Hitler's masochistic groveling with requests to be kicked
were highly unpleasant to his partners. Indeed, demands
which were even more emotionally painful than repulsive were probably made by Hitler during some of these
episodes (witness the large number of suicide attempts
among women connected with him). On the basis of Miss
Mueller's statement and the reports of Geli Rabaul, described below, and the study prepared for the OSS in
1943 edited by Dr. Langer, he concludes as follows about
Hitler's aberrant sexual behavior: "it is an extreme form
of masochism in which the individual derives sexual grat-

ification from the act of having a woman urinate or defecate on him" (Langer, 1972, p. 134).

By 1929, Hitler often appeared in public with his niece, Angela Maria Rabaul, called Geli. He brought her to live in his luxurious new Munich household, gave her the bedroom next to his own, had himself appointed her guardian, and asked her to call him "Uncle Alf." This name echoes the "Uncle Alois" used by his mother for his father. He always referred to Geli as "my niece Geli."

Hanfstaengl quoted a complaint from Geli to a girl friend that her uncle was "a monster," continuing, "You would never believe the things he makes me do." He also recalled an incident in 1931 in which Hitler cracked his dog whip to emphasize some political threat. This caused Geli's face to express "so much fear and contempt" that Hanfstaengl, thinking "whips as well," felt sorry for the girl despite a strong personal antipathy for her (1957, p. 165).

An account of Hitler's practice of perversion with Geli came from Otto Strasser, interviewed in Montreal in 1943. Strasser stated that Geli herself told him about Hitler's practices. She related that "Hitler made her undress . . . he would lie down on the floor. Then she would have to squat down over his face where he could examine her at close range and this made him very excited. When the excitement reached its peak, he demanded that she urinate on him and that gave him his sexual pleasure. Geli said that the whole performance was extremely disgusting to her . . . and it gave her no gratification" (OSS, 1943, p. 919).

Evidence which tends to support Strasser's information and Langer's conclusions concerns a sexual approach to Geli in a letter from Hitler in early 1929. It revealed his perverted sexual demands and was used in a blackmail incident. The blackmail was disclosed by a participant, Father Bernhard Stempfle, a Catholic priest who was also an anti-Semitic journalist and a Nazi, friendly to the Hesses and to Hitler. Although Stempfle had helped prepare the *Mein Kampf* manuscript, he was one of the old associates Hitler had ignored as he rose in power. The priest told the story in the early 1930s to a friend who had already learned a great deal from Geli herself. The disastrous letter in Hitler's own hand explicitly delineated his severely masochistic and coprophilic inclinations. It fell into the hands of a son of Hitler's landlady. In an attempt to retrieve it, Hitler had the Party Treasurer enlist the aid of a well-known collector of political memorabilia. Hitler's devious idea was that the collector get the letter back for him by buying it as though for his vast library of documents. The collector was a notorious eccentric named J. F. M. Rehse, who over years packed his rooms with cartons of political clippings, decrees, and posters. Father Stempfle happened to be Rehse's confidant. Together they exploited Hitler's vulnerability to exposure to extort from him the permanent financing of the entire accumulation, with the two as curators (Heiden, 1944, pp. 384–386).

Rehse, luckily for him, probably never handled the dangerous document; Father Stempfle delivered it to the Nazi Treasurer, and he to Hitler. The priest did not long survive telling the story to a friend. During the 1934 Blood Purge, Father Stempfle was shot to death. The Nazi Treasurer, Franz Schwartz, although never conspicuous, became an even more influential Party figure;

in 1935 Hitler made him sole executor of his personal will.

About the same blackmail incident or a similar one, Hanfstaengl (1957, p.163) recalled that early in the 1930s Schwarz confided to him that he paid blackmail to retrieve some pornographic drawings Hitler had made, "depraved, intimate sketches of Geli Rabaul, with every anatomical detail." Schwarz called them "the sort of thing only a perverted voyeur would commit to paper" and said he had not destroyed them because Hitler wanted them back, to be kept in the Brown House safe.

Extreme or bizarre as the nature of Hitler's perversion may seem, this very type of sexual behavior is part of the borderline personality syndrome. Otto Kernberg expressed this in the following terms:

> The more chaotic and multiple the perverse fantasies and actions and the more unstable the object relationships connected with these interactions, the more strongly is the presence of Borderline Personality Organization to be considered. Bizarre forms of perversion, especially those involving . . . primitive replacement of genital aims by eliminatory ones (urination, defecation) are also indicative of an underlying Borderline Personality Organization [1967, p. 649].

The multiple forms which Hitler's perverse sexual impulses took are clear in the reports. Even his masochistic behavior had a sadistic aspect because his partners were degraded, revolted, and frustrated by the parts they had to play. Hitler, of course, actually boasted of his sadism because he thought it evidenced masculinity. Unalloyed sadistic impulses were revealed by his pleasure in view-

ing films of executions, especially his zest for the film he
ordered to record the dying agonies of generals who
plotted to assassinate him; so, too, did his explicit order
to prolong these agonies disclose such impulses (Speer,
1970, p. 395; Toland, 1976, p. 927). Hitler's perverted
sexuality took still other forms. His voyeurism was demonstrated by his indulgence in pornographic pictures and
films, some especially made for him. Roehm exclaimed
scornfully about Hitler's sexual pleasure in viewing the
buttocks of women. His need to watch a woman bend
down and make up his bed before he could go to sleep
was noted by his royal Italian host. Coprolalia, or pleasure in uttering obscenities, and an exaggerated interest
in pornography indicate a combination of coprophilia,
exhibitionism, and sadism; witness the stream of vulgar
obscenities and sadistic threats Hitler uttered as he beat
a table or a wall during his temper tantrums, and his
lifelong preoccupation with thoughts of filth, dirt, and
putrefaction.

The behavior in a perversion is often a symbolic re-
enactment of a traumatic childhood experience, with the
sex partner representing an earlier important figure,
usually the mother. A common childhood trauma is the
witnessing of the primal scene. In the crowded quarters
of Hitler's childhood homes repeated primal-scene experiences were almost unavoidable. Because the child's
capacity to discharge the induced excitement of the primal scene is limited, it is transformed into anxiety and
provides an early fixation point to which regression may
later occur as the individual tries to master the anxiety.
Jacob Arlow (1980) believes that a more parsimonious
elucidation of the repetition of the primal scene, one

more clearly related to clinical observation, is the revenge motive, closely connected to a wounding of self-esteem experienced by the child. The deep narcissistic mortification, the feeling of being excluded and betrayed, understood as an oedipal defeat by the child, is often linked with an idea of anatomical inferiority. (In Hitler this idea probably had some reality reinforcement.) These elements lead to a persistent sense of personal unattractiveness, which, by way of compensation, elicits grandiose exhibitionistic wishes.

Another reaction to the humiliating feelings of being unloved and unlovable is the tendency of the narcissistically wounded observer of the primal scene to wreak vengeance on the offending parents. Arlow observes that in dreams, for example, the revenge motive in the primal-scene psychology may be expressed regressively in oral and anal terms. A common form is the demeaning or humiliation of the parents, with the role of one of them assigned to a participant in a re-enactment of the primal scene. In Hitler's perverted re-enactments, he was both observer and participant and forced another to be both observer and participant as well, thereby humiliating and disgusting the parental surrogate as he himself was humiliated and disgusted by witnessing the intercourse of his parents.

Hitler's urge to revenge himself on his father was due to other factors as well, including his unresolved oedipal complex and the harshness of Alois' behavior. Still another factor would have been seeing his father as a liberal, an admirer of the Hapsburg Empire, symbolized by its capital, Vienna. Vienna, we know, signified to Hitler "Jews and more Jews," whom he hated. A more direct connection between Jews and Alois was expressed in Hitler's preoccupation with the possibility that the father of his father was Jewish.

As to Hitler's paranoid attitude toward "The Jew," Freud's observations (1913, p. 50) on delusions of persecution are relevant:

> The importance of one particular person is immensely exaggerated and his absolute power is magnified to the most improbable degree, in order that it may be easier to make him responsible for everything disagreeable that the patient may experience. . . . The model upon which paranoics base their delusions of persecution is the relation of a child to his father. . . . When a paranoic turns another into a 'persecutor' he is raising him to the rank of a father. . . .

In other words, in identifying the hated Jew with his father, Hitler makes both the hated object.

Hitler's reported need was for the woman to squat over his head in such a way that he would "see everything," i.e., be able to peer into the vagina. Curiosity not only about the fate of the father's penis in the sex act but also about an imagined penis of the mother often figures in a perversion. A fantasy frequently connected with the image of the mother as dangerous and castrating is that she must have a penis hidden somewhere in her body—a fantasy that Hitler apparently retained. Characteristically for those who do so, Hitler became contemptuous of women and rejected them as normal sexual objects. The perverse ritual that he required of women included the appearance of a urinary stream as well as a fecal stick, both gratifying because they provided a reassuring discovery of the hidden penis, which both excretory products symbolize.

Still another feature of the symbolic re-enactment of the primal scene is the child's alternate identification with each of the parents. In his coprophilic sexual acts Hitler was both the passive, masochistic (mother) participant, and by demanding the degrading practices, the active, sadistic (father) one. But Hitler's dual image of his mother identified with himself is contradictory. In playing the passive role in this form of perversion, as well as in the form described by Renate Mueller where he demanded that she kick him, the identification with the castrated mother for the time overshadows any identification with the frightening phallic mother and the hostility toward her. Indeed, the aggression sought from the mother-substitute may also serve as a means of doing penance for the hostile feelings toward her. Such complex elisions are not uncommon in perversions. Beating fantasies could also have played their role in the form taken by Hitler's perversion. Freud regarded beating fantasies as an essential part of perversions and found that they represent unconscious wishes to be loved by the father.

A normal resolution of Adolf's oedipal strivings was prevented by his mother's efforts to bind her son to herself with overindulgence and by his father's long absences and harsh rejecting behavior. The father's aggressive behavior reinforced castration anxiety and discouraged Adolf from sufficient identification with him to further any normal tendencies of a son to repress his sexual fantasies about his mother. Thus all women, being equated with his mother, were unconsciously seen by

Hitler as incestuous and dangerous objects and therefore
tabooed as normal sex partners.

A perversion does not suddenly appear full-blown. The
permanent form of a person's sexual life is not established
before adolescence. In Hitler's life the basis for development of sexual aberration can be traced from the earliest probable sources of his castration anxiety in infancy
through a series of progressively intensifying factors,
some of them exaggerations of normal ones and others
special to Hitler. Monorchidism would lend an element
of reality to castration anxiety. Fear of his father's imagined castration threat because of the Oedipus complex
added to anxiety, as did identification with his mother
while she was also perceived as a phallic castrating figure.
All these converged in an unconscious acceptance of an
image of himself as castrated and also resulted in the
feminine passive inclinations which he disavowed so dis-
astrously. For all the disavowal, an extreme, even degrading form of the passive feminine inclination was
obviously expressed in the submissive situation Hitler
chose for himself in the perversion.

A perversion itself bespeaks extreme castration anxiety. Evidences of the persistence of the intense castration
anxieties in Hitler were his numerous phobias, most of
which clinical experience finds traceable to that condition. Fear of touching and of dirt, of exuding a bad odor,
of death, and especially of infection, all have been found
often to have their roots in castration fears. Hitler's sy-
philophobia was well documented by Hitler himself. In
Mein Kampf he spent almost a chapter on the disease
and seemed unable to keep from coming back to the
subject. As a constant danger connected with sexual re-

lations, fear of infection with syphilis is often found to be a rationalized fear of castration. The significance of so intense and pervasive a castration fear is that it blocks heterosexual expression of sexuality and thus impels the adoption of other means to gratify sexual needs. Indeed, it is always castration anxiety which interferes with the male's capacity to gain full genital sexual gratification. Through the perversion the individual unconsciously tries to prove to himself that his castration fear is baseless. (It should be noted that the interrelationship of masochism and sadism is reflected in phobias of infection, because infection by others also implies its opposite, the possibility of infecting them.)

That the inevitable resurgence of strong sexual preoccupation in Adolf broke through around puberty is evident in the sexual transgression involving a little girl mentioned by a teacher. Hitler's drawing of a teacher masturbating is another unusually frank expression of such preoccupation. By about age fifteen, however, he had so drastically repressed these interests that he never spoke to a girl, not even to his "Stefanie." An aspect of this imaginary love is that when Adolf talked of suicide he insisted that Stefanie would have to die with him. Adolf then exploded with an unprovoked and furious "reckoning" with Stefanie's mother. Since Stefanie was but a mirror image of Adolf, Stefanie's mother represented his own mother to him. Though Adolf used the term "reckoning" more than once in connection with his mother, it was easier for him to express hostile feelings toward her by attacking Stefanie's mother as her substitute.

Young Adolf's avoidance of women was absolute and

sometimes furious, as it was on the occasion when he found a girl consulting Kubizek, her music tutor. Kubizek observed that Adolf's character called for inhibitions in relations with women, that since the unforeseeable may happen in love, love is dangerous and to be guarded against. Obviously inhibitions and efforts to guard against drives would be unnecessary without sexual urges and their dangers to evoke them. Young Adolf discoursed on various unsanctioned forms of sexuality, prostitution, homosexuality, and incest, only to proclaim his disapproval of them with characteristic boundless rage. He acted as a knowledgeable guide to August through what he called the "Sink of Iniquity" and was also far more knowledgable than the older August about homosexuals. Kubizek stated that he himself had never even heard the term "homosexual," much less known what it meant, until Adolf explained it, saying that it had long been one of the problems he wanted to see fought against relentlessly (Kubizek, 1955, pp. 226–239). Again, something that presented no temptations would scarcely provoke such a campaign.

We can conclude that the perversion Hitler practiced later as an adult, served, in addition to providing revenge, to assuage his castration anxiety in the following way: his sadistic impulses toward his mother produced fear of her; to ward off her anticipated hostile retaliation, his masochistic stance in the perverse act *vis-à-vis* the sex partner or mother-substitute became a way of doing penance for these impulses, as well as a reversal of the hostile fantasies and thus a denial of them. The fact that the "mother" could be persuaded to give up the hidden penis was also reassuring, particularly since, in a sense, it was given to him. Insistence upon the closest examination of external female genitalia could also be a counterphobic reaction to aversion to the female genital. Hitler's fascination with the Medusa symbol also implies such a reaction.

The perverse act is an attempt to achieve other advantages as well. The anxiety which arises in carrying out its counterphobic aspect, as well as from the symbolic re-enactment of the childhood trauma, changes into sexual feelings that add to sadomasochistic excitement and pleasure. Another benefit sought is that the re-enactment of the childhood experience takes place under conditions which the person controls. This time, unconsciously, he expects that he will master the overwhelming anxiety. Perverse experience is thus sought not only for its erotic stimulation but also to try again and again to master the extreme anxiety which originally was traumatic to the child.

Like other defensive processes and substitutes for normal functioning, the perverse act does not succeed in the permanent control or diminution of anxiety. In Hitler, his perversion, colliding so directly with his glorious self-image, apparently induced further anxiety and shame, beyond the reach of the splitting defense. These feelings played an important role in the intensity of his epochal anti-Semitism, in a way examined in Chapter XIII.

CHAPTER XII

Guilt and Shame in Hitler

Hitler's destructiveness was colossal. Granted his anger, hate, and paranoia, how did any human conscience allow the cruel taking of so many innocent lives? Were he not psychotic, many ask, how could Hitler have felt sufficiently free of guilt to carry out his mass destructions, or, finally, to call for total devastation of his own country after choosing to destroy himself?

The question of conscience and guilt feelings is a knotty one, and not only as it relates to Hitler. Involved are questions of general usage of language as well as psychological issues about which psychoanalysts disagree. The concepts of guilt and shame are not sharply differentiated, either in ordinary discourse or in technical studies. Sometimes the terms guilt and shame are used interchangeably. Their referents are, however, better understood as separate phenomena.

The generally accepted conception of guilt feelings is that they denote the internal tension and pain caused by a transgression against conscience. Such transgressions include committing a crime or a moral offense or violating a taboo. Some moral offenses for which one might feel guilty are harmful acts to respected institutions or to other individuals whom one loves or respects and wishes to obey. Thus, one might feel guilty if, even in thought, one misuses another by attacking, humiliating, deceiving, cheating, or manipulating him.

Anyone even generally familiar with Hitler's history must have grave doubts that he had such feelings to a significant degree. We know that Hitler railed against conscience as a Jewish invention. He believed that the race will find internal peace only when it is no longer overshadowed by the consciousness of its own guilt. He believed that both intelligence and conscience should be distrusted (Langer, 1972, p. 190). But from these statements, one can infer that he must have been troubled to some extent by what he called conscience and guilt or he would not have been impelled to denounce them. This contradiction requires a closer examination.

The mental structure involved here is the superego, more specifically its critical, restrictive, and punishing function which, when violated by the transgression of moral attitudes, evokes pangs of conscience (in German, *Gewissensbiss*, the bite of conscience) and the feeling of guilt. Implicit in this process is the function of self-observation, for one cannot evaluate data against certain standards without observing both the acts and those standards. Standards of behavior are the products of numerous identifications, beginning with the parents in childhood and modified through adolescence and even into adulthood by identifications with moral aspects of admired individuals in the environment. These can be traced in Adolf Hitler.

Hitler's mother almost certainly attempted to inculcate respect for authority in him, especially religious authority and morality. She clearly tried to urge him to adhere to religious tenets by insisting on his confirmation. We know she urged him toward choosing work that would make him financially independent. These were Klara's conscious efforts. However, parents often unconsciously influence their children to behave contrary to their expressed wishes, so that they may vicariously experience some of their own repressed desires and ambitions (Johnson and Szurek, 1952, pp. 323–343). Indeed Stierlin built a major part of his study around the idea that Klara unconsciously "delegated" her son to carry out four major missions: avenging her, relieving her of shame, appeasing her guilt and redeeming her worth as a mother, and providing her with vicarious importance and power (1976, pp. 57–65).

Whether Klara actually did delegate her son to carry out these tasks or not, she allowed him to defy her as a symbol of family authority and to live a self-indulgent life free of the need to work and the discipline of earning a living. She obviously did not succeed in making him a God-fearing youth who adhered to religious tenets of behavior. Very likely, the early appearance of marked aggression interfered with any exercise of gentleness, Christian charity, or love of fellow man. Nor did Klara succeed in making her son an industrious and productive member of society. Nevertheless, most of any limited pangs of conscience that Hitler may have felt and fought against probably came from his mother as preceptor.

Theoretical reasons alone would lead to doubt that Adolf fully identified with his father's superego as a result of the resolution of the Oedipus complex, since there is much evidence that his Oedipus complex was not adequately resolved. There may have been some identification with the aggressor. Hitler showed his father's tendency to put the gratification of his own wishes before anything else, including the interests of others, especially women, and before truthfulness or religious considerations. Furthermore, identification with the aggressor would have encouraged Hitler's freedom to express hostile and aggressive impulses, condescendingly superior attitude toward others, and exhibitionism. On the relatively positive side, Adolf may have acquired from his father his punctilious attention to conventional forms of address and some aspects of the ambition that he found late in life, but little else that made for a conscience of any significance. He did not identify with his father's conscientious attention to work, with his tolerance of the preferences of others in certain areas, or with his respect for authority.

The outcome of parental influences on Adolf's superego in childhood is hinted at by his half brother's report that Adolf up to age seven was angry, arrogant, and willful, with little regard for the rights and feelings of others. The disregard for the feelings of others included those of his mother; Hitler himself admitted that he caused her bitter anguish by his behavior. During his early adolescence, his teachers noted that Adolf demanded the unqualified subservience of his fellow pupils, thus violating their right to their own wishes and needs. He showed no qualms about hurting the feelings of anyone, including his teachers, his landlord at Steyr, and even the kindly couple who tried their utmost to please him on the day they sponsored his religious confirmation.

During the Kubizek period, the deficient state of Adolf's superego manifested itself in his gratuitous and self-righteous discourtesy and abuse of former schoolmates and teachers, and even of Kubizek himself. In Adolf's fantasies about the allegedly beloved Stefanie, he ran roughshod over her preferences, such as her enjoyment of dancing. He even contemplated her murder. Adolf showed little concern for August Kubizek's interests or needs; indeed, he callously abused both throughout their relationship.

In his adolescence and young adulthood two figures influenced Adolf. One was Richard Wagner, whose music so often transported him and whose political and anti-Semitic ideas he incorporated. The other, he claimed, was his *Realschule* history teacher. Though he did not remember the teacher's name accurately, Hitler credited him with inspiring him to nationalism. German Nationalism centered in the idea of *"Deutschland, Deutschland ueber Alles,"* a sentiment evidently understood by Hitler as dominant over all. The idea goes back to the medieval title, *"Das heilige roemische Reich deutscher Nation,"* which referred to something that never actually existed but which expressed a longing for one mighty German nation. The influence of this myth on Hitler is illustrated by his plan to write a book in 1919 after World War I, to be entitled, characteristically, "The Monumental History of Humanity," setting forth the German task to establish "The German Reich of the German Nation," a new and racially pure empire (Waite, 1977, p. 56). Closely associated were vague ideas about the purity and uniqueness of German blood. To Hitler these ideas and ideals were concrete and literal, as his racial programs would reveal. '

Another contributor to Adolf Hitler's superego probably was Martin Luther. Though there is no evidence that Hitler read Luther, that cleric's considerable contribution to anti-Semitic as well as political ideas was part of the culture of Germany which Hitler absorbed and made his own (*ibid.*, pp. 117, 248–251). Luther preached that God had chosen the German people to perform a special mission in history and that the good Christian owed absolute obedience to the State because its rulers, right or wrong, were agents of God. As did Hitler centuries later, Luther opposed reason and trusted in instinctive action, with which Luther associated faith, feeling, and spontaneity of the heart. His idea that man's dual nature, the physical and the spiritual, called for two "governments," one secular and one spiritual, had a profound effect on the ethical code of most Germans. Luther's conception of the two "governments" separated private from public morality. Thus, Lutheran pastors preached for generations that the good Christian should be loving, forgiving, kind, and honest in his personal life whereas the State may be ruthless, cruel, harsh, and crafty. Hitler could excuse himself from the private morality by identifying himself with the State. Eventually, his psychopathology unrecognized, he virtually became the State.

Hitler expressed admiration for very few public figures of his time. All were anti-Semites. Thus the influence on Hitler's superego exerted by cultural anti-Semitism, a German prejudice for centuries, is strong and clear. In the German Reformation, which was dominated by Luther's ideas, we find demands that the Jews be harried from the land. Luther's tract "On the Jews and Their Lies" is both a scurrilous attack and a call for their elimination. The tract was reprinted through the centuries in numerous anti-Semitic pamphlets and quoted extensively by Theodor Fritsch, Guido von List, and Hitler's great hero, Richard Wagner. Contemporary anti-Semites whom Hitler admired were the Austrian politician Georg von Schoernerer and the pragmatic mayor of Vienna, Karl Lueger.

Hitler's superego was thus influenced by culture and environment to include as its standards certain cruel, paranoid, and prejudiced ideas that reinforced behavior characteristic of his personality. The very development of the narcissistic-borderline personality disorder described earlier makes for a defective superego. Thus a conscience in Hitler was at best weak and corruptible. Behavior which would be a gross transgression of a normal conscience would trouble Hitler very little if at all. In the observing function of the superego, Hitler as a narcissistic-borderline individual could use his capacity for primitive and complete denial of perceptions when it suited him. He could lie, acknowledge that he lied, indeed proclaim the lie as a great *desideratum,* and then vehemently deny that he ever lied. This element of his disorder again helped spare him the pain of any dim guilt feelings that may have resulted from the enormity of his acts.

Hitler was ashamed of his school failure because he lied about it, as we know. He was ashamed even into adulthood of his use of his school certificate as toilet paper. He was ashamed of his failures in his efforts to gain admission to the Vienna Academy of Arts. And he was ashamed of having allowed himself to deteriorate to the level of the dregs of society in Vienna and having to peddle "artistic" productions which he himself despised.

The more precise meaning of shame, as distinguished from guilt, can be understood in relation to the psychoanalytic concept of the components of the superego. In addition to its observing functions and the aspects manifested as conscience, the superego includes the *ego-ideal.* This is the image of himself to which a person both consciously and unconsciously aspires. The observing aspect of the superego measures the individual against this ego-ideal. When the performance of the actual self does not measure up to the ego-ideal, the tension which arises is experienced as lowered self-esteem, embarrassment, mortification, or humiliation—in short, shame. Thus shame arises from a shortcoming in the achievement of a level of excellence, a weakness, a rebuff, or a defeat, especially one that may be revealed to others. Behind the anxiety of shame is the fear of derogation and contempt, and ultimately, unconsciously, the fear of abandonment.

Manifestations cited by some authors as examples of

guilt feelings were feelings of shame and humiliation provoked by Hitler's glorified ego-ideal. For instance, Hitler's need repeatedly to assert his worthiness revealed his nagging doubts about it and his efforts to still them. In one of his speeches he exclaimed, "I carry my heavy burdens with dutiful thanks to Providence which has deemed me worthy" (Domarus, 1965, p. 2186). In another speech: "God continues to bestow His Grace only on him who continues to merit it" (Prange, 1944, p. 90). And in the New Year's Proclamation of January 1, 1944, he declared, "The Great Judge of all time . . . will always give victory to those who are the most worthy" (Domarus, 1965, p. 2076). Projecting his own feelings on the whole nation, as he frequently did, Hitler attributed Germany's impending defeat in 1945 to her unworthiness. In all of these statements one can see that he was not concerned about transgressions against his conscience but rather about falling short of his ego-ideal. The same is true whether the issue was his flatulence, his doubts about "Jewish blood" in his veins, about his Fuehrer-like appearance, his incestuous fantasies, or his perversion. When Hitler proclaimed, "I am freeing man . . . from the dirty and degrading modification of a chimera called conscience and morality," he was clearly speaking not of the pain caused by sinful transgressions against standards of ethical behavior but of shameful dirtiness and degradation.

Stierlin (1976) pointed out that in German the very word for shame, *Scham*, which, as *die Scham*, refers to the genital region, as *Schamhaare*, to pubic hair, and as *Schamteile*, to the genitals, indicates the relationship of shame to sexuality and the genital area. Shame is often the consequence of sexual shortcoming or deficiency. According to the demands of his ego-ideal, Hitler had ample sexual deficiencies and shortcomings to plague him. He practiced revolting perversions; he was probably monorchid; he had incestuous fantasies and extreme castration anxieties, as well as many grandiose fantasies about himself of which he fell far short. Therefore he was in a state of constant anxiety lest these deficiencies reveal themselves; he was ever anxious lest he make a *faux pas*, seem ridiculous, irresolute, inferior, betray weakness or ineptness, or suffer defeat or humiliation. All these real possibilities conflicted with his grandiose ideas about himself.

And behind all of them lurked a feeling perhaps surprising: the fear of abandonment by his followers and the loss of the power to dominate, control, and manipulate. The loyal adherence, admiration, and subservience of his followers, as we have seen, was practically the *raison d'être* of Hitler's whole existence. In order to deny any deficiencies which would shame him and also lose him his following, Hitler was constantly boasting of having characteristics he considered admirable, all in great measure. He proclaimed himself brave, superior, and possessed of brute strength and of unflappable dignity. Anxiety about the traits he could not adequately disavow in this way he tried to dispel by projection, primarily on Jews, as we see in considering his anti-Semitism in the next chapter.

Hitler's superego, then, certainly in its self-observing and conscience aspects, was poorly integrated and defective; its ego-ideal was distorted by megalomanic fantasy. Not surprisingly, the anti-social personality or sociopath, whose outstanding characteristic is that he is devoid of conscience, presents a typical borderline personality organization. Hitler's extreme narcissism, his pathologically grandiose ego-ideal, made for inevitable shortcomings and therefore shame. The efforts to overcome shame with distorted conceptions of strength and masculinity, together with defective self-observation and a very limited conscience, made Hitler's almost unimaginable excesses of destruction possible.

CHAPTER XIII

Behind the Intensity of Hitler's Anti-Semitism

A motif in a life, like most phenomena, results not from a single cause but rather from a convergence of factors, sometimes of many. The motif of anti-Semitism was the very watchword of Hitler, the man, as well as of Hitler, the German Dictator. His anti-Semitism long antedated the time when it came to have tactical political utility for him and may well have persisted beyond political usefulness. Once Hitler became Chancellor his hatred of Jews was both domestically and diplomatically counterproductive (Orlow, 1974, p. 137), and yet it became evermore deadly, accelerating until he began to

confront military defeat in 1942. Then he made the ultimate formulation of official anti-Semitism, his Final
Solution: to massacre all the Jews of Europe. The fury
of his anti-Semitism was retained to his last moments
and became his testament of hate "bequeathed" to
"heirs," the German people, whom he now also hated
enough to order their virtual destruction along with his
own.

As a phenomenon of mass psychology, anti-Semitism
has a long history in many parts of the world, including
the Austria and Germany that produced Hitler. The cultural, social, religious, historical, and economic factors
making up the mass psychological phenomenon unquestionably bear upon its appearance in an individual.
Still, the ultimate channel for the expression of all social
behavior including the phenomenon of prejudice is the
functioning of the individual's psyche. Hitler's own statements confirm the need for a personal investigation: he
told Helene Hanfstaengl that his anti-Semitism was "a
personal thing" and told his sister Paula that his failure
as an artist, always so galling to him, occurred because
"trade in works of art was in Jewish hands" (Toland, 1976,
p. 46).

It is true that Hitler hated not only Jews but also
Blacks, Poles, Russians, and ultimately Germans, indeed
all mankind including himself, as he indicated on rare
occasions, but his hatred of Jews was the most persistent,
the first and last he articulated. It had a phobic and
obsessive intensity and a paranoid quality different from
his attitude toward the others. The Germans he finally
rejected because they failed to achieve the military victories he wanted of them. For the Poles, Russians, and

other Slavic peoples he displayed a contemptuous antipathy, regarding them as inferiors fit only to be preserved as slave labor for the German "supermen." But Jews were to Hitler's way of thinking a concrete threat and uniquely dangerous. Individually, he believed, they corrupted the blood and purity of any German woman with whom they might have sexual relations. Collectively, they were not only a biological threat to the physical health and vitality of the German people but also a moral threat to their nobility of character. Very early he entertained thoughts of exterminating Jews "under poison gas," as he wrote in the last chapter of *Mein Kampf.* So great a danger must be removed from Germany, even from the face of the earth, as he indicated when he later decided to rescue the rest of the world as well.

The meaning of Hitler's anti-Semitism to his psyche has been sought by many commentators. Some have soon admitted defeat; others have offered complicated speculations to fit their preconceptions. If we review all of Hitler's biography, however, a general pattern appears. First, Hitler came to Vienna evidencing the anti-Semitism prevalent in his culture. Second, this prejudice became more intense in Vienna. Third, this more intense anti-Semitism soon revealed its underlying character as both a phobia and an obsession.

Again, the diagnosis here presented fits the observed facts about Hitler. The neurotic symptoms with specific peculiarities pointing to an underlying borderline personality often include certain multiple phobias and obsessive-compulsive symptoms which are rationalized and accepted by the ego and therefore become thoughts and actions whose value is exaggerated. Among the phobias

often found are those related to one's own body, those
involving severe social inhibitions and paranoid trends,
and those involving elements transitional toward obsessive neurosis, such as fear of dirt and fear of contamination. In addition to his dread of Jews, Hitler's known
fears were numerous: fear of physical contact with others,
especially of women until after he was thirty; fear of
infection, especially venereal infection; fear of contamination of his blood and also of moral contamination; fear
of dirt; fear of being sick, as with gastrointestinal disease
or cancer; fear of being ugly or repulsive, as by exuding
a bad odor; and fear of death. He also practiced compulsive hand-washing and other rituals rationalized in
various ways.

Two great fears experienced as revulsions stand out
in Hitler's life as a young man in Vienna. These are
manifested by his continued extreme avoidance of
women and his avoidance and increased fear and hatred
of Jews. A closer examination of these attitudes reveals
not only a probable chronological relationship but, more
significantly, a probable psychological one.

Hitler brought with him to Vienna the hatred of Jews
prevalent in his environment, intensified by his own
hostility toward almost everyone. Kubizek cited examples of Hitler's deepening anti-Semitism: his reluctance
to eat in the university canteen because Jews were present; his rageful refusal to consider work for a Jewish
editor; his testimony in court against the Jewish beggar;
and finally, his sole real political act as a youth, joining
an anti-Semite union. The last was a step unique for
Adolf in two ways: it was a concrete act, not a theoretical
proposition, and it was an act of affiliation with others.

Hitler joined the Anti-Semite Union of Vienna sometime in the spring of 1908.

The exact date is unknown, but the youths began to room together in March of 1908, and many events of their life in Vienna are reported before the day that Hitler announced to Kubizek that he had enrolled them both in the Anti-Semite Union. It could not have been during the Easter season in mid-April, since Kubizek was then visiting his parents in Linz. By the end of June, the two parted forever as roommates. Thus the day that Adolf formally joined the organized Anti-Semites must have been shortly before or shortly after the Easter holidays, a meaningful timing. The Easter holiday in a Catholic country is always a highly emotional festival, and that year it was especially significant to Hitler. It was the first Easter after the death of his mother, and Easter Monday fell on April 20, his nineteenth birthday, so that the Easter season also included his first birthday without her. In 1889, when he was born, Easter fell on the very day of his birth, something almost certainly mentioned by his doting Catholic mother and adding to its personal meaning.

Alone in Vienna at Easter time in 1908, Adolf was surrounded by celebrations of the resurrection of Christ. His megalomania was such that he would be able, thanks to the splitting mechanism, to identify with the glorious and glorified figure of Christ even while simultaneously eschewing Christianity and its constraints, as he said he had done by his fifteenth year. Later in life his identification with Christ, however paradoxical, persisted and he explicitly alluded to and encouraged it. In anti-Semitic Vienna in 1908 he was also surrounded with ample reminders of the Anti-Semitic idea that the Jews killed Christ. Thus he may have felt himself threatened by this identification. Among the accusations of Jewish perfidy encountered in Vienna around this time of the year, which more or less closely coincides with the Passover week, is the "ritual-murder" myth. As late as the 1930s, the ritual murder myth was still featured in anti-Semitic newspaper headlines in Vienna. The charge in this myth is that male Jews murder a Christian male child by dismemberment and mutilation (Loeblowitz-Lennard, 1947). The dismemberment motif and myths are interpreted by scholars as representations of castration in a disguised form. Here the direct charge was sometimes made that Jews castrated Christian boys; vague distortions about the Jewish rite of circumcision may be connected with this version of the myth. The effect on Adolf, with his intense castration anxiety, would be hard to exaggerate.

Hitler's feelings would have been strengthened by his identification with his recently dead mother, whom a Jewish doctor had failed to save. Consciously Adolf may well have felt the great appreciation he expressed for the professional ministrations to her by the highly regarded Dr. Bloch. But he could hardly avoid repressed hostility toward the doctor for "allowing" her to die, tantamount to killing her, an emotional attitude toward physicians not uncommon among the bereaved. In him, indeed, the first reaction to news of her terminal illness was a furious attack on doctors who call a malady incurable only because they are not capable of curing it. Klara's death was caused by ulcerated carcinoma of the breast (Kren, 1974, pp. 265–268). Her agony was a long one. Her son, although certainly absent for months of it, knew that his behavior was adding to her pain. He also hated as well as loved her. His identifications with Christ and with his mother, both "killed by Jews," would reinforce each other. The moment could not have been more propitious for focusing on the Jews as the vehicle to bear away the unwelcome anxiety-producing fantasies, and especially those perverse ones produced by sexual and aggressive stirrings, increasingly tormenting as his adolescence progressed.

The Easter season of 1908, then, seems to have been the moment when he actively transferred the raging feelings to the outside, to "The Jew." Having done so, he could, while the defensive projection worked with its usual partial and temporary efficacy, be fairly tranquil with August Kubizek for a few weeks. Kubizek described such an interval in a chapter the erotic quality of which bespeaks still another possible element in the situation. The course of events itself suggests that homosexual urges toward Kubizek may have emerged or come close to expression at this time. Such a threatening experience could reinforce the painful experience of envy of Kubizek's success in music and become another reason that Adolf broke so suddenly and cruelly from this companion.

The confluence of events described above may have triggered Hitler's joining the anti-Semitic organization, but it does not entirely account for the increased hatred of Jews. The adolescent Adolf was so excited and agitated by the sexually stimulating features he encountered, or sought out, in Vienna that he dragged Kubizek through the red light district not once but twice one evening. All of the young Hitler's sexual conflicts and fantasies were obviously stirred up in Vienna because, as Kubizek tells us, Adolf frequently inveighed against homosexuality, prostitution, incest, and related issues. He apparently had many troubling incestuous and other sexual fantasies to project onto the Jews for his own relief. No better example can be cited of Hitler's early proclivity for projection and projective identification than the episode which illustrates those defenses practically *in statu nascendi.* Kubizek described occasions when young Adolf wallowed deeper and deeper in self-criticism and then his self-accusations would abruptly become accusations against the times and against the whole world for setting tripwires against him.

Adolf's spoken and written products from adolescence onward point to the nature of some of the feelings he projected upon "The Jew." An early fantasy, the "Stefanie interlude," can readily be linked with another fantasy Hitler set down nearly twenty years later in *Mein Kampf.* After several pages of condemnation of "The Jewish Race," Hitler suddenly turned to the following image: "With satanic joy in his face, the black-haired Jewish youth lurks in wait for the unsuspecting girl whom he defiles with his blood, thus stealing her from her people" (1943, p. 325). And again: "Systematically these black parasites of the nation defile our inexperienced young blonde girls and thereby destroy something which can no longer be replaced in this world" (*ibid.*, p. 562).

No great leap of the imagination is required to see that these images interrupting Hitler's more general diatribes relate to some inner reality of his own, namely, his fantasies about "Stefanie." Indeed, a fantasy rather than an act in keeping with the part of the imagined "Jewish youth" who "lurks in wait" is undeniable, since he could hardly defile the girl by merely waiting for her, except in fantasy. Hitler knew so much about the imagined Jewish youth, even his fantasies, because that villain really represents young Adolf himself. Else why would he speak of joy in the Jew's face? Lust would have been more appropriate for this condemnatory picture. But joy is the emotion young Adolf felt most keenly at the anticipated appearance of "Stefanie." The sexual wishes were deeply repressed, so that even when the adult Hitler described the scene in the third person, the accompanying rape fantasies are alluded to only indirectly. Again, why the choice of the detail, "black-haired"? Certainly "hook-nose" or "beady-eyed" or any one of the commonly used traits in the caricature of the Jews would have contributed more to the unattractiveness of the picture he was painting. But Hitler himself had dark hair. Further, why a youth? A lecherous old Jew would have made the image even more repulsive. Again, why "lurks in wait," if not because that was exactly what the young Adolf used to do as he expectantly looked toward the appearance of his mirror image, "Stefanie?" And, of course, the real "Stefanie" was a completely "unsuspecting girl" whom he would not approach for many probable reasons, one of which could well have been that he feared to "defile her with his blood." Nevertheless, this did not keep him from fantasying—and sharing his fantasy with Kubizek—that he might "steal her from her people," by kidnapping her, it will be recalled. And, of course, "Stefanie" was blonde and he imagined her as completely inexperienced.

Subsequent periods in his life brought forth many

emotional elaborations of Adolf Hitler's sexual and sex-related fantasies projected onto the Jews. For instance, he projected his thoughts about incest. These, often in his mind, appeared in his speeches in an oddly conspicuous way (Waite, 1971a, pp. 205–206). Incestuous fantasies deriving from his unresolved Oedipus complex clearly contributed to his extraordinary attachment to his mother. He was old enough to be the father of most of the young women he used sexually. The difference in age was remarkably often close to the twenty-three years that his father was senior to his mother. Klara Hitler addressed her husband as "uncle." The woman who most affected Adolf was his young niece, Geli. He used the phrase, the "personification of incest," in writing about Vienna, which to him was the city of Jews and more Jews. In 1919 he declared that it was only by "thousands of years of incest" that the Jews had maintained themselves historically (Waite, 1971b, p. 234).

Adolf's idea of sexual relations, revealed in his words, seemed to be a bizarre one: a process in which the male introduces substances into the female which eventually reach "her blood stream"; when the relationship is an incestuous one or especially one between a Jewish male and an "Aryan" female, her blood becomes corrupted. Even if he meant her "blood line," Hitler showed himself obsessed with thoughts about blood and the quality of blood. Notions about the quality of blood appeared repeatedly throughout his writings, his speeches, his conversations, and thus, implicitly, his fantasies.

It may be that he believed his own blood was "poisoned" by Jewish blood because of the rumors that he had a Jewish grandfather. He may have considered his blood defective because of the alleged near-incestuous relationship between his parents. Perhaps he sought to understand on physical grounds his tensions, anxieties, fears, suspicions, sleeplessness, imperfect genitals, and general dissatisfaction with himself. We know the importance to him of the idea because he stated that "alone the loss of purity of the blood destroys the inner happiness forever; it eternally lowers man, and never again can its consequences be removed from the body and mind" (1943, p. 327). Hitler tried to deal with his anxieties about his "impure blood" in various ways. By claiming that the blood of all Germans was poisoned, he tried to universalize the fantasied defect, as he did so many others. The poisoning of the German blood became the "original sin" of all humanity. Universalizing apparently did not help much, so that eventually he had his physician, Dr. Morrell, draw blood out of his veins, either by syringe or by leeches, in the hope that he might thus be rid of his bad blood. Failing any help from this, the unconscious process of projection continued to operate. Not he, Hitler, had impure blood; the Jews harbored impure blood and with it defiled blonde young German maidens and all Germany.

Speculations have been offered about the possibility that as a child Hitler experienced an anal fixation, evidence for that idea abounding from his adolescent years on. At first the drives were manifested in his overcompensatory reactions to his anal impulses. He dressed with meticulous care and was remarkably fastidious about his person throughout the early period in Vienna with Kubizek. During the Vienna years following came a period of extreme regression. He dropped the over-compen-

sation and became conspicuously dirty in his person and
habits, even among the derelicts and downtrodden; he
remained dirty in habit for several years. Some improve-
ment in cleanliness was reported in 1912, and he was
remembered as clean in his person as a soldier in World
War I. By the time he took power he had fully resumed
his overcompensating defenses; the Chancellor washed
his hair at least once a day, frequently scrubbed his
hands, changed his underwear twice daily. He was always extremely concerned about his body odors and the
flatulence for which he took enormous quantities of "an-
tigas pills." His anality broke through directly in his
thoughts, as revealed in his conversations, speeches, and
writings and it focused upon the Jews. A few excerpts
from *Mein Kampf* make the point clearly:

> The cleanliness of this people, moral and
> otherwise, . . . is a point in itself.
> . . . later I often grew sick to my stomach from the
> smell of these caftan-wearers. Added to this, there was
> their unclean dress and their generally unheroic ap-
> pearance.
> . . . was there any form of filth or profligacy, partic-
> ularly in cultural life, without at least one Jew involved
> in it?
> . . . if you cut even cautiously into such an abscess,
> you found like a maggot in a rotting body, often dazzled
> by the sudden light—a kike.
> . . . the fact that nine-tenths of all literary filth, artistic
> trash, and theatrical idiocy can be set to the account of
> a people, constituting hardly one-hundredth of all the
> country's inhabitants, could simply not be talked away;
> it was the plain truth.

In discussing his hero's virtuous self-control and renunciation of all sexual gratification, Kubizek assured us
that Adolf never masturbated (1955, p. 237). The validity
of this statement is supported by two features of Hitler's
behavior. One is that after the repression of phallic masturbation, extragenital and sadomasochistic practices
may be substituted for the pleasure thus renounced, as
pointed out by Arlow (1953), citing Tausk (1951) and
Annie Reich (1951). We do not know when Hitler started
such extragenital practices, but that he did so is established. The other consequence of the renunciation of
masturbation is that phobic symptoms may develop when
the external object is regarded as a temptation or as a
reminder of the temptation to achieve sexual discharge
through masturbation. Hitler was quite explicit in describing woman as a temptress. With such an attitude
the ego defends itself against anxiety by avoidance, thus
establishing the basis for the formation of phobias. An
avoidance to the point of phobia of women was certainly
one of Hitler's traits for a long time. In fact, it was the
second major feature of Hitler's life in the Vienna period
and thereafter until he became involved in politics. We
know that phobias and obsessions are derivatives of unacceptable repressed impulses. These displace their energy onto connected ideas less objectionable to the
conscious ego and thus are eventually expressed consciously. Clinical experience teaches us that phobias and
obsessions like Hitler's usually represent fear of castration, a fear that would not be surprising in Hitler in the
light of the course of his childhood.

As early as his prepubertal or pubertal years Adolf
Hitler had an almost panicky reaction to the possibility

that his five- or six-year-old sister might give him a kiss. (The sexual conflicts that this bespeaks could well have been a factor in the onset of his poor school performance around this time.) Kubizek repeatedly referred to his companion's avoidance of females, extreme to the point of phobia, e.g., his inordinate rage on finding Kubizek tutoring a girl in music. This outburst occurred, of course, against the background of young Hitler's great preoccupation with his sexual fantasies, which he generalized and saw as social issues. In this he was helped by the pornographic themes conspicuous in the low form of anti-Semitic literature he devoured so avidly.

Hitler's phobia of women persisted through his adolescence and early adulthood as a soldier, only beginning to diminish to some extent when he became a politician. His need to finance his political activities made it expedient for him to play up to those who could provide him with funds. Among the most likely subjects for this purpose were rich elderly mother figures. They enjoyed mothering him and presented him with money and valuable gifts. As he came increasingly into the public eye, he must also have been aware of the need to avoid the appearance of a man who feared and avoided sexually attractive younger women. He therefore began publicly to approach such women also, playing a similar role with them of the pitiful little boy begging to be loved. These displays of interest in pretty young blondes Rauschning termed playacting during which Hitler remained "the same hopelessly unmature man, with the same morbid lusts" (1940, p. 266).

It was not that his fear of a woman's sexual approach disappeared entirely. At a New Year's Eve party in 1924, for instance, an attractive young woman managed to get Hitler under the mistletoe and gave him a good-natured kiss. "I shall never forget the look of astonishment and horror on Hitler's face," a witness recalled. In his table-talk the Chancellor decades later compared sexual intercourse to the trauma a soldier faces in battle. Characteristically for Hitler he projected the fear onto women, about whose actual fears in intercourse this man who was terrified of approaching them for intercourse obviously knew nothing. Something must have happened, however, to have made possible some diminution of his fear of women in the late 1920s. It might appear that external political needs entirely determined the change in Hitler. He needed money and he needed a single scapegoat on whom to focus the attention of his people. As he told Rauschning (1940, p. 237), if the Jews had never existed, they would have had to be invented. But that would not account for the increasing destructiveness of his paranoid and phobic hatred of Jews, which grew into a central part of his political credo as he rose in political importance. At the same time, his fear of women diminished. The juxtaposition of the two developments, increased intensity of the fear and hatred of Jews and decreased fear and hatred of women, is striking and readily suggests a relationship: a displacement of his fear from women to Jews.

Obviously these developments involved gradual processes which cannot be timed in split seconds. There are indications, however, of the general time period when these changes were taking place in Hitler's mind. Around 1928 Hitler was deeply, and more openly than ever, involved with a woman: his niece, Geli. About the same time he was preparing a work which became known as *Hitler's Secret Book*, published for the first time thirty-three years later. In this book he associated his hatred of Jews with ideas about blood and race for the first time. His sexual interest in his niece must have inevitably stirred in Hitler thoughts of incest and fears of harming her and possible progeny by what he believed might result: the corruption of her blood. All these ideas and wishes he projected onto the Jews, and by universalizing, as was his wont, he made the Germans, the Motherland, and the whole world their (his) victims instead of Geli. As if to justify his destructive fantasies after he had attributed them to Jews, he characterized them as a basic tendency for self-preservation which even Jews have. This rationalization doubtless helped him persist in his pursuit of Geli as much as did the displacement.

The most obvious bridge for this displacement was Hitler's idea that Jews were indeed like women in many respects. He described Jews as unheroic in appearance, meaning not manly but feminine. Like women, they were to him seducers and hypocrites; they were false—that is, liars and deceivers—inferior, and dangerous. When we consider these allegedly feminine traits, we see how well they fit Hitler himself. He disavowed them in himself by projective identification and projection onto the Jews. In so doing he facilitated the displacement of his paralyzing phobia of women onto them. As a result of the projection, he was at last able to approach women, although probably not for normal sexual relations.

Some observers saw in the Chancellor conspicuous feminine elements, even beyond the mincing gait and delicate hand gestures often noted. Karl Burckhardt told an English historian that Hitler was "the most profoundly feminine man" he had ever met, and that "at moments he becomes almost effeminate"; he imitated the gestures of Hitler's "white flabby hands." His walk was described in 1938 as very curious, ". . . very ladylike," with "dainty little steps." His Chief of General Staff mentioned "many proofs" of feminine characteristics being dominant in Hitler (Langer, 1972, p. 172; Toland, 1976, pp. 354–355, 720; Waite, 1977, pp. 5–6, 234–235). Indeed, it was these effeminate features, his misogyny, and his close relationship with known homosexuals that often raised the question of homosexuality in Hitler himself. Other suggestions of Hitler's own "unheroic" features are descriptions of him as "the stereotype of a headwaiter"; again, ". . . as he ranted, he had the look of a man trying to seduce the cook" (Reck-Malleczewen, 1970). Wrote a French diplomat (François-Poncet, 1949, p. 95), "Viewing him at close range while he was relaxed, I was struck as I was to be struck whenever I approached him later, by the vulgarity of his features and the insignificance of his face. . . ." He had a slouched posture, a half-hearted salute, and a stance in which he frequently held his clasped hands over his genitals.

But to Hitler it was always the Jew who presented the unheroic appearance. A detail confirmed the personal reference. A physical characteristic Hitler always stressed about Jews was the shape of the nose. Hitler insisted that one characteristic is common to all Jews from the ghetto of Warsaw to the bazaars of Morocco: the offensive nose, the cruel, vicious nostrils. As Robert Waite (1977, p. 6) noted, Hitler's persistent inclusion of this observation in his comments about Jewish people is revealing.

Many commented that his least attractive feature was his grossly shaped nose and unusually large nostrils: hence the bushy little mustache grown just wide enough to reduce the effect of its size. In effect, Hitler seemed to say, the Jew's nose is really the ugly, cruel, and vicious one, not mine.

To project the rest of his unacceptable features on the Jews was an easy step. When he found he could sustain increased contact with women, his incestuous and perverse fantasies and behavior became more intense. His defective superego permitted him to indulge in perverse sexual practices and other socially unacceptable behavior, but that behavior was inimical to his grandiose ego-ideal. No mental device could totally exclude from consciousness the disparity between his perversion and his image of himself as the highest representative of the pure, noble, virtuous German superman. With a certain degree of awareness of that disparity came shame. Because of the narcissistic aspect of his personality he had to search constantly for shameful behavior in others, in order to project onto them what he would disavow. He was able to find such behavior readily in Jews, given the prevalent ideas about them, especially in the pornographic anti-Semitic pamphlets so abundantly available in his Vienna days and in the anti-Semitic journalism he always encouraged Streicher and other Nazis to publish. He accused Jews of incest, prostitution, and the dissemination of syphilis among pure, clean-blooded Germans—indeed, of general degradation—all with deliberate destructive intent against Germans and all mankind. The indictment is elaborated in *Mein Kampf* in the passages that the historian Alan Bullock characterized as insane.

A surprisingly direct indication that he projected his perversions specifically on the Jew is an incident reported by Gisevius. When the Gestapo brought the Chancellor photographs, described as of the "most shocking depravity," of the bride of a general, he declared instantly that the male partner "must have been of Jewish extraction" and suddenly became "absolutely convulsed by the wildest anti-Semitic fulminations" (1963, pp. 383–384).

The displacement of his fear of women to the Jews, with the help of the projection of his own disavowed qualities on them, not only illuminates why, after avoiding women for so long, he was able after age thirty to approach them; it also helps account for the implacable progressive intensification of his anti-Semitic program. The displacement called for an ever-stricter avoidance of Jews, even useful Jews. But that was much more practical than continued avoidance of women. The political advantages of this emotional shift were enormous. Open hostility to Jews was culturally acceptable and welcome, whereas fear and hostility toward women were both unmanly and impolitic. Anti-Semitism even made him a hero among many, male and female, and for a long time early in his rise it was almost magically useful.

But although displacement of his fears of women onto the Jews made possible some heterosexual outlets, it did not completely relieve the castration anxiety associated with women. The enormously obsessive quality of Hitler's anti-Semitism can be better understood when seen as directed toward futile attempts to master this continuing and, for Hitler, basic anxiety. By attacking the Jew, Hitler tried with increasing frustration to eliminate the source of his castration anxiety. When verbal attacks were not enough, he decided to destroy all the Jews in Germany. But even this decision did nothing to diminish the anxiety. He then tried to destroy all the Jews in the conquered countries as well, but that did not help either. If he had succeeded in annihilating all the Jews on earth he would not have been satisfied, and his efforts to conquer his castration anxiety and his shame would have driven him to displace his fears onto other victims.

The defenses Hitler used were no solution to his problems; no defense mechanism works perfectly. This displacement of his revulsion and fear of women onto the Jews did not even make it possible for him to gain sexual gratification from normal heterosexual relations with women. Similarly, his projection did not completely relieve him of the awareness of those of his own features to which he objected.

Another psychological characteristic further aggravated other painful emotions. Persecutory delusions such as Hitler had are characterized as paranoid. Paranoid ideation is based on the very projection that Hitler's life embodied so clearly.

Additionally, Hitler's anti-Semitism was fueled by at least two other factors. One was that feature in his character which required constant denial of any trace of doubt in his masculinity, as well as of any feminine qualities whatever. He therefore found it necessary to keep proving that he was possessed of masculine qualities, among which he included merciless cruelty and brutality, so evident in the last years of World War II. A second factor was his capacity for cruel and brutal aggression, which was abundant, perhaps as a genetic heritage, and certainly as a developmental factor.

Two other factors facilitated Hitler's annihilation of millions of Jews. One relates to the inadequate resolution of his Oedipus complex and the resulting defective superego formation. This had many important consequences, as we have seen, one of which was the failure to learn to separate moral from other conflicts. Thus, Hitler never learned to separate what is dangerous from what is evil. Hence he felt motivated to destroy Jews, not only because he saw them as dangerous but also because he regarded them as evil. Secondly, in his great shame, he saw himself as a nonperson, an image which he tried to neutralize by boasts of being a superperson, almost divine. The objectionable nonperson image, with the dangerous and evil image, was also projected on the Jews, whom, indeed, he described as vermin, maggots, and bacilli. Their destruction, therefore, could be pursued with impunity as a virtue rather than a vice.

The enormous devastation to the Jews of Europe that resulted from Adolf Hitler's projection onto them of all that he disavowed in himself was made possible because he was given practically limitless political power. The nation was almost completely in his thrall. He could destroy any and all within his reach whom he wanted to destroy.

CHAPTER XIV

Psychopathology and Hitler's Political Career

A psychopathological condition unquestionably has disadvantages. Hitler's case is no exception. His intense anxiety, hypochondriasis, anger, hatred, paranoia, and shame were sources of torment. His impulsive outbursts, feminine inclinations, and perversion were sources of anxiety. His grandiosity, need for admiration, arrogance, lack of empathy with others, and obvious need to control and manipulate repelled many people, especially before he became a politician, when for a time he was able to work, to control himself, and to exploit his charm. Denial, splitting, and projective identification as well as par-

anoid trends made for defective perception of reality and
for poor judgment, even after he established himself as
a promising political figure. These defenses continued
to limit his relations with others, which again resulted
in isolation and inability to enjoy many of the pleasant
features of life, despite his incessant picnicking, touring,
and protracted meals with cohorts. The ultimate disad-
vantage of his disorder was evident in the catastrophic
end of his life.

Yet Hitler's successes raise the question of whether
a narcissistic-borderline personality cannot be exploited
in the making of a successful political leader. Some of
his pathologic features certainly provided advantages in
Hitler's phenomenal political ascent.

Narcissistic personality that he was, Hitler consciously
regarded himself as a creature almost divine, chosen by
Providence to lead the German people. He claimed to
be endowed for that purpose not only with superior intelligence but also with infallible intuitive insight into
politics, law, history, the arts, biology, genetics, and
almost every other phase of life. He also saw himself as
the most super of a race of supermen, not only having
extraordinary physical strength and courage but also
being morally pure and noble. Hitler was so completely
dominated by this delusional self-image that his conviction lent a highly contagious sincerity to his pronouncements of his absolute authority. Just as few can believe
in one who does not believe in himself, so many Germans
tended to believe in one who believed in himself utterly.
A public saturated in obedience to authority and desperate for direction responded with enthusiasm as well
as submission, thereby facilitating the gratification of

another of Hitler's narcissistic urges, his need to control and manipulate others.

Hitler's extreme narcissism gave him a useful way of presenting his faults as great virtues. He referred to his sadism and cruelty as his brutality, but he always spoke of brutality as one of the greatest virtues of man. He used the term to still his doubts about his masculinity by implying that it signified manly strength. Similarly, he was aware from his religious upbringing and probably also from his mother's precepts that one's conscience should not allow cruelty and murder. But since his conscience was distorted and defective, he was not deterred. Further, he made a virtue of the flaws in his conscience by denouncing conscience as a Jewish invention, *ipso facto* undesirable. He presented his rigidity as "iron" or "granite" resolve, will, or consistency. He explained away his incapacity for any close human relationship such as marriage as a deliberately planned disciplined abstinence. Such a notion became politically attractive, especially to female voters. The leader sacrifices himself, and women's fantasies about him flourish. Finally, his willfulness was presented as evidence of strength of character and strong will, instead of the remnant of infantile demandingness that it was.

In speaking of his intuitive and impulsive reactions to problems, he denigrated the importance of education. In this way he made a virtue of another of his deficiencies: his limited schooling. He scorned educated men because he could not admit anyone's superiority to him in any area. Rather, he asserted that education interferes with the superior evaluation of situations and decisions based upon intuition.

A related deficiency, his inability to apply himself and study dispassionately and in depth, Hitler simply concealed. He referred often to his "studies" of social problems, of history, of "the Jewish question." Actually, his teeming unconscious conflicts prevented him from applying himself to disciplined study of any subject that did not supply the immediate gratifications he sought: the confirmation of his prejudices or the excitement of fierce details about wars and fighting that held an abnormal fascination for him from childhood, reaching to "the depths of my being," as he put it. But there is scant evidence that he "studied" more than the cheap propagandistic tracts of pamphleteers with whom he agreed, those simplistic solutions to complicated problems for which the perplexed were only too hungry.

He professed that he had an ability to simplify complex issues. He was actually too misinformed in many areas to appreciate their complexities. He knew very little of science, economics, anthropology, evolution, or many another subject on which he made self-assured pronouncements and official decrees that determined the fate of millions. He could make his effective oversimplified statements about complex issues because he was unhindered by any knowledge of their complexities, details, and nuances. Joachim Fest wrote, for example, of Hitler's great trick of leaping over economic contradictions. Particularly in dealing with the masses, his propaganda effects around lofty but vague principles were actually facilitated by the capacity to deny inherent in his psychopathology. Not only the uneducated but also many others, hungry for quick, firm answers to questions that in fact were supremely difficult, joined the deceived.

Conflicting with his grandiose concepts and fantasies of omnipotence were his several personal realities: the limitations of his physique and probably defective genital apparatus, and the ignoble impulses and the fantasies they engendered. These were expressed in his perverted sex acts, in which he behaved as though he were so base and unworthy that the "inferior" woman should physically degrade and punish him by kicking him or urinating and defacating on his face. With the passage of time he seemed to have become more and more aware of his deficiencies, because his need to deny them with megalomanic claims to superiority became more extreme, even as his real situation was undeniably one of great power. He also dealt with many of the disturbing contradictions by projection, and often by projective identification.

A more detailed examination of these psychological processes is helpful in considering questions frequently asked about Hitler. During his lifetime and ever since, many have asked whether he could possibly have sincerely believed all those grandiose fantasies about himself. Just as baffling, how could an intelligent man accept all the patent nonsense he spewed out endlessly about the Jews and the other targets of his hate. His blindness to elementary facts is all the more puzzling to those who do not realize that intelligence like his is no obstacle to self-delusion or to any of the defenses that Hitler could exercise, given the pathologic personality organization here postulated.

Many individuals have grandiose ideas about themselves, but in few do they reach the fantastic dimension revealed in Hitler. This fortunate outcome is due at least in part to the fact that few achieve anything approaching the power that Hitler attained. He could carry out such fantasies and thus reinforce them. The fantasies increased in scope and outspokenness as Hitler acquired more and more power. One of the ways in which power corrupts even the most mature personality is precisely that it fosters ideas of omniscience and omnipotence. Great power in the hands of the distorted narcissistic-borderline personality serves to affirm and intensify the megalomanic concepts already so strong in the individual.

But still it is asked: if he were not psychotic, how could Hitler continue to entertain ideas about himself and about the Jews so far removed from reality? Here other borderline-personality aspects shed some light. He could maintain his own grandiosity and at the same time see all others, especially the Jews, as altogether inferior because of the defense mechanism of splitting, a basic part of the borderline personality, which permits the separation of people into the all-good and the all-bad. With his complete denigration of Jews and his glorification of so-called Aryans, Hitler demonstrated the defense clearly. He did the same in so passionately holding Communists, liberals, and Social Democrats as totally bad and Nazis as totally good. This very simplicity was politically useful, in that it provided clear targets for public anger in periods of chaos and frustration.

The violence of his hate for those whom he designated as all-bad relates to a result of splitting: impulses in particular areas become uncontrollable. Periodic break-throughs of primitive impulses, such as rageful outbursts, are perfectly acceptable to the borderline personality at certain moments. Although such eruptions were sometimes a source of embarrassment, Hitler soon perceived their utility in intimidating opponents: he would deliberately use one of these outbursts to force his will on statesmen (Toland, 1976, pp. 515–516).

Still another manifestation of splitting which the politician can put to effective use is the alternate expression of opposite sides of a conflict, along with bland denial and lack of concern over the contradiction in what he does or feels. The mechanism of splitting is reinforced by the mechanics of denial. The process has been described by Kernberg (1967, p. 670) in this way:

> The patient is aware of the fact that at this time his perceptions, thoughts and feelings about himself or other people are completely opposite to those he has had at other times; but this memory has no emotional relevance, it cannot influence the way he feels now. At a later time, he may revert to his previous ego state and then deny the present one, again with persisting memory, but with a complete incapacity for emotional linkage of these two ego states.

Such liberty to make opportunistic reversals of position is obviously an enviable convenience to a politician. From 1925 on, the swiftest shifts of viewpoint without a backward glance served Hitler constantly in his campaigns, becoming his "art of contradiction" (Rauschning, 1940, pp. 15, 85, 136), although at the same time he asserted and appeared to believe in the immutability of his principles. He could convincingly promise all things to all men, including such opposites as revolution and return to the good old days. A clear statement of Hitler's

use of these defenses was made during Hitler's lifetime
by a prominent Nazi from Danzig who fled the movement
in the 1930s. He noted on the basis of his many personal
conversations with the Chancellor that Hitler could totally reverse his position on a problem while remaining
completely oblivious that he had made any change. He
further noted that Hitler was "capable of entertaining
the most incompatible ideas in association with one another" (Rauschning, 1940, p. 245).

The splitting defense doubtless often made possible
the conviction with which Hitler used the Big Lie. The
Big Lie was, however, used many times quite consciously
and deliberately to create his myths, especially about
himself, and to deceive and overwhelm, as well, in order
to seize some immediate opportunity. Notorious examples of unabashed mendacity are Hitler's public claims
that the Czechs and later the Poles were the attackers
when he was the attacker—who had in fact begun his
preparations long before—in each case.

Moreover, with the defense of splitting supported by
that of denial, Hitler could sincerely believe in his own
grandiosity, despite the fact that at other times he had
entirely opposite views of himself. Other features of his
particular pathologic organization add more possibilities.
A man with the capacity for such denial and splitting who
also has easy access to projection and has a defective
conscience as well, operates with few hindrances. He
can be totally opportunistic and ruthless. With denial,
he can even ignore certain oppositional realities and with
his contagious self-confidence override them. Using the
splitting defense, Hitler could for years sanction the
homosexuality of Ernst Roehm, grant him the rare priv-

ilege of the familiar form of address, and benefit from his loyalty and often crucial support, and then when the political situation dictated, personally direct this old colleague and sponsor's bloody elimination, citing homosexuality as well as alleged disloyalty as a justification. Again, Hitler for many years accepted and used Jews whenever they provided some benefit to him. Yet when he needed a political scapegoat or a personal psychological one, his capacities for denial, splitting, and projection combined to permit him to destroy all Jews within his grasp.

In the borderline disorder, the absence of a realistic concept of other people as whole individuals in relation to the self, along with the defective conscience, permits the manipulation of people as mere pawns. Such an attitude can be the very basis of a political climb like Hitler's. Many of the other elements in the pathologic organization are all the more readily brought into play if other people are not perceived fully but seen as mere objects. The chronic denigration of others fosters exploitation of their every weakness as well, something of which Hitler openly boasted.

Among the unfavorable consequences of splitting is the absence of a stable, integrated self-concept. This results in weak ego boundaries, with poor discrimination between what is inside and what is outside the self. The contradictory partial identifications of self with the "good" and the "bad," dissociated from each other, manifest themselves separately at different times. The borderline individual may behave like either the all-good self or the all-bad self, and as though toward an all-good or an all-bad person—whichever at the moment is useful in his superficial adaptation to reality. Such shifting is facilitated because in close interpersonal involvement the borderline person's weak ego boundaries do not hold firmly. Thus his adaptability to others has a chameleon quality, and the self he presents to one person may be totally different from the self he presents to another.

This feature contributed much to the enigma that was Hitler. To different people at different times and in different situations he appeared diametrically different: either gentle, relaxed, charming, considerate, and the soul of reasonableness, or tense, anxious, violent, viciously vindictive, and irrationally fanatical. That is what his pathologic personality organization made possible. With good reason Hitler could pride himself on being "the best actor in Europe." And it is small wonder that his contemporaries saw him in different ways. Some of the wide differences among his biographers depend upon which of Hitler's contemporaries serves each biographer as the major source of information.

For Hitler this quality had significant advantages. He could be charming and engaging to an individual whom he wanted to win over, professing agreement with ideas totally opposed to his own avowed beliefs. For myth-making purposes, he could endlessly pose as the tender lover of children and dogs, as well as the gallant defender of womanhood. On the other hand, he could browbeat with vicious violence of word and manner those whom he wanted to bend to his will politically. In his oratory, the chameleon quality of a diffuse identity made it easy for him to say with conviction the things his audience wanted to hear.

The great aggressiveness inherent in the disorder can

be misinterpreted as inner strength and determination in a political leader and thus promise to save followers from imminent catastrophe. The very grandiosity that is central to the narcissistic personality found support in the enormous aggression of the borderline personality which Hitler harbored. It gave him the appearance of forcefulness and self-assurance which supported his own self-concept as a man of all-powerful will and at the same time permitted him to dominate others both as individuals and *en masse*. Very few individuals are ready instantly to muster the counteraggression necessary to resist the impact of the sudden flare-up of rageful aggression of which Hitler was capable.

As an administrator, Hitler would not have survived in any well-run business. Aside from a tendency toward slothfulness and undisciplined working habits, his paranoid trends diminished efficiency. But even this weakness helped him keep affairs in his control. One of his avowed methods was to reveal to any one follower only what was absolutely necessary for him to carry out a limited function. Such compartmentalizing obviously prevented integrated cooperative functioning among his subordinates. Although this *modus operandi* may have been deliberately chosen, underlying it was the paranoid element in Hitler's personality, as a result of which he trusted no one. Nevertheless, this element also helped him remain on top of the heap of his often incompetent, corrupt, and rivalrous subordinates. Hitler remained the sole essential figure, who alone knew all that the others knew partially and separately.

Paranoia accounts as well for an attribute that may seem paradoxical, his ability to perceive mood. Hitler's often-noted acute sensitivity to the moods of individuals and especially to the moods of masses of people was not the product of empathy, which clearly he lacked. Rather, it reflects the anxious paranoia that scans for dangers. Because of the paranoid quality of their relations with others, many individuals with narcissistic-borderline personality disorders become hypersensitive to the slightest stimuli in their environment. Such persons are keenly alert to every movement, gesture, facial expression, and sound that anyone makes, because they feel that everything has direct reference to them. Thus Hitler was known to dislike instantly all who would not become his unquestioning admirers, even when they gave no overt evidence of their feelings. He could, for instance, observe an audience, get the "sense" that they were not favorably disposed toward him, and turn on his heel and leave without delivering his speech. During World War II his swift discernment of those who would follow him and those who would resist was noted by a German army historian (Schramm, 1971).

Hitler's practice of delay, evasion, and equivocation may, again, have been in part deliberate. But much of it reflected his ambivalence and uncertainty, furthered by his lifelong slothfulness. As evidence one may cite the fact that his delays were sometimes disastrous, e.g., his procrastination in dealing with the conflict between Roehm's SA and the army. However, as he often did with other shortcomings, Hitler apparently convinced himself, and certainly persuaded many others, that he was merely awaiting mystic inspiration to guide his decision. His personal myth that Providence had sent him to lead the German people to glory was thus furthered.

His grossly unusual behavior had the advantage of taking an opponent by surprise. Many reporters originally saw the rising politician as a wild, hysterical demagogue who made impossible promises and improbable threats. Even when some of his predictions came to pass and he became Chancellor, far-better-informed people, e.g., Neville Chamberlain of Britain, persisted in regarding Hitler as just an aggressive leader who for effect made empty declarations of intentions which no decent man would carry out. Some statesmen could not imagine that a head of state would not be a gentleman. But when Adolf Hitler spoke of the extermination of the Jews, for instance, he was not indulging in hyperbole or symbolism. He was voicing the concretism that is part of the borderline personality. At first people did not fully recognize his concretistic way of thinking, any more than they could credit his capacity to lie or to destroy without a qualm. This ignorance of his pathologic traits, at that time not so clearly defined as it now is, permitted Adolf Hitler to consolidate his power to the point that it was too late for action against him to succeed.

Hitler could suggest to his followers the most violent measures, and he could sanction acts otherwise unthinkable, because of the defective conscience of the borderline syndrome, combined with his faith-inspiring grandiosity and forcefulness. The deeply exciting permission to act out forbidden drives becomes part of the leader's magnetism for the followers. Those with somewhat similar character structure, such as many of the near-criminal ruffians of Hitler's intimate circle, were most openly drawn to him by it.

Others were also affected, some concealing or able to

deny what drew them. The architect Albert Speer and his mother first joined the Nazis secretly, hiding their membership both from each other and from his father, an example of how Hitler's personality and his program touched off feelings that some seemed for a while unwilling to acknowledge in themselves. The phenomenon is not unknown. Dostoyevski in *The Possessed* (1962, p. 353), has the old intellectual Karmazinov, speaking to the young writer Verkovensky, declare, "The Russian people would enthusiastically follow a man who promised them the right to act dishonorably."

For those not drawn to crime, violence, and hostility, the same Hitler could simultaneously offer, through his ubiquitous Nazi organizations for every age and kind of person, a sense of belonging, contributing, and participating in the meaningful and patriotic. Here as everywhere untroubled by contradictions, Hitler seemed to understand that human behavior is not moved exclusively by the material but impelled as well by a craving for more altruistic goals. Hitler himself did not really share this idealism because, as he consistently showed, he could believe only in himself, but his personality left him entirely free to manipulate it in everyone else. Here again, many pathological elements combined to form qualities advantageous in his political life.

Hitler's negative personality traits also underlie a central, almost phenomenal, factor in his conquest of the masses and climb to power: his oratory. If Hitler could claim a unique talent it was certainly not one, as he long insisted, in the arts, but rather as "the greatest demagogue in history" (Bullock, 1964, p. 44), i.e., the greatest unprincipled mob orator. Without his unique oratorical gift he might well have been just one among the many nationalistic anti-Semitic angry men seeking political power in Germany.

All his achievements from beginning to end were linked to this endowment. Hitler was first recognized when his ability to hold a group spellbound by a harangue was noted by a professor instructing army undercover agents after the First World War. When this man recommended that Hitler be assigned to the promotion of nationalism in the ranks, Hitler (1943, pp. 215–216) was ecstatic: "For this I was at once offered the opportunity to speak before a large audience . . . I could 'speak' ['*reden*' in the sense of public speaking]. No other task could make me happier than this one."

The significance of this discovery for Hitler personally, as a means of dealing with his own feelings, is explicit. This spontaneous expression came before he was connected with any political organization at the time when he was doing army chores to keep alive. Despite his retrospective declaration that he dedicated himself to politics at the time of the 1918 defeat, the opportunity came before he had made any attempt at political activity on his own in the turmoil of Munich politics. When, in time, he began to apply his oratorical skills under army sponsorship in political meetings, he soon realized that in this talent to inflame mass passions he in truth had no peer.

This talent, fueled by his pathologic personality, found its true arena in sizeable groups of distressed, confused, and angry Germans. It worked best in groups larger than Adolf Hitler's earlier reluctant audiences in hostels and army camps. Its electric effectiveness in the post-war misery of defeated Germany explains why the man who in 1918 could not "make non-com" in the army for lack of leadership qualities found himself by 1922 swaying huge audiences. His rare gift was also attracting a fanatic personal following. The aimless thirty-year-old drifter became at thirty-three a political star performer with slavish disciples. Little else in him changed in the interval, not his ideas, not his tastes, not his erratic behavior and periodic rages, nothing but the discovery of this power in himself and the response it elicited from throngs of people in the social chaos of the time.

The gift also sealed his control over his cohorts. The growing party was unwilling to lose this magnet whose oratory brought thousands into what had been a tiny discussion group. Its leaders capitulated to his demands for dictatorial sway over them. With his gift he used his *Putsch* trial in 1924 as a theater, spellbinding his judges and reaching a world audience through the press. With more and more adherents, Hitler also became the man who spoke for the masses. This added to his authority, which his personality required be absolute. For his oratory, the masses gave him at last the total subservience he had earlier demanded in vain from his schoolmates and his auditors in the Vienna Home for Men.

His oratory had about it an "hypnotic quality." The term was used by contemporaries to describe Hitler's personal effect in individual encounters. To oversimplify somewhat, it can be said that the hypnotist like the parent arouses love and demands unquestioning submission. That these elements figured in Hitler's encounters with those he wanted to influence is not difficult to see. Goebbels and Ludecke (1938, pp. 13–16), two disciples who wrote extensively of Hitler's hypnotic effect upon them, both used terms of love and of giving themselves over to him.

From adolescence on, the dominating feature of Hitler's face was his eyes. Clinical experience shows that the eye(ball) is often unconsciously regarded as a symbol of the testicle. If Hitler were lacking a testicle, an aspect of his behavior is illuminated: his aggressive use of his eyes, beginning in his youth. Hitler, at first probably unconsciously and later quite deliberately, practiced an effective use of his conspicuous and somewhat bulging eyes, so like his mother's. The often cruel stare, as clearly demonstrated in the "stare-you-down" games he liked to play even as Chancellor, was intended to dominate others. Some people, notably including Francisco Franco, Benito Mussolini, President von Hindenburg, and the American journalist Dorothy Thompson, were not at all cowed by the little man or his angry staring eyes. But the fearfully susceptible were both cowed and enthralled. When he wished to impress or to dominate someone in an individual encounter he could use his eyes both aggressively and libidinally, two aspects of hypnosis.

With large crowds he could not use his eyes alone to achieve his hypnotic effect. Here he used his gifts for oratory primarily through the way he used his body and his voice. By the time he was in his thirties Hitler's voice was recognized as a most arresting one, capable of the widest range of tone and volume, and with great variety in qualities, from harsh to sweet. His dramatic talents for enacting roles, weeping, bullying, wheedling, and mimicking were extraordinary. The passionate energy he could expend in oral expression, involving his whole body, was almost boundless. Beyond the gifts, the record shows the careful preparation which he applied to this part of his political work and to this part only: the writing and rewriting, the outlining according to a deliberate scheme like a musical composition, the systematic preparation of written notes, the cue words behind the seeming spontaneity, the scrutiny of audience mood even before his precisely staged arrivals. On his speeches, uniquely, Adolf Hitler worked.

To further the receptivity and suggestibility of his audiences, Hitler quite deliberately used masterly psychological or theatrical devices. For his immediate audiences in large halls or stadia or open-air squares, he provided awe-inspiring spectacles tending to stimulate a sense of smallness and helplessness in the individual and more readiness to accept the promises of rescue and glory from the speaker, who represented himself as the wise, strong, fearless savior. Together with the martial music chosen, the spectacles also promoted in each hearer a welcome feeling of kinship with the rest of the crowd. On the radio, Hitler followed other tactics. He often scheduled his speeches for broadcast at night when members of the audience were tired after the workday and least alert and critical.

In his early oratory, as so often in his career, Adolf Hitler had pure luck on his side. All the contrivance and control he mustered in his public speaking happened to be backed by a pervasive sincere emotion in him on one theme that he shared with his hearers. He truly felt, like each of his hearers, that society and its institutions had been unjust to him. This happened, as Joachim Fest pointed out, to coincide exactly with an almost universal feeling of resentment in the whole post-war population (1973, p. 7).

But more reason for that magic, that hypnotic quality to which so few were immune, must be sought beyond the gifts, beyond the rare application to the task, and beyond the luck. Three psychological elements illuminate the extraordinary emotional relationship between this speaker and his hearers: (1) the affinity between his narcissistic-borderline psychological state and the psychological state of his hearers as a crowd; (2) his expression and sanction of aggression and rage in himself and them; and (3) the intensely sexual nature of his speeches and the reaction they induced.

The parallels between Hitler's psychopathology and the psychology of the crowd as described by the French sociologist LeBon in his work, *The Crowd* (1895—published in German in 1908), are striking. To summarize LeBon's analysis: the crowd operates at a regressed level of emotional development; it is "feminine" (i.e., to LeBon, erratic); it has grandiose ideas of omnipotence; it is irritable and easily stimulated to cruel and ruthless aggression; it is impulsive and its emotions are changeable and contradictory; it is blind to certain realities, especially those that oppose the gratification of its drives, so that its judgment is often impaired; it readily overidealizes individuals, notably its leaders; its fantasies often have the force of reality; it is stubborn and demanding; its moral level is low. Thus, Hitler when speaking to throngs spoke to "brothers under the skin." The crowd understood him as he understood it. The crowd stimulated him as it was stimulated by him and therefore

readily found in him its spokesman. The congruence
between the two was remarkable (LeBon, 1895).

The abundant, almost unheard-of expression of hate
and rageful anger that is at work in the narcissistic-borderline personality fired his successful orations. This outpouring from Hitler's personality found responsive
resonance in his audience's anger born of the frustration
and deprivation of unemployment, inflation, and vascil-
lating political leadership. The oral filth he poured out,
incidentally, can be seen as the reverse of his perverse
sexual behavior, where Hitler was the passive recipient
of the woman's excretions. When he gave his hearers
their scapegoat, he gave them not only the relief of
expression but also the thrill of speaking the unspeakable
for them. His practice of touching off hostile emotions
rather than conveying mere critical ideas was wildly successful. Logic had little if any part in his moving of an
audience. Even the sound of his speeches, their shrieks
and guttural sounds, signalled pure emotion. Indeed, his
sometimes poor enunciation, further obscured by choking rage, made some of what he said incomprehensible.
But the crowd always responded to the rageful invective,
the threats, and the promises of annihilation of the enemies, be they the Jews, French, British, Russians, or
Americans.

The most telling psychological element in Hitler's tor-
rential orations was probably their unconscious sexual
meaning, both to him and to many of his hearers. Hitler
considered the masses as feminine in their nature and
likened them to women who needed to be overwhelmed,
not won by intelligent argument. In keeping with this
idea he actually treated each audience as though it were

a woman, a woman to be conquered. In *Mein Kampf* (1943, pp. 42–43) he put it specifically as follows:

> The psyche of the broad masses does not respond to anything weak or half-way. Like a woman whose psychic feeling is influenced less by abstract reasoning rather than by undefinable sentimental longing for a complementary strength, who will submit to the strong man rather than the suppliant. . . . They neither realize the impudence with which they are spiritually terrorized or the outrageous curtailment of their human liberties, for in no way does the delusion of this doctrine dawn on them. Thus they see only the inconsiderate force, the brutality and the aim of its manifestations to which they finally always submit.

On another occasion he put part of this concept more succinctly (1953, p. 391): "Someone who does not understand the intrinsically feminine character of the masses will never be an effective speaker."

More than one contemporary described a speech of Hitler's as resembling a sexual act. He would begin his oration slowly and tentatively, as though to feel his way. Then the tempo of his speech and his rhythmic hand movements increased. This phase was followed by a stormy outpouring of shouting, during which all objectivity disappeared and he was completely possessed by passion. Hanfstaengl (1957, p. 69) wrote that "the last eight or ten minutes of a speech represented an *orgasm of words*, because the crowd was to Hitler "a substitute medium for a woman" (his italics). This realization "made the phenomenon of his oratory more intelligible" to Hanfstaengl, who felt both overcome and baffled by what he observed. Hitler, after this climax, was covered with perspiration. Finally, he was spent and relaxed in utter exhaustion. Nevertheless, he often said that he was never so happy or fulfilled as after he had delivered a successful speech.

The sexual effect of his oratory on an audience was most vividly and frequently mentioned. Men were driven into a frenzy of eagerness to follow him, women to hysterical sobbing in the height of passive surrender, "slack of mouth and breathing heavily as if in the grip of sexual excitement" (Fest, 1970, pp. 36–37) or fainting away.

One observer described him significantly as a limp little man whom the stream of speech stiffened, "like a stream of water stiffens a hose" (Waite, 1977, p. 208); he might as well have said that the stream of speech stiffened him as the stream of blood into the *corpora cavernosa* stiffens the penis.

A distinguished German historian (Reichmann, 1950, p. 264) reported Hitler's spontaneous exclamation to his audience after he had reached the climax of his speech at a Nazi Party rally she attended in 1933: "Aren't you as enthralled by me as I am by you?" Eva Reichmann observed that "the erotic character, not only of the words but also the accompanying gestures, was unmistakable."

The function Hitler's oratory served for his own psyche is apparent. In symbolically ravishing the collective "woman," the crowd, he was able to deny and, unconsciously, magically undo his castration anxieties and genital anomaly and assert that he did not fear copulation with a woman. Indeed, he was demonstrating a superiority to most men, in that he could have his way, both literally and figuratively, with many individuals simultaneously. Feeling whole, complete, physically and functionally perfect, he was therefore uniquely happy and fulfilled after a speech, as he himself said.

The critical element in Hitler's oratory may well have been this symbolic sexual ravishing of his audience. With elements of the hypnotic phenomenon, he not only manipulated his hearers to do his bidding but also held them in thrall and commandeered a nation. Thus for Hitler his sexualized oratory was an essential exploitation of aspects of his psychopathologic personality.

Helpful as were all these features in his rise to power, they had even greater force for a considerable time after he attained it. When he became in reality the figure of immense power, most of those who met him were already overawed before he brought his "hypnotic" stare to bear on them. When that did not work, however, the Chancellor did not have to hesitate to set loose his enormous rage; it was now backed up by real threats often irresistible in themselves. In time, even his closest collaborators did not dare to bring up unpleasant realities, much less to contradict his distorted perception of realities. And so, late in this war, the disadvantageous or maladaptive aspects of his psychopathology came to predominate.

Such impediments in fact emerged when his task was no longer to amass power but to use it to govern. For this he was not helped by his disorder but hampered. Even before his final near-delusional state, in which he refused to accept reports of realities, megalomania and paranoia combined to reduce his use of the assistance of genuine experts and specialists. Speer describes how

". . . the principle of negative selection . . . governed the composition of Hitler's entourage. Since he regularly responded to opposition by choosing someone more amenable . . . he assembled . . . associates who more and more surrendered to his arguments." These translated Hitler's arguments "into action more and more unscrupulously" (1970, p. 198). Finally he could replace opposition only with one completely amenable person: himself. In the end he could not supervise his Nazi leaders in the separate rival fiefdoms he had encouraged to preserve his unique control. The official bureaucracy became an administrative nightmare. The Nazi leadership in less than a decade became so corrupt that even the extreme crisis of a losing war in 1942 could not persuade them to restrain their costly excesses. Clearly, the narcissistic-borderline personality so advantageous for the rising politician does not have the same utility in leadership once the rise to power is complete. The disorder ordained Hitler's fall, when aggression, rage, and need for ever greater successes drove him to defeat and death.

In considering the political advantages that psychopathological features provided Adolf Hitler, one must not forget that without his real skills, and his luck in time and place, his psychopathology would not have made him the historical figure he became. His hypnotic oratory and his skill in devising coercive propaganda effects to influence both individuals and crowds were real talents. His lifelong absorption in things warlike, fueled by his aggression and his audacity, resulted in the mastery of military strategy during the early stages of World War II with which he is credited. And however banal Hitler's mentation, his memory was prodigious, especially for details, from bicycle registration numbers to armament statistics, an ability he used to the hilt for purposes of control. Recall is an aspect of intelligence not necessarily affected by an emotional disturbance such as his. And, in general, the more emotionally disturbed, the less effectively can a person use his intelligence. Hitler displayed this consequence. While he was always strongly pragmatic and usually remarkable in foreseeing the value of new technology and in mustering it to his purposes, he was blind to the possibilities of nuclear research: he associated it with hated Jewish scientists and so fortunately eschewed it, to his detriment.

In sum, what is inherent in any such abnormal personality that is advantageous in a rise to political leadership? The megalomania of the narcissistic-borderline personality, reinforced by his aggression, permits the climbing politician to present a believable image of the strong, self-confident, and determined authority figure. He can attract followers hungry for simple answers and single enemies. His sanction releases them to act upon their own otherwise forbidden impulses. He can exploit the violence he engenders. He can, because of his suspiciousness, perceive the emotional attitudes of hearers, and freely shift to enact the different roles he sees as welcome. The borderline has few if any checks from conscience, and so he can think and do what for most would be unthinkable. He can stun adversaries with surprises. He can freely manipulate others as pawns. The defenses and traits of the disorder permit him to be a consummate opportunist, shifting and changing without hindrance.

Unique to Adolf Hitler was the combination of his extraordinary talent as a public speaker, his boundless aggression, and his incessant need to deny his feminine tendencies. Power was his sole program; all the rest was window dressing. Whatever his rationalizations for his insatiable drive for power, it was propelled by that urgent need to disavow his feminine inclinations. He sought relief from this anxiety by demonstrating what he considered masculine characteristics: brutal aggression and power to subjugate and control others. But complicated unconscious tendencies are not eradicated by a conscious show of so-called masculinity, however vigorous the conscious acts may be. Hitler's vain efforts to disavow unacceptable tendencies by demonstrating "masculinity" in ever more power and in greater conquests persisted and became more unrealistic until he overreached and brought about his own ignominy and self-destruction.

References

Adler, G. (1981), The borderline-narcissistic personality disorder continuum. *Amer. J. Psychiat.*, 138:46–50.

Arlow, J. A. (1953), Masturbation and symptom formation. *J. Amer. Psychoanal. Assoc.*, 1:45–58.

———— (1980), The revenge motive in the primal scene. *J. Amer. Psychoanal. Assoc.*, 28:519–541.

Baynes, N. H. (1942), *The Speeches of Adolf Hitler: April 1922–August 1939*, Vol. I. London: Oxford University Press.

Bezymenski, L. (1968), *The Death of Adolf Hitler: Unknown Documents from Soviet Archives*. New York: Harcourt, Brace & World.

Bloch, E. (1941), "My patient, Hitler." *Collier's*, March 15 and March 22, 1941 (no. 1, no. 2).

Blos, P. (1960), Comments on the psychological consequences of cryptorchism. *The Psychoanalytic Study of the Child*, 15:395–429. New York: International Universities Press.

Brady, K. (1974), "Interview with Joseph Rottenburger." *Boston Globe*, January 26, 1974.

Bromberg, N. (1960), Totalitarian ideology as a defense technique. In: *The*

Psychoanalytic Study of Society, Vol. 1. New York: International Universities Press.

————— (unpublished), The psychotic character as political leader, I.: A psychoanalytic study of Adolf Hitler. Read at the Annual Meeting of the American Psychoanalytic Association, Chicago, 1961.

————— (unpublished), The psychotic character as political leader, II: Hitler as leader of Germany. Read at the Annual Meeting of the American Psychoanalytic Association, Toronto, Canada, 1962.

————— (1971), Hitler's character and its development: Further observations. *Amer. Imago*, 28:289–303.

————— (1974), "Hitler's childhood." *Internat. Rev. Psycho-Anal.* 1:227–244.

Bullock, A. (1958), Foreword. In: Jetzinger, F. (1958), *Hitler's Youth*.

————— (1964), *Hitler, A Study in Tyranny*, Comp. rev. ed. New York and Evanston: Harper & Row.

Bursten, B. (1973), Some narcissistic personality types. *Internat. Psycho-Anal.*, 5:287–300.

Dawidowicz, L. S. (1975), *The War Against the Jews: 1933–1945*. New York: Holt, Rinehart and Winston [text citations are to Bantam edition of 1976].

Dietrich, O. (1934), *Mit Hitler in Die Macht*. München: Franz Eher Verlag.

————— (1955), *Hitler*. Translated by Richard and Clara Winston. Chicago: Henry Regnery.

Domarus, M. (1965), *Hitler: Reden und Proklamationen, 1932–1945*. Süddeutscher Verlag, München.

Dostoyevski, F. (1962), *The Possessed*. Translated by Andrew R. McAndrew. New York: New American Library.

Fest, J. C. (1970), *The Face of the Third Reich: Portraits of the Nazi Leadership*. Translated by Michael Bullock. New York: Random House, Pantheon Books.

————— (1973), *Hitler: Eine Biographie*. Frankfurt: Verlag Ulstein.

————— (1974), *Hitler*. Translated by Richard and Clara Winston. New York: Harcourt Brace Jovanovich.

François-Poncet, A. (1949), *The Fateful Years: Memoirs of a French Ambassador in Berlin, 1931–1938*. Translated by J. LeClerq. New York: Harcourt, Brace and Co.

Frank, H. (1955), *Im Angericht des Galgens*. München: Eigenverlag Brigitte Frank/Neuhaus bei Schliersee.

Freud, S. (1900), The Interpretation of Dreams. *Standard Edition*, 5. London: Hogarth Press, 1953.

————— (1913), Totem and Taboo. *Standard Edition*, 13. 1–161. London: Hogarth Press, 1955.

————— (1916), Some character types met with in psycho-analytic work. *Standard Edition*, 14. London: Hogarth Press, 1957.

————— (1922), Medusa's head. *Standard Edition*, 18. 273–274. London: Hogarth Press, 1955.

Frosch, J. (1970), Psychoanalytic considerations of the psychotic character. *J. Amer. Psychoanal Assoc.*, 18:24–50.

Gilbert, G. M. (1950), *The Psychology of Dictatorship.* New York: Ronald Press.

——— (1961), *Nuremberg Diary.* New York: Farrar, Straus and Cudahy.

Gisevius, H. B. (1963), *Adolf Hitler, Versuch Einer Deutung.* München: Rütten & Lening Verlag, p. 383.

Gitelson, M. (1958), On ego distortion. *Internat. J. Psycho-Anal.*, 39:245–257.

Grinker, R. R., Sr., Werble, B., & Drye, R. C. (1968), *The Borderline Syndrome.* New York: Basic Books.

——— & ——— (1977), *The Borderline Patient.* New York: Jason Aronson.

Gun, N. E. (1968a), *Eva Braun-Hitler: Leben und Schicksal.* New York and Bruchsal/Baden: 1968.

——— (1968b), *Eva Braun: Hitler's Mistress.* New York: Meredith Press, 1968.

Gunderson, J. G., & Singer, M. T. (1975), Defining borderline patients. *Amer. J. Psychiat.*, 132:1–11.

Hanfstaengl, E. (1957), *Hitler: The Missing Years.* London: Eyre & Spottiswoode.

Hartocollis, P., ed. (1977), *Borderline Personality Disorders.* New York: International Universities Press.

Heiden, K. (1936), *Hitler.* New York: Alfred A. Knopf.

——— (1944), *Der Fuehrer: Hitler's Rise to Power.* Translated by Ralph Manheim. Boston: Houghton Mifflin Co.

Heyst, A. (1940), *After Hitler.* London: Minerva Publishing Co.

Hilberg, R. (1973), *The Destruction of the European Jews.* New York: Franklin Watts.

Hitler, A. (1943), *Mein Kampf.* Translated by Ralph Manheim. Boston: Houghton Mifflin Co., Sentry.

——— (1953), *Hitler's Secret Conversations: 1941–1944.* Translated by N. Cameron & R. H. Stevens, with introductory essay, "The Mind of Adolf Hitler," by H. R. Trevor-Roper. New York: Farrar, Straus and Young.

——— (1961a), *Hitler's Secret Book.* Introduction by Telford Taylor; translated by Salvator Attanasio. New York: Grove Press.

——— (1961b), *Testament of Adolf Hitler, Hitler–Bormann Documents.* ed. F. Genoud. London: Cassell Co.

——— (1973), *Hitler's Briefe Und Notizen.* ed. Werner Maser. Düsseldorf: Econ Verlag.

Hitler, P. (1959), Interview. *The New York Times,* March 5.

Hoffmann, Heinrich (1935), *Hitler wie ihn Keiner Kennt.* Berlin: Zeitgeschichte-Verlag.

Hughes, R. (1973), Essay. In: *Time,* May 21, p. 6.

Jacobson, E. (1964), *The Self and the Object World.* New York: International Universities Press.

Jenks, W. A. (1960), *Vienna of the Young Hitler*. New York: Columbia University Press.

Jetzinger, F. (1958), *Hitler's Youth*. Translated by Lawrence Wilson. London: Hutchinson.

Johnson, A. M., & Szurek, S. A. (1952), The genesis of antisocial acting out in children and adults. *Psychoanalyt. Quart.*, 21:323–343.

Kaltenborn, H. V. (1950), *Fifty Fabulous Years*. New York: G. P. Putnam's Sons.

Kernberg, O. (1966), Structural derivatives of object relationships. *Internat. J. Psycho-Anal.*, 47:236–253.

———— (1967), Borderline personality organization. *J. Amer. Psychoanal. Assoc.*, 15:641–685.

———— (1970), Factors in the psychoanalytic treatment of narcissistic personalities. *J. Amer. Psychoanal. Assoc.*, 18:51–85.

———— (1974), Further contributions to the treatment of narcissistic personalities. *Internat. J. Psycho-Anal.*, 55:215–240.

———— (1975), *Borderline Conditions and Pathological Narcissism*. New York: Jason Aronson.

———— (1976), *Object Relations Theory and Clinical Psychoanalysis*. New York: Jason Aronson.

Knight, R. (1953), Borderline states. *Bull. Menninger Clin.*, 17:1–12.

Koenigsberg, R. A. (1975), *Hitler's Ideology*. New York: The Library of Social Science.

Kohut, H. (1971), *The Analysis of the Self*. New York: International Universities Press.

Kren, G. (1974), Comment on previously published paper. *Hist. Childhood Quart.*, 2:265–268.

Kubizek, A. (1955), *The Young Hitler I Knew*. Translated by E. V. Anderson. Boston: Houghton Mifflin Co.

Kurth, G. M. (1947), The Jew and Adolf Hitler. *Psychoanal. Quart.*, 16:11–32.

Langer, W. C., ed. (1942–1943), *OSS Source Book*. National Archives, 58, Documents collected by OSS.

———— with the collaboration of Henry A. Murray, Ernst Kris, and Bertram D. Lewin (1943), *Psychological Analysis of Hitler*. Secret typescript declassified March 12, 1968. Washington, D. C.: National Archives, Record Group #226, "Records of the Office of Strategic Services."

———— (1972), *The Mind of Adolf Hitler: The Secret Wartime Report*. New York and London: Basic Books.

LeBon, G. (1895), *The Crowd*. New York: The Viking Press, 1960.

Lidz, T. (1976), Foreword. In: *Adolf Hitler: A Family Perspective*, by H. Stürlin. New York: Psychohistory Press.

Lochner, L. P. (1948), *The Goebbels Diaries*, 2nd ed. Translated by L. P. Lochner. New York: Doubleday, 1971.

Loeblowitz-Lennard, H. (1947), The Jew as symbol. *Psychoanal. Quart.*, 16:33–38.

Lorant, S. (1974), *Sieg Heil!* New York: W. W. Norton and Co.

Ludecke, K. (1938), *I Knew Hitler: The Story of a Nazi Who Escaped the Blood Purge.* New York: Charles Scribner's Sons.

Mahler, M. S., Pine, F., & Bergman, A. (1975), *The Psychological Birth of the Human Infant.* New York: Basic Books.

Maser, W. (1973), *Adolf Hitler: Legende, Mythos, Wirklichkeit*, 5th ed. München and Esslingen: Bechtle Verlag.

———— (1974), *Hitler's Letters and Notes.* New York: Harper & Row [text references are to Bantan edition of 1976].

Masterson, J. F. (1976), *Psychotherapy of the Borderline Adult.* New York: Brunner/Mazel.

McRandle, J. (1965), *The Track of the Wolf: Essays on National Socialism and Its Leader, Adolf Hitler.* Evanston, Ill.: Northwestern University Press.

Müllern-Schönhausen, J. von (no date), *Die Lösung des Rätsel's Adolf Hitler.* Vienna: Verlag zur Förderung wissenschaftlicher Forschung.

Niederland, W. G. (1965), Narcissistic ego impairment in patient with early physical malformations. *The Psychoanalytic Study of the Child*, 20:518–534. New York: International Universities Press.

Norden, E. (1971), "Interview of Albert Speer." *Playboy*, 18:69–203.

O'Donnell, T. F. (1969), "The devil's architect." *New York Times Magazine*, October 26, p. 48.

Orlow, D. (1974), The significance of time and place in psychohistory. *J. Interdisciplinary History*, 1:137.

Ostow, M., ed. (1974), *Sexual Deviation: Psychoanalytic Insights.* New York: Quadrangle/The New York Times Book Co.

Payne, R. (1973), *The Life and Death of Adolf Hitler.* New York and Washington: Praeger.

Picker, H., & Hoffmann, H. (1973), *Hitler Close-Up.* Compiled by Jochen von Lang; translated by Nicholas Fry. New York: Macmillan Co.

Prange, G. W., ed. (1944), *Hitler's Words (1942–1943).* Washington: American Council on Public Affairs.

Rangell, L. (reporter), (1955), The borderline case: A symposium. *J. Amer. Psychoanal. Assoc.*, 3:285–298.

Rauschning, H. (1940), *The Voice of Destruction.* New York: G. P. Putnam's Sons.

Reck-Malleczewen, F. P. (1970), *Diary of a Man in Despair.* Translated by Paul Rubens. London: Macmillan & Co.

Recktenwald, J. (1963), *Woran Hat Adolf Hitler Gelitten?* München: Ernst Reinhardt Verlag.

Reich, A (1951), The 1912 discussion on masturbation and our present-day views. *The Psychoanalytic Study of the Child*, 6:80–94. New York: International Universities Press.

Reichmann, E. G. (1950), *Hostages of Civilization*. London: Victor Gollancz.

Roiphe, H. (1969), On an early genital phase with an addendum on genesis. *The Psychoanalytic Study of the Child*, 23:348–365. New York: International Universities Press.

―――― (unpublished paper, 1972), The castration complex and object loss.

Schilder, P. (1950), *The Image and Appearance of the Human Body*. New York: International Universities Press.

Schramm, P. E. (1965), Introduction. In: *Hitler's Tischegespräche im Führerhauptquartier*, 2nd ed. Stuttgart: Seewalt Verlag.

―――― (1971), *Hitler: The Man and the Military Leader*. Translated by Donald S. Detwiler. Chicago: Quadrangle Books.

Shirer, W. L. (1960), *The Rise and Fall of the Third Reich: A History of Nazi Germany*. New York: Simon and Schuster.

Smith, A. M., Lattimer, J. K., & Masoud, R. (1973), Current therapy for undescended testicle. *New York J. Med.*, 73:2557–2560.

Smith, B. F. (1967), *Adolf Hitler: His Family, Childhood and Youth*. Stanford, Calif.: Hoover Institution on War, Revolution and Peace.

Speer, A. (1970), *Inside the Third Reich: Memoirs*. Translated by Richard and Clara Winston. New York: Macmillan Co.

―――― (1976), *Spandau*. New York: Macmillan Co.

Stein, G. H., ed. (1968), *Hitler*. Englewood Cliffs, N. J.: Prentice-Hall.

Stierlin, H. (1976), *Adolf Hitler: A Family Perspective*. New York: Psychohistory Press.

Stolk, P. J. (1968), Adolf Hitler and his illness, *Psychiat., Neuro., Neurochir.*, 71:381–398.

Stone, M. H. (1980), *The Borderline Syndromes*. New York: McGraw-Hill Book Co.

Tausk, V. (1951), On masturbation. *The Psychoanalytic Study of the Child*, 6:61–79. New York: International Universities Press.

Toland, J. (1976), *Adolf Hitler*. Garden City, N. Y.: Doubleday & Co.

Trevor-Roper, H. (1953), Introduction. In: *Hitler's Secret Conversations*. New York: Farrar, Straus and Young.

Waite, R. G. L. (1971a), Adolf Hitler's anti-Semitism: A study in history and psychoanalysis. In: *The Psychoanalytic Interpretation of History*, ed. B. B. Wolman. New York: Basic Books.

―――― (1971b), Adolf Hitler's guilt feelings: A problem of history and psychology. *J. Interdiscip. Hist.*, 1:229–249.

―――― (1977), *The Psychopathic God: Adolf Hitler*. New York: Basic Books.

Walters, J. H. (1975), Hitler's encephalitis: A footnote to history. *J. Operational Psychiat.*, 6:99–112.

Waugh, M. (1964), National socialism and the genocide of the Jews. *Internat. J. Psycho-Anal.*, 45:386–395.

Wykes, A. (1971), *Hitler*. New York: Ballantyne Books.

Zoller, A., ed. (1949), *Hitler Privat: Erlebnisbericht seiner Geheimsek-retärin*. Düsseldorf: Droste Verlag.

Index

327